"This book makes an important contribution to the literature on Fair Trade and hybrid organizations. The author uses rigorous research to offer new thinking in both these topic areas which will be of interest to both scholars and practitioners working in ethical and Fair Trade, as well as to managers concerned with creating more effective organizational models in hybrid market spaces."

*Alex Nicholls, University Lecturer, Skoll Centre for Social Entrepreneurship, Saïd Business School, University of Oxford*

"A very stimulating analysis of the Fair Trade sector, at the crossroads of economics and organization theory. This book will be a very useful reference for researchers and practitioners, based on solid data and insightful case studies."

*François Pichault, Professor in Organizational Change and Human Resources, HEC Management School, University of Liege*

"This book is one of the most competent and insightful contributions in terms of comparative analysis of Fair Trade organizations and strategies in different European countries. It reflects a long-term, careful and detailed investigation of how social enterprises in the North are competing by selling bundles of goods including ethical characteristics and conquering the "vote with the wallet" of socially and environmentally concerned consumers."

*Leonardo Becchetti, Professor in Economics, University of Rome "Tor Vergata"*

"What impresses me most in this book is the remarkable integration of both theoretical and empirical analysis: all the theoretical approaches are used to explain and shed light on empirical findings and the relevance of each of them is very finely discussed thanks to the author's deep knowledge of Fair Trade organizations"

*Jacques Defourny, Professor in Economics, HEC Management School, University of Liege EMES European Research Network on Social Enterprise*

# Fair Trade Organizations
# and Social Enterprise

# Routledge Studies in Management, Organizations, and Society

This series presents innovative work grounded in new realities, addressing issues crucial to an understanding of the contemporary world. This is the world of organised societies, where boundaries between formal and informal, public and private, local and global organizations have been displaced or have vanished, along with other nineteenth century dichotomies and oppositions. Management, apart from becoming a specialized profession for a growing number of people, is an everyday activity for most members of modern societies.

Similarly, at the level of enquiry, culture and technology, and literature and economics, can no longer be conceived as isolated intellectual fields; conventional canons and established mainstreams are contested. **Management, Organization and Society** addresses these contemporary dynamics of transformation in a manner that transcends disciplinary boundaries, with books that will appeal to researchers, student and practitioners alike.

# Fair Trade Organizations and Social Enterprise

Social Innovation through Hybrid Organization Models

**Benjamin Huybrechts**

Routledge
Taylor & Francis Group

NEW YORK   LONDON

First published 2012
by Routledge
711 Third Avenue, New York, NY 10017

Simultaneously published in the UK
by Routledge
2 Park Square, Milton Park, Abingdon, Oxon OX14 4RN

*Routledge is an imprint of the Taylor & Francis Group,
an informa business*

*Library of Congress Cataloging-in-Publication Data*
Huybrechts, Benjamin, 1981–
  Fair trade organizations and social enterprise : social innovation through
hybrid organization models / Benjamin Huybrechts.
    p. cm. — (Routledge studies in management, organizations and
society 17)
Includes bibliographical references and index.
  1. International trade—Moral and ethical aspects.   2. Competition,
Unfair—Moral and ethical aspects.   3. Fair trade associations.   I. Title.
    HF1379.H89 2012
    382—dc23
    2011041971

ISBN13: 978-0-415-51745-4 (hbk)
ISBN13: 978-0-203-12191-7 (ebk)

Typeset in Sabon
by IBT Global.

Printed and bound in the United States of America on acid-free paper by
IBT Global.

# Contents

**PART III**
Managing Hybridity in Fair Trade

# Figures

# Tables

# Abbreviations

| | |
|---|---|
| AB | Advisory Board |
| ADM | Artisans du Monde |
| AGICES | Assemblea Generale Italiana del Commercio Equo e Solidale |
| AIES | Associazione dei Parlementari per il Commercio Equo e Solidale |
| ASBL | Association sans but lucratif |
| ATO | Alternative Trading Organization |
| BAFTS | British Association for Fair Trade Shops |
| BFTF | Belgian Fair Trade Federation |
| CIC | Community Interest Company |
| CLACE | Coordination lyonnaise des acteurs du commerce équitable |
| CNC | Conseil national de la coopération |
| CSR | Corporate Social Responsibility |
| CTM | Cooperazione Terzo Mondo |
| DGD | Directorate-General for Development |
| EFTA | European Fair Trade Association |
| FINE | FLO, IFAT, NEWS, and EFTA |
| FEB | Fédération des entreprises de Belgique |
| FLO or FLO-I | Fairtrade Labeling Organizations (International) |
| FT | Fair Trade |
| FTAO | Fair Trade Advocacy Office |
| FTSE | Fair Trade Social Enterprise |
| FTE | Full-time equivalent |
| GA | General Assembly |
| IFAT | International Fair Trade Association (now WFTO) |
| MDM | Magasins du Monde |
| MMH | Miel Maya Honing |
| MFT | Maya Fair Trade |
| NEWS! | Network of European Worldshops |
| NGO | Non-Governmental Organization |
| ONLUS | Organizazzione non lucrativa di utilità sociale |
| PFCE | Plate-forme française pour le commerce équitable |
| PLC | Public Limited Company |

| | |
|---|---|
| RES | Roma Equa e Solidale |
| SA(RL) | Société anonyme (à responsabilité limitée) |
| SAW-B | Solidarité des alternatives wallones et bruxelloises |
| SCIC | Société coopérative d'intérêt collectif |
| SCOP | Société coopérative de production |
| SFS | Société à finalité sociale |
| SPRL | Société privée à responsabilité limitée |
| SME | Small or Medium Enterprise |
| TDC | Trade for Development Centre |
| WFTO | World Fair Trade Organization |
| WW | Wereldwinkels |

# Foreword

## ROOTS OF THE JOURNEY

This work is the result of a long journey initiated in 2005 and tracing back its roots much before then. My interest in Fair Trade began during my studies as a volunteer in an Oxfam worldshop. As a student in management sciences not very interested in traditional for-profit management, I wished to integrate my citizen's commitment into my studies. Lacking classes on how to orient the economic activity to serve social and environmental purposes, I took the opportunity of a student exchange in Chile to write my master's thesis on Fair Trade producers. The thesis explored the preparation of a Fair Trade partnership between a Belgian importer and a Chilean cooperative of winegrowers (Huybrechts and Manigart 2003). Next, in the context of master in development studies, I examined the impact of Fair Trade on Bolivian coffee growers (Huybrechts 2005).

After such a focus on the Southern side of Fair Trade, I wished to better understand the actors who pioneered and still (at least partly) run the initiative. Little is known about the organizations concretely connecting the producers in the South with the consumers in the North. Descriptions of Fair Trade in the North have often been restricted to issues of consumer interest, labeling process, and market growth. Yet, as a recent special issue in the *Journal of Business Ethics* has shown (Huybrechts and Reed 2010), differences among countries are very often linked to different histories and strategies of Fair Trade organizations.

## WHAT THIS BOOK IS ABOUT

How do entrepreneurs concretely connect the North and the South? What are the organizational solutions through which a social movement such as Fair Trade can enter markets while trying to transform these markets? Is it (still) possible to run a viable business while complying with the Fair Trade principles? What types of organizational models enable the pursuit of the hybrid goals associated with Fair Trade? Has the identity and the objectives of the organizations importing and distributing Fair Trade goods become less relevant since a label certifies the compliance of the practices with the stated goals?

These are few of the questions that this book will deal with through exploring the organizational dimensions of Fair Trade in the North. This work particularly tries to connect the reality of Fair Trade organizations with emerging literatures on the "social economy," "social entrepreneurship," or "social enterprise," as well as with the broader field of organization studies. This was possible thanks to an international journey featuring different ways of practicing Fair Trade, embedded in different economic and cultural contexts. Meeting so many entrepreneurs, volunteers, and other organizational actors totally involved in—and generally convinced by—their ventures was exciting, both from an academic and from a personal point of view.

This book seeks to show the richness of and the complementarities among the diverse models and practices of Fair Trade. It thus aims to provide a richer picture than that of a monolithic movement, often depicted either very positively (thereby lacking credibility) or very negatively (thereby bringing exaggerated skepticism).

More fundamentally, I wished to emphasize how the simultaneous articulation of economic, social, and political dimensions is both possible and welcome, in a context in which the market logic is becoming increasingly dominant. To articulate these dimensions, organizational actors in the Fair Trade sector have developed innovative and hybrid organizational models that may serve as a source of inspiration for other social enterprises that combine an economic activity with the pursuit of social goals.

## WHAT THIS BOOK IS NOT ABOUT

Lots of fascinating research topics are available when examining a unique and complex initiative such as Fair Trade. This book, however, rather than proposing a general overview of the field, chooses to focus on social enterprises active in the North. Hence, it ignores other perspectives which are of interest but do not correspond to the author's choice and expertise. Production processes and strategies, consumption patterns, product-based supply chain analyses or corporate strategies toward Fair Trade will not be covered, or at least not directly, in this book. Readers interested in these other issues should consider either general books on Fair Trade (e.g., Nicholls and Opal 2005; Raynolds, Murray, and Wilkinson 2007; Hutchens 2009) or books and articles on specialized topics (see www.fairtrade-institute.org for a list of articles). Moreover, entrepreneurs looking for concrete tools to manage Fair Trade Social Enterprises (FTSEs) beyond the organizational models analyzed here should refer to toolkits, which are increasingly provided by Fair Trade networks or consultants.

# Acknowledgments

This work would never have been achieved without the help of a large number of people whom I would like to thank. Here is a nonexhaustive list:

My PhD jury:

- Jacques Defourny, for his confidence, frequent advice, inspiration, and motivation to pursue this journey until the end and even beyond.
- François Pichault, for helping me to structure my work and to consolidate its foundations by guiding me into the labyrinths of organization theory.
- Alex Nicholls and the Skoll Centre for Social Entrepreneurship team at the University of Oxford, for welcoming me in Oxford and sharing their knowledge of and enthusiasm about social entrepreneurship.
- Leonardo Becchetti, for his involvement in the Italian part of this study, his warm welcome in Rome, and our exciting writing collaboration.
- Corinne Gendron, for helping me to better understand and analyze the Fair Trade movement.

The members of the Centre for Social Economy at HEC Management School of the University of Liege:

- Julie Rijpens, for having joined me along the road, thereby making it much more pleasant and less lonely.
- Sybille Mertens and Rocio Nogales, for their frequent advice, constant confidence, and numerous doses of motivation, especially during the most difficult stages of the journey.
- Sophie Adam, Catherine Davister, Anne Dujardin, Hyung-Sik Eum, Julie Failon, Nadine Gentile, Caroline Lovens, Michel Marée, Hugues Mouchamps, Charlotte Moreau, Chantal Nicks, Françoise Navez, Nathalie Vrancken, and all the other past, present, and future colleagues that make the CES [KES] such a wonderful place to work.

Other academics:

- Marthe Nyssens, for her useful advice for studying social enterprises.
- Bob Doherty, Mark Hayes, Geoff Moore, and Darryl Reed, for helping me to better understand Fair Trade organizations both from an academic and a practitioner perspective.
- All the young academics working on Fair Trade and involved in the "Fairness" network, for the advice and the mutual motivation; I particularly thank Amanda Berlan, Iain Davies, Virginie Diaz-Pedregal, Aurélie Carimentrand, Matthieu Gateau, Ronan Le Velly, Jean-Frédéric Lemay, Nil Ozcaglar-Toulouse, and Alastair Smith.
- The co-organizers of the FTIS 2008 and 2012 conferences.
- The academics of the EMES European Research network and the members of the EMES PhD student network.

All the Fair Trade practitioners (entrepreneurs, supporters, network coordinators, etc.) I met during the study, and in particular:

- In Belgium: Eric Dewaele (BFTF), Benoît Olivier, and Maurice Lambert (MMH-MFT), Samuel Poos (Trade for Development Centre), Sophie Tack, François Graas, and Jérôme Chaplier (Oxfam-MDM), and Joël Van Cauter (Citizen Dream)
- In France: Guihem Papelard (Equisol) and Emilie Sarrazin-Biteye (PFCE)
- In the UK: Paul Chandler (Traidcraft) and Geoff Moore (Gateway and Traidcraft)
- In Italy: Hassan Bajaj, Laura Saponaro (Esprit Equo), and Gaga Pignatelli (Pangea-Niente Troppo and Agices)

Sophie Adam and Christina De Schepper, for their precious help in reviewing and editing the text.

My friends and family, particularly Claire-Anne, Noé, and Lucie, who have never ceased to encourage me, and without whom this journey would be absolutely meaningless.

# Introduction

Among the recent initiatives that promote more ethical and sustainable production and consumption modes, Fair Trade (FT) is probably one of the fastest growing and most promising. Although the sales of FT products still represent a marginal proportion of the total trade in the world,[1] their size,[2] growth rate,[3] and symbolic content make them much more than an anecdotic phenomenon (Krier 2005; Nicholls and Opal 2005). FT, of course, is not just about trading figures. Indeed, the idea of FT is to use trade as a means to achieve the social mission of supporting small-scale producers in the South. And, beyond such support to producers, FT also aims to educate citizens and lobby governments and corporations to make international trading rules and practices fairer. From a conceptual standpoint, FT can be seen as a hybrid concept entailing at least three dimensions: an economic, a social, and a political one. In various aspects, FT appears as a "social innovation" (Phills, Deiglmeier, and Miller 2008; Mulgan et al. 2007; Martin and Osberg 2007): through the reactualized ambition of using the market to pursue social and political aims; through the range of concrete devices (re)invented to achieve this goal; and through the organizational models experienced by Fair Trade Social Enterprises (FTSEs) to implement these devices.

For several decades, FTSEs—broadly defined as organizations specialized in FT—have been involved in the import and distribution of FT products. While developing their own commercial capacities, FTSEs have been instrumental in the development of standards for FT. These standards led to the emergence of FT certification. The main certification model, the Fairtrade[4] label has enabled corporations to engage in FT at the different levels of the supply chain[5]. The emergence of the FT label has had a deep influence on the whole FT movement, including FTSEs, whether using the label or not. Hence, there has been an increasing diversification of the organizational landscape, not only through the coexistence of FTSEs and corporations, but also among the FTSEs. This book focuses on the latter diversification process and on its influence on the practice of FT as a hybrid concept.

Several authors describe the FT movement as divided in two oppos- ing strands, one with pragmatist and the other with radical visions of FT (e.g., Raynolds and Long 2007; Renard 2003). The pragmatic vision puts the emphasis on increasing the FT market share to have more impact on the producers in the South. It is worth noting that several pioneer FTSEs have adapted their structure and functioning to collaborate and to compete with corporate players; new FTSEs have also been launched specifically to address mainstream markets.[6] The more radical vision sees FT mainly as a *"tool for modifying the dominant economic model"* (Renard 2003, 91). While selling FT products is important to support the producers, it is, in the first place, the concretization of a broader political project aiming to transform international trading rules and practices. A merely quantitative extension of FT is viewed as a threat to this transformational aim.

Typical descriptions of the FT movement associate the organizations dealing with labeled food products (Fairtrade International) to the prag- matic vision and those working with handicraft products (many of whom are members of IFAT-WFTO[7]) to the radical vision. This is an overly sim- plified picture. The main aim of this book is to show that FTSEs are situ- ated all along a continuum between, put simply, "market" and "solidarity". This is due to the evolution of FTSEs in very different directions, as well as to the emergence of new FTSEs whose structures and visions do not necessarily fit into the existing categorizations. Moreover, the latest years have brought new debates and thus new divides among FTSEs, which have complexified the landscape and blurred the pragmatist-radical divide. As a consequence, we can observe a rich organizational diversity in the FT sec- tor, even when focusing only on FTSEs. The purpose of this work is to look at how FTSEs, whatever their affiliation, concretely deal with the hybrid— economic, social, and political—nature of FT. Organizational models are chosen here as the main—albeit not exclusive—entry to examine how FTSEs manage such hybridity.

## RESEARCH ON FAIR TRADE

Simultaneous to the commercial success of fairly traded products, research on FT has started to lift off from the end of the 1990s. Some of this work has been rather descriptive, presenting the principles and actors of FT (e.g., Moore 2004), its different supply chains (Warrier 2011), and the history and challenges of implementing FT in different countries (e.g., Davies 2009; Krier 2008; Becchetti and Costantino 2010; Özçağlar-Toulouse et al. 2010; Huybrechts and Reed 2010). From the early 2000s, several books have been written to digest the knowledge gathered on FT (e.g., Nicholls and Opal 2005; Raynolds, Murray, and Wilkinson 2007; Warrier 2011; Özçağlar- Toulouse and Béji-Bécheur 2008; Macdonald and Marshall 2010). A grow- ing number of articles have been written[8], and several academic journals have published special issues on FT.[9] FT is also increasingly discussed in academic conferences; a conference specifically focused on FT (the Fair Trade International Symposium) and organized by a network of scholars researching FT is also gaining increasing attention.[10]

Most of the recent academic work around FT can be categorized into a number of key issues and levels of analysis, five of which seem particularly salient. A first series of studies examine the *concept* of FT, typically in the light of broader frameworks such as (business) ethics, sustainable development, or economic theory (e.g., Maseland and de Vaal 2002; Hayes 2006; Zehner 2002; Steinrücken and Jaenichen 2007; Becchetti and Adriani 2002; Balineau and Dufeu 2010).

Second, we find numerous analyses of the FT *movement*, often viewed as a social movement. This work looks at the evolution and challenges facing FT, with a focus on the changes and possible paradoxes induced by mainstreaming (e.g., Gendron, Bisaillon, and Rance 2009; Hira and Ferrie 2006; Moore 2004; Charlier et al. 2007; Raynolds, Murray, and Wilkinson 2007; Renard 2003; Low and Davenport 2005a).

Related to the FT movement is the study of FT *certification*. Several authors look at how standards are constructed (and contested), how pioneer actors interact with corporations and public authorities, and how this influences distribution of value from producers to consumers (Reed 2009; Muradian and Pelupessy 2005; Smith 2010; Raynolds 2008; Jaffee 2007, 2010; Renard 2005; Hutchens 2009; Ballet and Carimentrand 2010).

A fourth issue, which has developed under the impulse of FT practitioners, is the strategies of *producers* and the impact of their participation in FT (e.g., Hopkins 2000; Ronchi 2000; Utting 2009; Ronchi 2002; Lake and Howe 1998; Jones et al. 2000).

Finally, a fifth major topic is that of *consumers*: their profiles and buying behavior as well as the marketing strategies aiming to increase FT consumption (e.g., Nicholls and Alexander 2007; Becchetti and Rosati 2005; De Pelsmacker, Driesen, and Rayp 2005; Moore, Gibbon, and Slack 2006; Nicholls 2002; Özçağlar-Toulouse, Shiu, and Shaw 2006).

This is, however, one categorization among others, recognizing that many other issues are dealt with in the FT literature, which has been developing fast over the last years.[11] In terms of participants in FT, there has been a lot of work on the two ends of the FT chain—producers and consumers. The intermediaries of the chain, mainly FTSEs in the North,[12] have received less attention. This does not mean that there has not been any work on FTSEs. Indeed, most work on FT involves, at a certain moment and to a certain extent, analyses of FTSEs. For instance, most impact studies start by examining the standpoint of the importing FTSE (e.g., Lake and Howe 1998); several consumer studies start by describing FTSEs' marketing strategies (e.g., Doherty and Tranchell 2007); and any analysis of the FT sector as a whole requires commenting on the role of a number of key FTSEs. Nevertheless, taking FTSEs themselves as the central object of investigation is less common. What Davies and Crane (2003, 80) observed some years ago still seems valid at this date: "*there has been virtually no academic research focusing on the implementation of fair trade principles in [FT] companies.*" These authors provide an interesting study on ethical decision-making in the British FTSE Divine Chocolate. Moore and his colleagues (2009) take the case of FTSEs to illustrate SMEs' responsible business practices. Nicholls and Opal (2005) cite a number of studies on different fields of management in FTSEs, including: marketing, strategy, operations, and finance.[13] Finally, several case studies focus on the description of particular FTSEs (e.g., Otero 2007; Hervieux 2008; Tadros and Malo 2002).

Still, the study of the structure and functioning of FTSEs appears as a much under-researched issue. The reason might be that these organizations are supposed to link the demand (consumers) and the supply-side (producers) under precise criteria fixed by the FT label or by a network to which they belong (Davies and Crane 2003). But as there is much latitude in this regard, the implementation of these criteria is likely to depend on the nature and the vision of the FTSEs. Different types of FTSEs have been highlighted in the context of more global descriptions of the movement (e.g., Diaz Pedregal 2007; Becchetti and Huybrechts 2008; Raynolds and Long 2007). However, most of these typologies are based on general observations of the sector; they assume particular goals or visions based on the FTSE's affiliation or distribution strategy and often lack a systematic and in-depth observation of the organizations. FTSEs are far from being black boxes that conduct FT activities in a homogeneous way. As already mentioned, they can be located along one, or even several, continuum(s). One entry to discriminate among FTSEs is their hybrid and innovative organizational models. This book departs from the observation of these different models. All these models seem hybrid in that they seek to combine, to various extents and with different priorities, the various goals and dimensions inherent in FT. This book wonders whether these different models reflect and enable different ways of practicing FT and managing its hybrid nature (including the tensions that such hybridity may involve). In other words, it explores the different organizational avenues to the social innovation that FT embodies.

## BOOK OUTLINE

This book is structured into three main parts. Part I is devoted to describing FT and FTSEs in an international (mainly European) perspective and to introducing their diverse organizational models. In Chapter 1, the FT concept is examined and decomposed into an economic, a social, and a political dimension. Such a hybrid nature is not new. Indeed, other concepts and initiatives to which FT, and, more specifically FTSEs, can be affiliated, highlight specific ways for organizations to combine these three dimensions, suggesting that such combination requires—or is better achieved through—specific organizational models. Chapter 2 then presents the FT landscape in the North, particularly focusing on four countries in which FTSEs will be examined: Belgium, France, Italy, and the United Kingdom. Chapter 3 introduces the different organizational models of FT identified throughout the study, examining similarities and differences among countries, and suggesting possible explanatory factors. Different elements of the organizational model are first presented and categorized separately: the legal form, the architecture, and the governance model. These three elements are then combined through a global taxonomy. The different categories obtained from this exercise are analyzed, as well as the possible evolution of FTSEs from one category to another.

Part II uses theory and is made of four chapters (Chapters 4–7). Chapter 4 provides a global theoretical overview, introducing the three perspectives which will be used to interpret the observations. First of all, using *economic* new institutionalism, Chapter 5 tries to understand how the different organizational models constitute efficient institutional arrangements, in the sense that they enable the minimization of a number of transaction costs. Chapter 6 uses *sociological* new institutionalism, focusing on two dimensions to examine organizational diversity: a historical one and a geographical one. Chapter 7 departs from the case studies to introduce agency-based insights; it examines how FTSEs conceive their organizational models as "institutional bricolage" hybridizing different logics in the context of *institutional work*.

Part III, consisting of the last chapter, examines how organizational actors concretely shape their organizational model, give a meaning to it, and use it as a strategic tool to gain power and promote particular visions of FT. Recommendations on how to articulate the hybrid dimensions of FT and deal with the possible tensions among them are then provided.

The findings of the study show how five types of organizational models co-exist in the FT field and seem to correspond to different stages of the organizational trajectories but also to different visions of FT. While the organizational models can be interpreted in terms of aiming efficiency, they can be even better understood as devices whereby entrepreneurs seek to garner legitimacy from different audiences and thus to integrate different and possibly conflicting logics within their organization. Using different theoretical lenses, the main contribution of this book is to show the different ways through which FT social enterprises in various countries experience FT as a hybrid concept and orient their models to achieve what they consider the best fit between its economic, social and political components.

Part I

# Diverse and Innovative Organizational Models in a Hybrid Field

# 1 Fair Trade
## A Hybrid Concept and Practice

In this first chapter, the history and notion of Fair Trade (FT) are examined as well as its affiliation with other concepts and initiatives that have inspired it. FT is interpreted as being composed of three interrelated dimensions: an economic one, a social one, and a political one. Then, the need for innovative organizational models allowing for the pursuit of these hybrid goals is highlighted based on the study of the affiliated concepts.

## THE EMERGENCE OF THE FT MOVEMENT[1]

Most authors situate the origins of the FT movement just after the Second World War, with experimental initiatives of import and distribution of handicraft, led by NGOs and charitable organizations with a religious background (e.g., Nicholls and Opal 2005; Raynolds, Murray, and Wilkinson 2007; Diaz Pedregal 2007; Moore 2004). The most often mentioned initiatives include Oxfam UK, SOS Wereldhandel in the Netherlands, the Mennonite Central Committee (MCC; later Ten Thousand Villages), Self-Help Crafts program in the US, as well as the Church of the Brethren's Sales Exchange for Refugee Rehabilitation and Vocation (SERRV) program (also in the US). A number of authors describe these initiatives as successive waves having inspired FT, together with the cooperative movement (Gendron, Bisaillon, and Rance 2009a). The various names used to refer to these initiatives—charity trade, solidarity trade, developmental trade, alternative trade, etc.—each emphasized a particular dimension (Gendron, Bisaillon, and Rance 2009; Low and Davenport 2005a). Charity trade emphasized the charitable logics that were often inherent in religious groups during that period (Low and Davenport 2005a). Solidarity trade had a more political meaning; trading was considered as a means to support producers from countries excluded from the international trading arena (socialist countries at the time, such as Cuba, Nicaragua, and Vietnam). Developmental trade focused on the assistance provided by NGOs to producers in the production and exportation processes.

While several authors locate the birth of FT in these initiatives, others highlight the striking differences that distinguish them from the current practice of FT. Often, these trading initiatives were punctual and constituted only a small part of the NGOs' activities (Anderson 2009b; Tallontire 2000). Moreover, the producers whose products were sold, were not necessarily those who were basically supported by the NGOs (Gendron, Palma Torres, and Bisaillon 2009). Finally, contrary to a common view on these initiatives as being noncommercial and partnership based, Anderson (2009b) emphasizes how Oxfam UK and other pioneers organized such trading in order to generate profits and thus revenues for the developmental activities.

According to Anderson (2009b), it is only in the 1970s that fair trading partnerships were set up as a model with explicit rules and that organizations were created specifically for this purpose. These organizations were called alternative trading organizations (ATOs), "a name stemming from the early days of Fair Trade where 'fair' seemed too weak a description of the vision that these companies had" (Moore 2004, 76). Products were sold through worldshops and volunteer-based networks. After two decades of practice and rule-setting, a first step[2] of institutionalization and consolidation was achieved in the late 1980s with the creation of several international networks (Diaz Pedregal 2007; Moore 2004; Crowell and Reed 2009; Raynolds and Long 2007). In Europe, the largest FT pioneers (CTM in Italy, Gepa in Germany, Oxfam in the UK and in Belgium, etc.) joined together in the European Fair Trade Association (EFTA) in 1987. Two years later, the International Federation for Alternative Trade[3] was launched; it gathered producer organizations, importers, and worldshops in a worldwide network. The international networks formalized the practices of the ATOs, which had been active for several years or decades.

It was during that same period that labeling initiatives appeared, starting in the late 1980s with "Max Havelaar"[4] in the Netherlands. This label emerged from the joined efforts of a Dutch priest involved in a Mexican coffee cooperative (UCIRI) and Dutch NGOs (Roozen and van der Hoff 2001). Standards were set up and implemented through different national initiatives. These initiatives joined together into Fairtrade Labeling Organizations International (FLO or FLO-I), now Fairtrade International, in 1997. Most academics and practitioners agree that the emergence of certification[5] brought a fundamental change in the evolution of FT (Moore, Gibbon, and Slack 2006; Reed 2009; Raynolds and Long 2007). Indeed, the possibility of having products recognized as meeting the FT standards by an external certifying body and not by the importer (or distributor) itself, as was the case previously with ATOs, opened the door of the FT sector to any type of company. Mainstream businesses, including supermarkets and food multinationals, started selling FT products. This resulted in a huge increase in the volume of FT sales but also in debates about the possible "dilution" or "capture" of FT. Much of the literature on FT has been analyzing the consequences of mainstreaming on the FT movement

(Moore, Gibbon, and Slack 2006; Nicholls and Opal 2005; Raynolds and Wilkinson 2007; Jaffee 2010).

The formalization of the international networks and the emergence of labeling constituted two steps of institutionalization during the late 1980s, period that can thus be seen as a crucial momentum in the FT movement (e.g., Reed 2009; Raynolds and Long 2007; Gendron, Bisaillon, and Rance 2009). Following the distinction relayed by Gendron and her colleagues (2009), while the first institutionalization step was a rather political one, the second step was closer to an economic one. This concretized into two distribution strategies: the historical, alternative one, consisting of worldshops and volunteer networks; and the mainstream one, consisting of supermarkets and other nonspecialized shops. It is common in the practice[6] and in the FT literature to divide the movement into two main spheres according to these two distribution strategies (e.g., Renard 2003; Gendron 2004b; Moore 2004; Nicholls and Opal 2005; Raynolds, Murray, and Wilkinson 2007).

The first sphere, integrated FT, is mainly composed of craft producers and importers, and is often associated with a radical or political vision of FT, embodied by a large part of the pioneers grouped in the WFTO network as well as in other local networks of worldshops (e.g., NEWS: Network of European World Shops), importing FTSEs (e.g., EFTA in Europe) and WFTO-member producer organizations (COFTA in Africa, IFAT-LA in Latin America, AFTF in Asia) (e.g., Raynolds and Long 2007; LeClair 2002; Renard 2003; Gendron 2004a). WFTO differentiates itself from the Fairtrade labeling model in various aspects. First, it boasts its membership, the majority of which is composed of producers, and its democratic functioning, to claim a stronger representation and thus legitimacy (Raynolds and Long 2007). Second, it has developed a more demanding definition of FT, based on a trust relationship rather than on standardized control (e.g., Wilkinson 2007). Such differentiation has translated into the development, in 2004, of its own certification scheme, namely the Fair Trade Organization Mark. The FTO Mark applies to organizations rather than products and aims to help consumers and FT supporters identify the "*true* Fair Trade organizations,"[7] 100% dedicated to FT and complying with standards that include fairness within the organization (e.g., democratic decision-making) and involvement in education and advocacy.

The second sphere, certified FT, mainly deals with food products[8] and is associated with a more commercial or pragmatic vision of FT (e.g., Diaz Pedregal 2007; Gendron, Bisaillon, and Rance 2009; Renard 2003). The focus here is on expanding the FT market as the main strategy to improve the producers' livelihoods. The rise and legitimacy of the labeling sphere is linked to several factors. Crowell and Reed (2009) point out that several NGOs and FTSEs have supported the development of labeling and mainstreaming, beyond labelers themselves. Moreover, it is often suggested that most producer organizations have welcomed positively the perspective of reaching the mainstream and thereby increasing their production volumes.

Although producers' visions are far from homogeneous (Poncelet, Defourny, and De Pelsmacker 2005; Lemay 2007), the latter's assumed positive attitude toward mainstreaming is a key argument put forth by labelers and stakeholders to justify mainstreaming (Low and Davenport 2005b).

Despite their diverging orientations, these two spheres and visions of FT dialogue with each other at the institutional level through FINE.[9] The goal of FINE is to maintain a minimal consensus around FT principles and orientations. For that purpose, a common definition was established in 1999, revised in 2001 and completed by a charter of FT principles in 2009 (see next section). Beyond the definition of FT, a major issue for the four international networks constituting FINE is advocacy. In order to coordinate the advocacy activities, particularly toward the European Union, FINE created the Fair Trade Advocacy Office (FTAO)[10] in Brussels in 2004.

While this dual picture of FT is useful insofar as it explicitly reveals the fundamental tension in the FT movement (e.g., Wilkinson 2007), it has become insufficient to capture the whole diversity and complexity of the current FT landscape (Özçağlar-Toulouse et al. 2010). Certain authors call for a reconciliation of the two spheres (e.g., Gendron, Bisaillon, and Rance 2009; Nicholls 2010). As Wilkinson states (2007, 220), "[i]n spite of the more obvious tensions, there are also unexpected synergies and, it is, precisely, the multifaceted nature of the movement that has accounted for its success to date." Furthermore, recent work also brings nuances to the distinction between the two spheres, observing that several organizations and supply chains are based on both distribution strategies (Wilkinson 2007; Ballet and Carimentrand 2008). For instance, Traidcraft in the UK or Oxfam Fairtrade in Belgium sell their products—some of which are labeled, and others not—both through specialized channels (worldshops, catalogs, etc.) and through supermarkets. In the same way, some businesses launched by pioneer FTSEs themselves, such as Cafédirect or Divine Chocolate, have a strong positioning in the mainstream market while at the same time being WFTO members and being partially owned by FT pioneers as well as by producer organizations (Davies and Crane 2003; Doherty and Tranchell 2007).

The distinction between the two spheres seems even less adequate when considering the local level (Özçağlar-Toulouse et al. 2010; Sarrazin-Biteye 2009). In many places, new FT-focused businesses are emerging, selling nonlabeled FT products through a variety of channels, both mainstream (e.g., B2B sales) and specialized. In recent years, many small businesses have engaged in a "100% FT" practice[11] without belonging to one of the traditional FT systems (Özçağlar-Toulouse et al. 2010): they constitute what some have started calling a third wave or third institutionalization of FT, after the foundation of FT by pioneers (first wave) and the certification-mainstreaming process (second wave) (Poos 2008). These new companies have often established links with other FTSEs leading to the emergence of local "bottom-up" networks that cannot be captured through the classical distinction in terms of affiliation to a particular sphere. Before further exploring the current organizational landscape, the next section defines and analyzes the concept of FT as well as that of FTSE.

## FAIR TRADE AND ITS PARTICIPANTS

### Fair Trade as a Hybrid Concept

The definition developed by FINE, which is based on a consensus among several FT networks, is the one that is most commonly used in practice and in the academic literature (e.g., Moore 2004):

> *Fair Trade is a trading partnership, based on dialogue, transparency and respect, that seeks greater equity in international trade. It contributes to sustainable development by offering better trading conditions to, and securing the rights of, marginalised producers and workers—especially in the South. Fair Trade organizations (backed by consumers) are engaged actively in supporting producers, awareness raising and in campaigning for changes in the rules and practice of conventional international trade.*

A first draft of this definition was written in 1999. It focused on producers (not on workers) and insisted on FT as being an alternative to conventional trade. The evolution of the definition toward a less radical standpoint has been seen by some as an adaptation of FT "aimed at making it more palatable to corporations" (Crowell and Reed 2009, 148). In 2009, FLO and the WFTO completed the definition of FT thanks to a common charter of Fair Trade principles.[12] The goal was to be more explicit about the implementation of FT through the two types of distribution strategies embodied by the two networks. Besides the statement of a common vision of FT and a comparison with the ILO standards,[13] five core principles were identified and detailed: market access for marginalized producers, sustainable and equitable trading relationships, capacity building and empowerment, consumer awareness raising and advocacy, and long-term commitment "in the context of a social construct" (as stated in the charter).

Since the FINE definition and the charter of principles result from compromises among different approaches to FT, they remain relatively general, allowing for a wide range of interpretations and practices. What clearly appears in these definitions is that FT is an innovative and highly hybrid concept[14], which is made of paradoxes (e.g., Renard 2003; Schümperli Younossian 2006). The study of these paradoxes, which will further be examined here at the organizational level, first requires to define more precisely the different dimensions of FT and the elements that they entail. Among the various possible categorizations, three dimensions are identified here: producer support (the ultimate goal); trade (the means to achieve this goal); and education, regulation, and advocacy (the actions to scale up the initiative and influence the broader context).[15]

### Producer Support

FT aims to practice trade under conditions that are "fair" for producers, in order to support them beyond what they would obtain from a traditional trading exchange. These conditions constitute the core of the FT concept: fair price, social premium, pre-financing, provision of market access, long-term relationship, and so on (Raynolds and Wilkinson 2007; Moore 2004; Nicholls and Opal 2005). Such tools are supposed to orient the trading relationship in a way that genuinely improves the livelihoods of the producers in the South. The content and the impact of producer support may, however, vary across FTSEs, even when a label aims to homogenize practices.[16]

The ambition of fairness in FT partnerships can be considered as a social dimension, and more precisely as the heart of FT as a social innovation. "Social" means that FT aims to serve a specific category of people considered as disadvantaged.[17] In other words, an FTSE aims, at least as one of its goals, to provide benefits to people who would normally not—or only to a very small extent—enjoy the fruits of equitable trading partnerships. The idea of improving the livelihoods of certain producers in the South is central to FT, and FTSEs' practices and decisions are often justified in the light of this central goal (Davies and Crane 2003). It is mainly through their social mission that FTSEs distinguish themselves from traditional businesses. The importance of producer support does not mean that this is the only social dimension of FT. For instance, FTSEs may seek to provide employment to low-skilled people or to provide ethical products to poor consumers in the North. But producers in the South are generally the primary declared beneficiaries of FTSEs' activities. Specific to FT, compared to development projects, is the idea of pursuing the social aim through an economic partnership with these producers.[18]

### Trade

Trade refers to all the market activities (import, transformation, distribution), which are similar to those carried out by any company. Albeit "fair," FTSEs are running trade and using market mechanisms: FT as a whole relies on the market to achieve its social goals (Nicholls and Opal 2005). The positioning of trade within the overall strategy of FTSEs, however, can vary on a continuum between "trade as a means" and "trade as a goal" (Gendron 2004b).

Such a trading activity can be described as the economic dimension of FT. It is often used to distinguish FT from traditional charity or development cooperation initiatives. There may be confusion, however, on the term "economic." Indeed, in the broad sense, "economic" refers to the production of goods and services, which does not necessarily take the form of trading on the market. In a more restricted sense, "economic" may mean "market-oriented." Nicholls and Cho (2006) suggest a number of concrete elements to characterize market orientation: risk-taking, cost recovery, efficient deployment of resources, strategic operations, and so on. The importance of the market in the discourse and practice of FT has strongly increased in recent years, which has resulted in vivid debates about the relationships of FT actors with mainstream market players (Renard 2003; Gendron 2004b; Raynolds, Murray, and Wilkinson 2007).

Although both the "fairness" and "trade" dimensions are intertwined in the practice of partnerships with producers in the South, they may be distinguished from a conceptual point of view. This dual nature is observed by most authors who have studied the FT movement, albeit with various foci and names.[19] As we will see further, the combination of economic and social dimensions also lies at the heart of other movements or concepts. It is suggested here, however, that these two dimensions are not sufficient to fully describe the scope of the FT concept and practice. Indeed, they leave aside the ambition of acting for a fairer world beyond the specific partnerships with FT producers. Such ambition can be viewed as the political dimension of FT and finds concrete expressions through education, regulation, and advocacy.

### Education, Regulation, and Advocacy

At the origins of FT, there is the intent of creating a new regulation framework for commercial exchanges. The creation of such a framework, its continuous adaptation, and its promotion in front of national and international public authorities is a fundamental element of FT that falls under the term of "regulation," i.e., using FT as a new governance system for international trade (Gendron, Palma Torres, and Bisaillon 2009; Renard 2005; Macdonald and Marshall 2010).

Closely linked to regulation is the advocacy work undertaken by FTSEs, networks, and support structures. This action is aimed not only at public authorities but also at corporations. It may be the denunciation of unethical trading practices and rules, and/or the promotion of FT as a source of inspiration to raise the global ethical standards. Education is slightly different from—although closely linked to—advocacy in the sense that it aims the people (citizens/consumers). Education campaigns are intended to change consumption habits toward FT and, more generally, toward more respect for people and for the environment. They are different from marketing campaigns if they do not aim to promote one organization's specific products but rather to foster change in consumers' overall behavior. Education, regulation, and advocacy mainly have a political focus: the purpose here is not so much to support particular producer communities, but to influence the broader economic system. It is in fact the translation of the "fairness" dimension at the macro-level, with the goal of transforming the context of international trade by scaling up the FT principles.

Naming this the "political" dimension follows authors such as Laville and Eme (2003, 1994), themselves drawing on Polanyi (1944) and Mauss (1950). While these authors' approach to the political dimension in the context of the "solidarity economy" will be detailed further in this chapter, it should be mentioned that "political" will be used here to refer to the ambition of societal change inherent in FT. The "political" goals and activities are those that explicitly aim to change the society by influencing consumption habits and making international trading rules and practices more favorable for small-scale producers in the South. These goals and activities may take three inter-related forms: educating and informing citizens about the context, rules, and consequences of international trade and the economic system in general; lobbying public and private institutions and advocating for fairer trade (either directly or indirectly; e.g., through campaigns, writing, conferences, etc.); and participating in the formulation of new rules for trading relationships (in the context of FT but also aimed at other economic and political actors).

### Synthesis

The three dimensions can be viewed as the three edges of a triangle (see Figure 1.1).

Three observations should be made about the distinction and characterization of these dimensions. The first is that each of the dimensions is ambivalent: there is no single way of conceiving and applying the economic, social, and political dimensions. Different organizations may, for instance, develop political visions that are totally incompatible. The remainder of

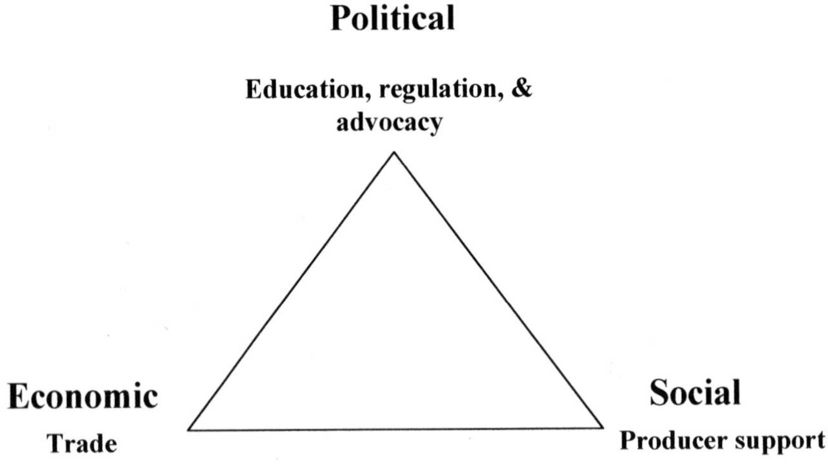

*Figure 1.1*   The FT triangle.

this work will try to take such ambivalence into account (see, e.g., Nicholls and Cho's discussion of the social mission later in this chapter). The second observation is that FT hierarchizes these three dimensions. In particular, the economic *activity* is presented as a tool to serve the social *goal*. The term "dimension" is purposively chosen here to avoid hierarchies and keep these elements as neutral as possible. Indeed, from a critical perspective, partnerships with producers, for instance, could in some cases be seen as tools to serve economic or political goals. Third, it should be noted that these three dimensions are difficult to distinguish from each other in practice. As previously mentioned in this chapter, most FT authors would, indeed, describe the pragmatist vision of FT as one that emphasizes the extension of the economic activity as a vehicle to pursue the social mission, and the radical vision as one that submits the economic activity to social goals and to a broader political project. Instead, this work focuses on the micro, organizational level, rather than the macro, field perspective. In other words, individual FTSEs should not be considered based only on their "affiliation" in terms of international networks or on their distribution strategies. This work rather follows Gendron, Palma Torres, and Bisaillon (2009, 190, author's translation) who suggest that "Fair Trade is translated into chains, structures and organizations that are far more numerous and varied than what a simplistic analysis [ . . . ] restricted to the sole labels [and networks] grouped within FINE might suggest." Rather than restricting FT to its most institutionalized components, it is preferable to "recognize the plurality of practices likely to underlie the Fair Trade project in the context of a dialogue between pioneer and newcomer organizations" (Gendron, Palma Torres, and Bisaillon 2009, 191, author's translation; see also Sarrazin-Biteye 2009).

This requires deconstructing FT into its elementary building blocks, to see how individual FTSEs reassemble these blocks through their organizational model and practices. Considering these dimensions as necessarily intertwined and complementary would, furthermore, neglect both the fundamental tensions that may appear among them and the differences among FTSEs in the way in which they balance and combine them. Several authors identify FT as being simultaneously "in the market" and to a certain extent "against the market" (Renard 2003; Le Velly 2004; Fridell 2003). This inevitably leads to a tension in the sense that FTSEs wish to use market mechanisms as a tool to increase their social impact, but at the same time promote a political project that questions the functioning of the market. While this and other tensions have been at the center of numerous analyses of FT (Bisaillon, Gendron, and Turcotte 2005b; Schümperli Younossian 2006; Haynes 2006), a key question that has only little be examined is the way in which the three dimensions and their inherent tensions are managed *within each individual FTSE*. In order to focus on the organizational level, it is important to first define what types of organizations can be referred to as FTSEs.

## FAIR TRADE SOCIAL ENTERPRISES

Originally, as previously mentioned, pioneer FTSEs were referred to as "alternative trading organizations." This term, however, is used less and less, simply because the term "alternative trade" has been replaced by that of "fair trade." Moreover, many organizations that recognized themselves as such (including, in Europe, most of the historical importers members of EFTA) have become less "alternative." The frontiers between "ATOs" and "businesses" and the historical distribution of roles between import (ATOs) and distribution (worldshops) have also become increasingly blurred.

Whatever the name, several authors find it useful to distinguish 100% FT companies from corporations involved only to some extent in FT (Reed et al. 2010; Nicholls and Opal 2005; Raynolds and Long 2007). A first criterion is the focus on FT as a "100% commitment." Such a commitment is central in the previously mentioned WFTO definition. The Charter of FT Principles also defines FTSEs as "organizations of which Fair Trade is part of their mission and constitutes the core of their objectives and activities." Reed and his colleagues (2010) distinguish four types of "FT businesses": "FT co-operatives (including buyer and worker coops), FT social enterprises (established by NGOs as not-for-profit businesses to promote FT), FT social entrepreneurs (who have set up their own SMEs with the purpose of promoting FT) and mixed FT enterprises (with ownership by a group of businesses dedicated to promoting FT)" (155).

These authors propose a second discriminating element: FTSEs (or ATOs) are engaged in education and advocacy. This might be linked to the FINE definition, which ends by stating: "Fair Trade organizations (backed by consumers) are engaged actively in supporting producers, awareness raising and in campaigning for changes in the rules and practice of conventional international trade." But this definition of FTSEs insists *only* on education and advocacy, thereby referring to the whole range of structures supporting FT (networks, NGOs, labelers, etc.) rather than to the organizations and businesses engaged in a trading activity. On the contrary, the World Fair Trade Organization (WFTO) defines FTSEs as "organizations directly engaged in Fair Trade through their trading activity."[20] As involvement in education and advocacy may take many forms and include organizations supporting FT but not directly dealing with FT products, it seems more logical to apply the "100% FT" commitment to the trading activity when defining FTSEs.

Both Nicholls and Opal (2005), and Reed et al. (2010), each propose a third criterion, but not the same one. The former consider that, if a label exists for the products, the organization should have it on its products. The latter suggest that FT businesses are characterized by personal relationships with the producers. These two criteria are not unambiguous. The first one leaves aside the organizations that, for financial or ideological reasons, have no labels on their products. In France, for instance, certain

FT shops consider that the Fairtrade label offers an insufficient ethical guarantee and prefer not to use it. In Italy, most of the products (including food) sold by the pioneer FTSEs are not labeled. Without judging the adequacy of bearing a label or not, it should be acknowledged that labeling is a highly political process, entailing normative issues which may be a weak basis to discriminate between FTSEs. Second, while the criterion of a personal relationship with producers proposed by Reed and his colleagues is interesting, the notion of personal relationship is, again, subject to debate. Indeed, large FTSEs that have partnerships with a high number of producer groups do not always have direct and regular personal relationships with these groups, either because of time constraints, or because the FTSEs rely on intermediate structures (other FTSEs, corporations, NGOs, local networks, etc.).

It is suggested here that the "100% FT" commitment seems the most solid criterion to identify FTSEs. "Fair Trade" is considered here as involving a trading activity, at one or several steps of the FT supply chain: import, transformation, wholesale, retail and/or labeling/certification. Previously mentioned definitions speak of FT organizations, which is a neutral term but may refer to actors not necessarily dealing with FT products. Reed et al. (2010) describe trading organizations as FT *businesses*. Davies and Crane (2003) speak of FT *companies*. Following Doherty and Tranchell (2007), this book uses the term FT *social enterprises*, precisely to highlight the hybrid nature of these organizations, as will be justified further in this chapter.

## FAIR TRADE IN A BROADER CONTEXT

FT is certainly not the first concept trying to reconcile economic activity, social purpose, and political involvement. FT can be seen as one of the latest of a series of ideas and experiments that stem back to the origins of humanity. It is important, thus, to place FT (and FTSEs) in a broader context, linking it to the concepts and initiatives that have inspired it. It is impossible, however, to mention all these initiatives, such as previous versions of FT known as charitable and solidarity trade (Gendron, Bisaillon, and Rance 2009; Low and Davenport 2005a). Nor will FT be compared with more general trends such as sustainable development (e.g., Bisaillon, Gendron, and Turcotte 2005a; Le Velly 2009) or corporate social responsibility (CSR) (e.g., Bezençon and Blili 2009; Low and Davenport 2005b)—this lies beyond the scope of this book. The focus will be laid on notions and movements that have proposed innovative organizational models and practices to combine hybrid dimensions. Among these, four notions to which FT can be affiliated will be explored here: the cooperative movement, the social economy, the solidarity economy, and social enterprise/social entrepreneurship. These are partly overlapping concepts and movements, which have influenced each other, while also influencing—and, in turn, being influenced by—the emergence and development of the FT movement.

## Cooperative Movement

### Definition and Principles

A cooperative is defined by the International Cooperative Alliance[21] as "an autonomous association of persons united voluntarily to meet their common economic, social, and cultural needs and aspirations through a jointly-owned and democratically-controlled enterprise." The origins of the cooperative movement date back to the nineteenth century, with thinkers such as Robert Owen and pioneering initiatives such as the Rochdale Society of Equitable Pioneers, founded in 1844.

From an economic standpoint, cooperatives are economic organizations owned by their "users" (e.g., Hansmann 1999; Platteau 1987; Levi 2005). For instance, consumer cooperatives differ from mainstream shops in that the consumers are also the owners. However, unlike shareholders in a traditional business, members of a cooperative do not enjoy an unlimited profit distribution and have a voting power not linked to the shares they hold— most cooperatives apply the "one member, one vote" principle (ICA 1996). From a socio-political standpoint, cooperatives have joined into a social movement that has historically aimed to challenge the dominant capitalist logics (for recent analyses, see, e.g.,Schneiberg, King, and Smith 2008; Reed and McMurtry 2009; Birchall 1997).

### Fair Trade and Cooperatives

Several principles of FT (fair price, economic democracy, suppression of intermediates, etc.) have been directly inspired by the cooperative principles (Gendron, Bisaillon, and Rance 2009). The term "Fair Trade" was even used to describe the trading relationships among cooperatives since the nineteenth century (Develtere and Pollet 2005; Anderson 2009a). Crowell and Reed (2009) see FT as a model for international cooperation among cooperatives. Develtere and Pollet (2005) identify a number of convergences between FT and the cooperative movement, *inter alia*:

- both notions were initially conceived as alternatives to the dominant capitalist model, while at the same time being integrated in the market;
- equitable income is central in both concepts;
- in both cases, the economic activity serves—or at least coexists with— social and political purposes; both cooperatives and FTSEs try to balance ethical standards, on the one hand, and survival in a competitive market environment, on the other.

However, several differences can be observed between the FT and cooperative movements. FTSEs necessarily operate in an international context, while cooperatives may be active at the local and/or at the international level. Moreover, while FT mainly locates fairness at the level of the producers in the South and not necessarily within FTSEs, cooperative principles are mainly applied to the members within the organizations and not necessarily at the suppliers' level (except in producer cooperatives where the members *are* the suppliers).

In practice, the FT movement includes numerous cooperatives (Develtere and Pollet 2005; Anderson 2009a; Crowell and Reed 2009). In the South, historically, producer ownership often implied the cooperative model for producer groups, although this requirement was gradually relaxed. The centrality of cooperatives particularly decreased since the certification of plantations—i.e., not producer-owned companies—as producing partners (Crowell and Reed 2009). In the North, the cooperative form was chosen by several FTSEs, especially in the 1980s and 1990s (Crowell and Reed 2009), as will be described further.

The promotion of the cooperative form obviously has a political content. As in the case of FT, there is the intent of scaling up the cooperative idea and having its values pervade the traditional business world. Concretely, the cooperative principles focus on educating members to the cooperative ideal and on empowering them. Nevertheless, in many countries, the evolution of cooperatives toward a stronger business focus has seemed to dilute some of the political and educational dynamics (e.g., Monaci and Caselli 2005). Certain cooperatives have become very business-like, while others have been bought over by business corporations (e.g., in the retail and banking sectors). Yet, some authors suggest that, even in these cases, the cooperative form still constitutes an alternative to the dominant capitalist model (Reed and McMurtry 2009), especially when the business is backed by a citizen movement (Vienney 1997). The commercial evolution of FT might be seen as similar to what happened for cooperatives, in that the challenges of maintaining the original features of the concept and the debates that have opposed radical and pragmatist streams of actors, are quite similar. Such debates will also be commented upon in subsequent sections on the social and solidarity economy. In conclusion, the FT and cooperative movements have much in common, both conceptually and in practice. Nevertheless, FT is more than just a re-actualization of the cooperative idea. It integrated itself in and was inspired by other movements seeking to ally economic activity and social and/or societal goals without necessarily focusing only on one particular organizational form.

## The Social Economy

### Definition and Principles

The social economy has been partly inspired by the cooperative movement, which constitutes one of its major components (Defourny and Develtere

1999). Another major component is that of nonprofit organizations, around which a whole stream of literature has emerged, particularly in the US (for a literature review, see, e.g., Anheier 2005; Steinberg 2006). The social economy refers to a wider range of organizations, located between the public sector and the for-profit business sector. Characteristic of a social economy organization is "to provide services to its members or to a wider community, and not serve as a tool in the service of capital investment [ . . . ]. The generation of a surplus is therefore a means to providing a service, not the main driving force behind the economic activity" (Defourny, Develtere, and Fonteneau 2000, 16). It is possible to define the social economy through a legal/institutional approach, including all the organizations with an associative, cooperative, or mutual form,[22] and through a normative approach, emphasising the values common to these organizations (Defourny and Develtere 1999; Defourny 2001). One example of a definition combining both approaches is the one co-constructed by academics, field operators and the government in the Walloon region (CWES 1990, cited in Defourny and Develtere 1999):

*The social economy is composed of associations, cooperatives and mutuals whose activities are guided by the following principles:*

- *placing service to its members or to the community ahead of profit;*
- *autonomous management;*
- *a democratic decision-making process;*
- *the primacy of people and work over capital in the distribution of revenues.*

The Charter of Principles of the Social Economy promoted by the European Standing Conference on Cooperatives, Mutual Societies, Associations and Foundations (CEP-CMAF) extends this definition by adding an emphasis on solidarity and sustainable development as guiding values (Chavez and Monzón Campos 2007).

There seems to be a broad consensus on the general meaning of the social economy in the countries and regions where the term is used, i.e., in Latin Europe, Scandinavia, Canada, the UK, and many other parts of the world (Chavez and Monzón Campos 2007; Defourny and Develtere 1999). When it comes to circumscribing the field of the social economy, however, there are diverging interpretations. We can particularly highlight the distinction between one broad and several narrower views of the social economy. In a broad perspective, the social economy is referred to as the "third sector" that is located between the state and the private for-profit world (Anheier and Seibel 1990; Defourny and Monzón Campos 1992). This third sector encompasses a broad range of organizations, including all types of nonprofit organizations (nonprofit hospitals, schools, museums, sport clubs, NGOs, etc.), cooperatives, mutuals and foundations. Although these organizations do not necessarily recognize themselves as social economy organizations (but rather, e.g., as a "hospital" or a "museum"), they share the four previously mentioned criteria in common.

In a narrow sense, however, the social economy is sometimes restricted to a range of sectors in which the organizations generally do recognize themselves as belonging to the social economy. In such a context, the term "social economy" is used to designate the nonprofit, cooperative and mutual organizations engaged in a commercial, market-based activity ("economy" being restricted to the production of goods and services that can be exchanged on the market). Chavez and Monzón (2007) refer to this as the "market or business sub-sector of the social economy." Market-oriented actors often share this narrower view and are reluctant to be included in the same category as nonmarket organizations such as NGOs and social action associations, but the narrowing may also be caused or reinforced by public authorities. It is striking to observe how the definition of the social economy differs according to the specific attributions and philosophy of the politicians who wish to support it. In Belgium, for instance, the Walloon minister of economy has long supported only social economy initiatives with a commercial content.[23] In Flanders, the social economy has traditionally been restricted to the integration of handicapped or low-skilled people. Such a focus on work integration also characterized the financial support brought to the social economy by the European Union, typically in the context of the EQUAL program. In other cases, though, public support or recognition embraced the larger view of the social economy.[24]

*Fair Trade and the Social Economy*

In both the broad and the narrow view, FT can be linked to the social economy "through the nature and the goals of the main organizations that have launched it" (Gendron, Palma Torres, and Bisaillon 2009, 128, author's translation). Reed and his colleagues (2010) consider that organizations totally devoted to FT and engaged in advocacy are necessarily social economy organizations. FT is regularly presented as one of the social economy fields of activities, among others such as recycling, work integration, microfinance, and so on.[25] With the growing success of FT and the need to establish partnerships among movements with similar aims, social economy networks have been increasing their efforts to collaborate with FTSEs and to promote the link between the two concepts. This is especially observed, for instance, in French-speaking Belgium and Canada, through, respectively, the networks Solidarité des Alternatives Wallonnes et Bruxelloises (SAW-B)[26] and Chantier de l'économie sociale.[27] However, little work examines the conceptual convergences between the two concepts (attempts can be found, e.g., in Lévesque 2004; Poncelet, Defourny, and De Pelsmacker 2005). As suggested by Gendron and her colleagues (2009, 129, author's translation), "the integration of FT actors in the movement of the social economy is more often an intuitive approximation than the result of an in-depth analysis of the respective natures of FT and the social economy."

The four elements of the definition of the social economy can be applied to the FTSEs in the North.[28] Placing service to the members or the community ahead of profit was central in the initial FT project. The payment of a fair price, completed with a FT premium and prefinancing, can theoretically be seen as a transfer to the producers of the potential profit that would be realized by FTSEs if the products were bought at market prices and conditions. In some cases, however, sales of FT products may allow corporations to increase their profits by capturing ethical consumers, ready to pay a higher price, and making them loyal. In such case, the transfer of value to the producer is exclusively due to the higher prices paid by the consumers, and not to the corporations' commitment to reduce their profits to serve the community (Smith 2010). The social economy legal forms adopted by pioneer FTSEs formally prevented such opportunistic behavior (profit appropriation), although, as will be explained further, other devices than legal forms may fulfil the same safeguarding role.

The second criterion, namely the autonomy of the organizations vis-à-vis other actors, typically the state, seems valid for Northern FTSEs. While states have been increasingly interested in recognizing and promoting FT[29] and have been involved in the creation of certain FTSEs,[30] they are not supposed to control FTSEs.

Third, the democratic decision-making process was a central element in the initial FT project and in the organizational models of pioneer FTSEs, especially through the involvement of volunteers.[31] Again, the participation of corporations, in the context of mainstreaming, and the creation of FTSEs under forms that do not impose democratic decision-making, lessened the importance of economic democracy. While democracy is promoted at the producers' level, it is not a requirement within Northern FTSEs, which are free to integrate or not the principles of FT into their own governance (Gendron, Palma Torres, and Bisaillon 2009; Davies and Crane 2003). At the movement's level, economic democracy has been a driving principle of IFAT/WFTO[32], but it has not always been a priority in FLO (now Fairtrade International), which has led to criticism (González and Doppler 2006; Hutchens 2009).[33]

Finally, the primacy of people and work over capital in the distribution of revenues can be examined in the same way as for the first criterion. The fair price and the other mechanisms inherent in FT precisely aim at giving primacy to producers and to their work in the distribution of revenues. Of course, other intermediates benefit from the revenues of FT according to the type of supply chain, and some of them are remunerating capital over work: transporters, retailers, transformation companies (e.g., chocolate, cosmetics, garments, etc.), and so on. While the FTSEs and the labeling organizations are supposed to guarantee that a significant part of the value is transferred to producers, actual practices are diverse and the interpretation of "primacy" is subjective. At the organizational level, only FTSEs with nonprofit and cooperative forms formally impede giving primacy to the remuneration of capital. But adopting a "business" form does not necessarily mean for FT entrepreneurs to give primacy to capital and expect high profitability, as will be examined in the Chapter 3.

In conclusion, although it is impossible to generalize at this stage, three out of the four principles of the social economy seem applicable to the majority of FTSEs: autonomy, service to the community ahead of profit, and primacy of people and work over capital in the distribution of revenues. These two last criteria may differentiate most FTSEs from traditional businesses. Economic democracy, however, does not seem automatic in all FTSEs, especially the newer ones. The remainder of this work will help to clarify this basic observation. While nonprofit and cooperative forms (juridical/institutional approach) tend to favor the respect of all four principles of the social economy (normative approach), these forms are (1) not an absolute guarantee that the principles are effectively implemented, and (2) not the exclusive depositories of a social economy dynamic. We thus tend to follow Reed and his colleagues (2010) when they suggest that 100% FT organizations are naturally close to the social economy.

## The Solidarity Economy

### *Principles*

The concept of solidarity economy is close to that of social economy but it adopts a slightly different perspective. Rather than considering a number of legal forms and governance principles that put people ahead of profit, the authors of this approach insist on the citizen roots of the economic initiatives and on their political role of democratization (Laville 1994; Eme and Laville 1994; Laville 2003; Evers and Laville 2004). These authors suggest that solidarity organizations reintroduce the political dimension in the very heart of the economic activity. Through the creation of "public spaces" of citizen participation,[34] decision-making in the economic domain is submitted to a political deliberation. Solidarity economy organizations emerge from a "co-construction" of supply and demand. The integration of beneficiaries and other stakeholders in the very design of the production of goods and services is thus particularly central in this approach.

The "embeddedness" of the economic activity in a broader socio-political project exceeding the sole market logic is borrowed from Mauss (1950) and Polanyi (1944), as is the notion of "hybridization" of market, reciprocity, and redistribution logics (Laville 1994). These are three of the economic principles distinguished by Polanyi's economic theory (1944). The market principle "refers to the matching of supply and demand for goods and services with a view to exchange, facilitated by a price-setting mechanism" (Laville and Nyssens 2001, 324). Unlike the two other principles, the market principle is based on contractual relationships and is not necessarily embedded in the social system (Evers and Laville 2004). Redistribution is "the principle on the basis of which the results of production are handed over to a central authority responsible for managing it" (Evers and Laville 2004, 17). Such a central authority is typically the state, but it may also be nonstate institutions (e.g., private foundations). Finally, reciprocity is "an original non-contractual principle of economic action in which the social link is more important than the goods exchanged" (Evers and Laville 2004, 18); it is a specific type of spontaneous giving and counter-giving mechanism constituting "a complex mix of selflessness and self-interest" (Laville and Nyssens 2001, 324).

Polanyi's work is based on a historical perspective. He analysed various combinations of the three logics throughout history, with the market logic, initially confined to specific spheres of economic life, progressively imposing itself upon the other spheres. In the contemporary economy, while the three logics remain present, they have been prioritized in the following way: the market principle is considered as primary, redistribution as supplementary, and reciprocity as residual (Evers and Laville 2004). Solidarity economy initiatives try to reconcile these three principles through an economic activity embedded in logics of reciprocity and redistribution, with a strong emphasis on solidarity and political involvement. For that purpose, these initiatives tend to "hybridize" different goals as well as different resources, from the market (sales), the state (subsidies), and the sphere of reciprocity (through gifts, voluntary work, etc.). In this sense, the solidarity economy is not a clear-cut "sector" but rather a space for hybridizing different economic principles.

Through taking into account the reciprocity principle, rather than only the redistribution and the market principles, when characterising economic organizations with social and political goals, the solidarity economy puts forth a whole range of citizen initiatives that are not—or not properly—covered by the social economy approach. Hybridization is presented as a tool that allows organizations to resist the trends toward institutional isomorphism, i.e, the progressive attraction by and resemblance to one of the three poles, particularly the market and the state. It is through a constant combination of goals and resources that solidarity organizations manage to preserve their uniqueness (Laville and Nyssens 2001; Evers and Laville 2004). Such combination attempts, nevertheless, may involve tensions within and around these organizations (Evers 1995).

## Fair Trade and the Solidarity Economy

FTSEs offer an interesting example of "co-construction" of the supply by diverse "demand-side" stakeholders. We can indeed consider most of FTSE's founders and workers as people who were themselves interested in the provision of FT in its different dimensions: economic (as consumers of FT products), and socio-political (as citizens desiring a fairer trading system). The hybridization of goals and the re-embedding of the economic activity in a wider socio-political project lied at the heart of the initial FT concept (see, e.g., Bisaillon, Gendron, and Turcotte 2005b; Auroi and Yepez del Castillo 2006). The combination of economic, social, and political dimensions is borrowed from the same intuition of re-embedding of the economic activity in a socio-political context.

Nevertheless, the three dimensions identified in this book are slightly different from the three types of economic principles. Indeed, the social dimension of FT, although it relies on certain logics of redistribution, is specific to each partnership and is thus not centralized (only the basic principles are common to all FTSEs). This is thus quite different from the redistributing role of a central authority such as the state, as emphasized in the solidarity economy. Moreover, while certain FTSEs aim to establish a direct relationship of reciprocity between producers and consumers, the FT principles and practices have often tended to describe producers as the beneficiaries of FT, thereby distancing themselves from the principle of reciprocity and from the idea of co-construction of supply and demand. Indeed, despite the close partnerships established between certain FTSEs and producer groups, the FT standards have been designed and monitored in the North, and it is only recently that producers have been associated to a certain extent to the definition and implementation of these standards (Gendron, Palma Torres, and Bisaillon 2009; González and Doppler 2006).[35]

The goal of "political transformation" through public spaces of citizen participation (Laville 2003) is close to the definition of the political dimension of FT. In FT, these public spaces are concretely visible, for instance, through worldshops in which the purchase of FT products takes place within a social relationship between the volunteers and the customers, and within a broader political project. This project partly relies on reciprocity resources, such as voluntary work and donations. The focus on the political role advocated by the supporters of a solidarity economy approach sounds very appealing to the FTSEs with a strong political involvement, especially in France and in Italy, as will be examined later.

Finally, the economic dimension of FT is linked to the market principle. But with the mainstreaming of FT and the increasing importance of market resources for FTSEs, several authors consider that the market principle is gaining dominance over the other principles. Certain of these authors view this as a welcome extension that situates FT "along a continuum from corporate social responsibility to [ ... ] the solidarity economy" (Wilkinson 2007, 220). Others consider that the logic of "re-embedding" of the economic exchange in a socio-political project, as introduced by the initial advocates of FT, is jeopardized by the increasing emphasis on the market as the dominant logic. This translates into giving priority to volume, control and quality of the products at the expense of economic democracy, personal relationships, and political objectives (Bisaillon, Gendron, and Turcotte 2005b; Charlier et al.

2007; Gendron, Palma Torres, and Bisaillon 2009). This view is shared by some politically involved FTSEs, which find in the concept of the solidarity economy a way to distinguish themselves from market-oriented FTSEs and mainstream companies, all of which are seen as contributing to the "disembedding" of FT from its political and social background (e. g., Minga 2005).

## Social Enterprise, Social Entrepreneurship, and Social Innovation

Recently and increasingly associated with FT is a set of interrelated notions that still lack solid ground: social enterprise (Huybrechts and Defourny 2008; Doherty and Tranchell 2007), social entrepreneurship (Nicholls 2006; Hervieux 2008), and social innovation (Phills, Deiglmeier, and Miller 2008; Mulgan et al. 2007). These different terms are often mixed in the literature. At first sight, they might simply refer to different levels of analysis: individuals (social entrepreneurs), organizations (social enterprises), processes (social entrepreneurship), and outcomes (social innovation). Put simply, "social entrepreneurship" would be the dynamic process through which specifics type of individuals deserving the name of "social entrepreneurs" create and develop organizations that may be defined as "social enterprises" in order to produce a set of outcomes defined as "social innovation" (Mair and Marti 2006; Defourny and Nyssens 2008b). However, the use of one term or the other is often linked to a different focus and/or understanding of the phenomenon. As the most encompassing notion, social innovation can be found in any sector (public, private for profit, nonprofit, etc.) and may refer to both outcomes and processes (Phills, Deiglmeier, and Miller 2008; Mulgan et al. 2007). Social entrepreneurship then restricts social innovation to those initiatives undertaken in an entrepreneurial, market-oriented way. These initiatives include but are not limited to social enterprises (Nicholls 2006; Thompson 2008), as social entrepreneurs can also be found in "for-profit" businesses (Austin and Reficco 2005).

This book does not have the ambition to clarify all the debates around these terms and the definitions they encompass. The idea is to use the notions that seem most useful in this context. As this book is about the *organizations* involved in FT, the term social enterprise will be used in priority, as well as the literature relating to the organizational level. But as the organizations are means rather than ends, and as the idea here is to look at how the different FTSEs innovate in their practice of FT, social innovation will also have a central place, in terms of both process and outcomes.

The literature relating to these notions is recent and heterogeneous. It has evolved in different ways, with, on the one hand, a first stream mainly based in North America[36], and on the other hand, a stream based in continental Europe and represented by the EMES network (Kerlin 2006; Defourny and Nyssens 2008a; Kerlin 2008). It seems that the former have rather used the perspective of *social entrepreneurship*, despite several exceptions[37], while the latter have mainly developed an organizational analysis of *social enterprises*. Although the two schools have initially developed separately, bridges have recently been established, revealing more convergences than what might have been expected (Defourny and Nyssens 2008a).

## North American Literature

Within the North American literature, Dees and Battle Anderson (2006) propose to distinguish two schools of thought. The first one focuses on earned income strategies developed to support the organization's social mission. Dees and Battle Anderson call it—although reluctantly[38]—the "Social Enterprise" school. At its origins, the focus was on nonprofit organizations increasingly looking for new resources from the market and seeking to adopt more efficient and market-oriented behavior (Skloot 1987; Emerson and Twersky 1996). Later, as for-profit companies were increasingly including social purposes in their basically economic missions, they were also integrated in this approach. Social enterprises are thus seen as emerging either from the social or from the business sectors. The boundaries between these sectors are described as increasingly blurring. Central to social enterprises in this approach is the idea of using the market and generating one's own incomes to achieve sustainability and thus pursue the social mission more effectively.

The second school of thought, called the "Social Innovation" school, is based on the theories of entrepreneurship (mainly Schumpeter, but also Drucker) and focuses on innovation rather than on income generation. Dees and Battle Anderson (2006, 45) state this as follows: "[t]he use of the term 'social entrepreneurs' to describe innovators pursuing social change helped to reinforce the idea that social entrepreneurship needs not to be framed in terms of income. It could be more about outcomes, about social change." Battle Anderson and Dees (2006) are particularly critical about the links made in the previous school of thought between market incomes and efficiency. The focus on outcomes rather than incomes seems to be embraced by various foundations supporting social entrepreneurs (e.g., Ashoka).

Dees and Battle Anderson (2006) point out the convergences between the two schools. Indeed, the first approach they identify is also concerned about innovation and outcomes, while the second is not opposed to incomes exclusively originating from the market: it is rather the idealization of market resources and the idea that such resources necessarily imply independence, self-sufficiency or greater impact that has been criticized (Battle Anderson and Dees 2006). Dees and Battle Anderson (2006) propose to call this intersection "Enterprising Social Innovation," including all the innovative initiatives that seek to create sustainable social change by blending methods from both the business and the social sectors. This intersection is described as the most promising research area.

Several contributions can be located in this intersection, covering both the process of social entrepreneurship and the nature of social enterprises, highlighting both the potential of market incomes and its limits (e.g., Nicholls 2006).

Nicholls and Cho (2006) define social entrepreneurship as composed of three elements: sociality, innovation, and market orientation. The social nature of social entrepreneurship may seem obvious, through "a context, process and/or set of outputs that might reasonably be considered to be in the public benefit" (Nicholls 2010). Nicholls and Cho (2006), however, warn about the often ill-defined and descriptive nature of social change, which may lead to ignoring the heterogeneity of interests and favoring particular social groups at the expense of others. The second element is innovation. Drawing on the Schumpeterian view of innovation, the emphasis is laid on new combinations of goods, services, and organizational forms. Three types of social innovation can be distinguished (Nicholls 2010, 247; Gardner, Acharya, and Yach 2007): "in new product and service development (institutional innovation); in the use of existing goods and services in new—more socially productive—ways (incremental innovation); in reframing normative terms of reference to redefine social problems and suggest new solutions (disruptive innovation)." Finally, market orientation involves a stronger emphasis on competition, performance, rational cost recovery strategies, and accountability. Despite a stronger market orientation, certain authors, nevertheless, suggest that social entrepreneurship re-embeds the economic exchange in its social context, vesting it with "ideas of reciprocity and the public good" (Nicholls 2010), hereby converging partly with the view of the solidarity economy.

### EMES Approach

In Western Europe, the dominant approach to social enterprise is based on the work developed by the EMES Network since the second half of the 1990s (Defourny 2001; Nyssens 2006). EMES defines social enterprises as "not-for-profit private organizations providing goods and services directly related to their explicit aim to benefit the community. They rely on a collective dynamics involving various types of stakeholders in their governing bodies, they place a high value on their autonomy and they bear economic risks linked to their activity" (Defourny and Nyssens 2008b, 5). But more than a definition, the EMES approach aims to provide an "ideal type," i.e., an abstract construction, or a "compass," that "can help anyone to locate the position of the observed entities relative to one another and [ . . . ] to establish the boundaries of the set of organizations that he or she will consider as that of social enterprises" (Defourny and Nyssens 2008b, 5).

The EMES approach sheds light on some features of social enterprises that seem underestimated or ignored by the North American approaches (Defourny and Nyssens 2008a). First of all, based on extensive empirical research carried out across EU countries, EMES authors suggest that most social enterprises do actually belong to the social economy or "third sector." In other words, they are generally nonprofit or cooperative organizations in which profit distribution is limited. This does not mean that traditional business forms are automatically excluded from the social enterprise area, but rather that the primacy of social goals is better guaranteed by legal provisions than by the sole appraisal of managers or owners. Such legal provisions include not only limitations on profit distribution, but also specific governance models oriented toward a participatory management process as well as a democratic decision-making. In this sense, the EMES approach does not entirely subscribe to the idea of increasingly "blurred frontiers" among organizational forms, as suggested by much of the North American literature.

In line with the participatory and democratic nature of social enterprises' governance, the authors of the EMES network observe an increasing involvement of various stakeholders in the decision-making processes, leading to "multi-stakeholder" configuration. Such a configuration is associated with the variety of goals pursued by social enterprises—economic, social, and political—and the variety of resources raised (Campi, Defourny, and Grégoire 2006; Defourny and Nyssens 2006; Petrella 2003). The insistence on the possibility of combining various types of resources—rather than on their sole market origin—contrasts with part of the previously mentioned approaches that focus on the market as the main or even exclusive source of incomes. Finally, the EMES approach converges with the "Social Innovation" school through its shared Schumpeterian view of innovation, although EMES authors have mainly described such innovation at the theoretical level (Defourny 2001).

### Fair Trade and Social Enterprise

FT has not only been cited as an *example* of a successful social innovation (Phills, Deiglmeier, and Miller 2008; Mulgan et al. 2007); the socially innovative processes and outcomes have also been central in several in-depth *analyses* of the FT concept (e.g., Hervieux 2007). At the organizational level, FT businesses have been used from the start as examples of social enterprises and have contributed to the shaping of the social enterprise concept. Such a link has been made in a particularly explicit way in the UK, by both academics (e.g., Nicholls 2006; Doherty and Tranchell 2007) and practitioners[39]. It is worth noting that the Social Enterprise Unit, part of the former Office of the Third Sector of the British government (now Office for Civil Society), proposed a definition that situates social enterprises in the social economy,[40] similar to what is suggested by the EMES approach.

In her taxonomy of social enterprises' "mission and money" models, Alter (2006) describes FTSEs as mission-centric and embedded: the social enterprise is not just a device to raise resources to achieve a distinct social mission, but "the enterprise activities are 'embedded' within the organization's operations and social programmes" (212). FT is described as a typical example enabling the simultaneous pursuit of economic and social benefits. The political dimension of FT, however, finds fewer echoes in the social enterprise approaches.[41] One link, however, may be made with the idea of "systemic change": social enterprises try to scale up their model and influence their broader environment in a sense that fosters global social change (e.g., Grenier 2006; Nicholls and Cho 2006).

A more encompassing analysis is found in Nicholls (2010), who extends Dees and Battle Anderson's (2006) distinction of social entrepreneurship conceptions ("social enterprise" versus "social innovation") to describe FT. He suggests that the first type of social entrepreneurship is useful to characterize FTSEs and corporations that focus on market mechanisms as the main vehicle to develop FT. On the other hand, FTSEs that rather focus on education and advocacy to influence the conventional market are closer to the vision of "social innovation." As others, Nicholls (2010) sees a high potential in the combination of these two types of social entrepreneurship, which might enable "both current exploitation of extant [market] institutions and future reframing of their meaning and functions" (247).

Following Nicholls' analysis and translating it to the organizational level, the diversity of FTSEs, and, more broadly, FT visions, echoes the rich diversity of practices and conceptualizations of social enterprise. Indeed, FTSEs with a nonprofit or cooperative form, a collective dynamic, democratic decision-making and a hybridized resource mix are probably closer to the EMES ideal type, as well as to the "social innovation" school in the North American literature. Conversely, newer FTSEs, which rely exclusively on market resources and strategies to achieve social change, might be better described by the North American "social enterprise" approach. In certain cases of small, entrepreneurial FTSEs, a characterization of the distinctive features of the social entrepreneur may be the most useful perspective. It seems clear that each conception may shed light on a particular dimension of FT, from the more market-based approaches to those that emphasize the socio-political role of social enterprise, from the broad, "blurred boundaries" vision to the more narrow situation of social enterprise in the social economy, and from the entrepreneur-centered conceptualization to those that emphasize the collective, citizen-based and democratic dynamics.

In the meantime, it is useful to highlight a number of features of FT and FTSEs that seem to fit into most of these conceptions:

- The FT concept corresponds well to the general idea of using (and adapting) market mechanisms to pursue a social purpose in an innovative way.
- The apparent diversity of FTSEs' organizational models seems embraced to a certain extent in all the conceptualizations of social

enterprise, even the EMES one, insofar as they are less explicitly limited to one or a few legal forms than, for instance, the cooperative and social economy approaches.

- Most FTSEs seem to rely heavily on market resources, either as the exclusive or as the main source of incomes, and are not averse to risk-taking.
- The development and growth of FT, particularly through labeling and mainstreaming, constitute an illustration of the idea of "scaling up" social innovation to achieve more global social change (e.g., Dees 2001).

## CONCLUSION

In this chapter, FT was analyzed as a hybrid concept entailing an economic, a social, and a political dimension. FT and the organizational avenues to practice it were characterized as socially innovative, in terms of both processes and outcomes. FTSEs were then defined as organizations totally focused on FT in their trading activity.

To introduce the study of FTSEs, four concepts and movements were chosen to highlight the existence of specific, "alternative" *organizational models*. Indeed, whereas several authors examining recent trends in social entrepreneurship stress the importance not to focus too narrowly on specific organizational forms, it is suggested here is that the pursuit of multiple— and sometimes conflicting—dimensions should not be examined regardless of the organizational vehicle used.

Different organizational models are put forth by the different concepts. The cooperative movement is centered on one specific legal form: the cooperative. Two radically distinct features characterize this form. First, the cooperative form gives the ownership to categories of stakeholders other than the shareholders. Second, the formal power (voting right) is distributed equally among the owners (economic democracy). This induces specific challenges in terms of governance, with one or several particular stakeholder categories (customers, producers, employees, etc.) taking part in governance structures such as the General Assembly and the Board of Directors (Cornforth 2004).

The social economy stresses the common features of four "alternative" (noncapitalist) legal forms: nonprofits, cooperatives, mutuals, and foundations. The ideal of economic democracy is also implemented through the "one member, one vote" principle. This raises a number of governance challenges be it in cooperative or in nonprofit organizations (Cornforth and Edwards 1999; Miller-Millesen 2003; Ostrower and Stone 2006).

The authors adopting the solidarity economy approach do not explicitly mention particular legal forms. However, their focus on the citizen roots of solidarity organizations and on the hybrid nature of these organizations' goals and resources lead to favoring "alternative" legal forms with participatory governance models and leaves little room for comparison with the traditional model of mainstream profit-seeking companies (Laville 1994).

The organizational model of social enterprises can be interpreted differently according to the approach chosen. While EMES authors see most social enterprises at the interface between nonprofits and cooperatives (Defourny 2001), others argue that social entrepreneurship may be found in all types of private and public organizations (Austin, Stevenson, and Wei-Skillern 2006; Mair and Noboa 2003). Some suggest, however, that even these authors mainly take nonprofit and cooperative initiatives when giving examples of social enterprises (Weerawardena and Mort 2006; Dart 2004). It is worth noting that the development of the notion of social enterprise has given birth to specific legal forms across Europe, such as the Community Interest Company in the UK, the Social Cooperative in Italy, and the Social Purpose Company in Belgium (see, e.g., Defourny and Nyssens 2008b for other European examples such as France, Denmark, Portugal, etc.). These legal forms hybridize to various extents the legal features of nonprofit, cooperative, and business companies. Still regarding the social enterprise approach, many authors studying these organizations put a strong emphasis on governance features such as multi-stakeholdership and participation (Campi, Defourny, and Grégoire 2006; Malo and Vézina 2004).

The four concepts show some complementarities to describe FT and FTSEs. The width of the largest approaches, such as social enterprise and the social economy, is completed by the depth of narrower ones, such as the solidarity economy and the cooperative movement. The latter bring a historical perspective allowing the concept and mechanisms of FT to be linked to older quests for fairness in and social embeddedness of the economic activity. The social economy approach brings a perspective that emphasizes the role of economic democracy and limited profit distribution in securing the social mission. The solidarity economy approach brings a focus on the political and citizen dimensions of FT and explicitly describes the combination of logics and the possible tensions within organizations. And the social enterprise approach, as the most recent concept, enables to better understand the increasing market orientation that seems to characterize FTSEs, although such an orientation seems to translate into diverse organizational practices and models.

The social enterprise approach seems the one that most broadly embraces the spectrum of organizational models observed in FT. This approach also pays particular attention to the "hybrid" organizational models that cannot be understood properly through extant classifications (Nicholls 2006, 11). To summarize, while the roots of FT may be found in the cooperative, social economy and solidarity-based economy movements, and while certain FTSEs still identify themselves with one or several of them, the current, diversified landscape of FTSEs seems best described by the social enterprise approach, which has precisely been fed by the practice of FTSEs. In any case, the study of the affiliation of FT to other concepts and movements shows that FT should not be studied as a separate and new initiative.

It must be understood as a recent and successful illustration of a much larger and older quest aiming to reconcile the economic activity with social purposes and political involvement. All four concepts contributed to shed light on specific features of organizational models that express such combination and that contrast, although to various extents, with the traditional model of the "for-profit" corporation.

In this context, the next chapter will more concretely present the reality of FTSEs in a comparative international perspective.

# 2 Fair Trade Social Enterprises Worldwide and in Europe

This chapter introduces the reality of FTSEs in the world and then more specifically in four European countries: Belgium, France, the United Kingdom, and Italy. The history and organizational landscape of FT are described in each of the four countries. Then, a few methodological elements are introduced as to how the study feeding this book has been led and which FTSEs have participated in this study, either at the sample level (interviews) or through case studies.

## FTSES IN THE WORLD

Although this book focuses on Europe, FTSEs can be found all over the world. In the South, producer groups can be found in Latin and Central America, in the Caribbean, in Africa and in Asia; whether organized as cooperatives or through other democratic-based models (thus excluding for instance plantations), they can also be considered as Fair Trade social enterprises. They lie, however, beyond the scope of this book. For analyses of the structure, challenges, and impacts of producer FTSEs in the South, an increasing number of case studies and analyses are available (e.g., Hopkins 2000; Ronchi 2000; Utting 2009; Ronchi 2002; Lake and Howe 1998; Jones et al. 2000). It should be noted that a number of countries traditionally linked with the production side of FT have recently engaged into local retailing, thereby fostering ethical consumption in these countries. The most famous example is Mexico—precisely the country where FT production started: local FT retailing has been developed there together with the launch of a producer-owned label, Comercio Justo Mexico (see Renard and Pérez-Grovas 2007). Similar schemes have emerged in Brazil, South Africa, and India, blurring the North-South divide in the FT field.

In the traditional "North," import and distribution FTSEs are mainly active in Europe and in North America, but also in other countries such as Australia, Japan, New Zealand, and Russia. In the latter countries, although FT is growing rapidly, labeled sales are still marginal compared with Europe and the US (FLO-I 2010). The US is, together with the UK, the largest national FT market, with over $1 billion sales and a still impressive growth (FLO-I 2010; Jaffee 2010). Parallel with this huge commercial development, disputes have been intense around the extent and conditions of corporate participation (Jaffee 2010). Jaffee suggests that, while American FTSEs such as Equal Exchange have been instrumental in bringing FT to the forefront of public (and corporate) attention, they have not been much involved in the governance of the FT label (Transfair USA). As a consequence, there has been a disconnection between Transfair, which has developed corporate alliances to increase the FT turnover (e.g., with Starbucks), and pioneer FTSEs, which have advocated to maintain the ethical integrity of the FT standards. The commercial orientation of Transfair (now Fairtrade USA) led it to withdraw from Fairtrade International in 2011, after witnessing diverging visions on producer certification. FT is also very developed in Canada, although the sales per capita are still lower than in most European countries (Krier 2008). FT in Canada has emerged from joined efforts by civil society, regional governments, and academia in the context of promoting the social economy. The largest FTSEs include Equittere, Oxfam Québec, and Equal Exchange (Reed et al. 2010). While corporate participation has been increasing and also contested (Fridell 2009), it does not seem to have marginalized the social movement, which remains involved in the governance of the labeling initiative and still has an instrumental role, together with other social economy actors, in promoting and developing FT (Reed et al. 2010).

The importance of Europe in worldwide FT is not only historical (see Chapter 1) but also factual. On the €3.4 billion labeled sales for FT in the world, nearly three quarters were generated in Europe (€2.5 billion, see FLO-I 2010). To look at the situation of the different European countries, beyond the global sales, the most valuable source resides in the DAWS-FTAO reports compiled by Jean-Marie Krier. The latest report (2008) indicates that FT is growing in most of the European countries. FT initiatives have also emerged in Eastern Europe and in the Mediterranean area (Cyprus, Malta, etc.). As will be discussed further, however, while Krier's reports provide an excellent overview of European FT in terms of labeled sales and main actors, it ignores part of the local dynamics in each country and the smaller or less aligned actors that are not associated with the international FT networks. By providing in-depth studies of four European countries, this book aims to provide a more detailed picture of the landscape and dynamics of FTSEs in particular regional and national settings.

## FOUR EMBLEMATIC EUROPEAN COUNTRIES

In order to reach this goal, the focus was laid on four countries, or more exactly four regions, with a high density of FTSEs: Belgium, the Rhône-Alpes region in France, England, and the Roman area in Italy. These four regions cannot pretend to be representative of the European FT landscape. Important countries such as the Netherlands (where FT certification started) and Switzerland (where market shares are outstanding) are missing. Yet, the four regions include different cultures (Latin and Anglo-Saxon), different histories, and different market configurations (see Huybrechts and Reed 2010). As such, they seem to cover a broad diversity of patterns in terms of FT history, landscape, and market. In terms of organizational models, moreover, the study on the four regions enables to examine a large number of FTSEs representing different ways of practicing FT.

## Belgium[1]

FT in Belgium finds its roots in the experience of Oxfam in the 1960s. Following the international development of the Oxfam Movement after the Second World War, the NGO Oxfam-Belgium was created in 1964. The focus was on famine relief in former colonies, particularly in Africa. The first worldshop (*wereldwinkel*) was opened in 1971 in Antwerp, and several other cities followed. In 1975, the Flemish worldshops formalized into vzw Oxfam-Wereldwinkels (hereafter Oxfam-WW). The French-speaking worldshops launched Magasins-du Monde Oxfam asbl (hereafter Oxfam-MDM) one year later. The number of worldshops and volunteers increased rapidly and the name Oxfam became particularly famous and synonymous with Fair Trade in the public opinion, a situation which remains to a large extent to this date.

Other pioneer FTSEs emerged in the 1970s and also played an important role in the diffusion of the movement. Miel Maya Honing (hereafter MMH) was created in 1975 as an NGO helping honey producers in Central America. MMH did not create a new network of worldshops, but launched honey-based products sold by volunteers. In the late 1970s, a pioneer FTSE in the Netherlands, the Fair Trade Organisatie (now Fair Trade Original) created a subsidiary near Leuven. Fair Trade Original Belgium grew to become a wholesaler for worldshops but also, inaugurating a future trend, for mainstream buyers. In the German-speaking part of Belgium, Weltladen ("worldshop" in German) was created in 1978. After opening its first worldshop in Eupen, Weltladen developed a partnership with Rwandese handicraft producers and launched several NGO-related activities (logistics, communication, etc.).

In the 1980s, the pioneer FTSEs continued developing their networks of worldshops and diffusing the FT concept. Yet, FT awareness and consumption remained restricted to a small part of the population. Like in other countries, the development of certification strongly contributed to the development of FT sales and awareness. In 1989, just one year after its creation in the Netherlands, Max Havelaar was launched in Belgium. Several development NGOs were at the basis of Max Havelaar Belgium and some of them are still involved in its governance. Max Havelaar Belgium, a founding member of FLO, started certifying the products of the FTSEs and of a small but growing number of corporations.

During the 1990s, the Belgian FT sector developed further, while remaining relatively homogeneous: nonprofit, anchored in civil society, relying mainly on voluntary work and selling FT products through worldshops. In 1994, Oxfam-WW decided to give a new impulse to its commercial activity by creating a specific cooperative structure for it. Such restructuring announced the major evolution that took place in the end of the 1990s. At that time, nearly all pioneer FTSEs were actively involved in extra-economic producer support, through development projects with the producers' communities or even beyond these communities. This activity was subsidized to a large extent by the Belgian Directorate-General for Development Cooperation (now DGD). However, with the commercial development of these FTSEs, the DGD became reluctant to give subsidies to a business. It only accepted to fund the socio-political part of the activity. As a result, several pioneer FTSEs had to split up their structure into two entities: a business and an NGO. MMH and Max Havelaar followed the example of Oxfam-WW. Only Oxfam-MDM[2] managed to remain a single entity, even if it had to clearly distinguish the two activities in its accounting. The creation of a specific commercial structure gave a boost to the economic development of Oxfam-WW, MMH, and Max Havelaar. The latter attracted a growing number of mainstream companies, including supermarkets, to invest the FT niche.

During the same period, another important event was the creation of Citizen Dream in 1998. Citizen Dream differentiated itself sharply from the pioneer FTSEs through a stronger commercial approach and marketing strategy aiming to reach consumers less aware of FT. With this purpose, Citizen Dream established a dozen shops in city centers. The design of the shops and the quality of the products were intended to attract mainstream consumers who were not familiar with the worldshops. In its marketing, Citizen Dream highlighted the quality of the products rather than their FT dimension, even if information on the producers was available on request. Thereby, Citizen Dream inaugurated a new way of "doing FT" which would later be followed by several other companies.

In the late 1990s, FT became officially recognized and supported by public authorities, mainly through the creation of the Fair Trade Centre (now Trade for Development Centre, hereafter TDC). The center was hosted by the Belgian Technical Cooperation, a public agency for development cooperation. It aimed to support the FT operators in the North as well as in the South and to foster the growth and promotion of the sector. Such a promotion included the organization of an annual Fair Trade week (in October), the ordering and publication of reports on FT awareness and sales in Belgium, and the creation of a dynamic website.[3]

The success of Citizen Dream, together with the commercial development of FT, pushed FT pioneers to professionalize—a trend that is still currently widespread in FTSEs' discourse and practices. These developments were intended to change the image associated with FT, from a charitable to a (social) entrepreneurial image combining high-quality products and demanding ethical standards. In 2002, Oxfam-WW decided to sell its products in supermarkets. Starting with the Delhaize chain, many supermarkets began to offer Oxfam food products. Simultaneously, Oxfam-WW decided to make its cooperative entity totally autonomous and called it Oxfam Fairtrade, which also became the brand name of the products.

Recently, certain supermarkets developed their own line of products, often coexisting with FTSEs' products. Delhaize, for instance, now has twenty products of its own line, along with another twenty Oxfam Fairtrade products. Lidl launched its own FT product range called Fair Globe. Supermarket FT products were sometimes developed in collaboration with FTSEs, for instance, some of the Solidair products imported by Fair Trade Original for Carrefour.

Following the development of Citizen Dream, but on a smaller and more focused level, several FT companies were created after 2000, and particularly since 2004, at a rhythm of several new FTSEs each year. The emergence and the development of small FT companies was favored by several factors: growth of the FT market, interest of idealistic entrepreneurs, existence of niches uncovered by the pioneer FTSEs in terms of products (e.g., wine, chocolate, etc.), distribution channels (Internet sales, B2B, etc.), and so on. Examples include Satya-Pure Elements (clothing), Vino Mundo (wine), Emile (home sales following the Tupperware model), Tout l'or du monde (shops), and so on.

The emergence of new FT businesses found additional support through the TDC. Besides other missions previously mentioned, the TDC wishes to stimulate new FT initiatives with the Be Fair Award. Each year, during Fair Trade week, two new FT companies are given awards. Beyond the monetary prize, such an award increases the recognition and the credibility of the nominees. Another stimulator for entrepreneurship in FT is the Belgian Fair Trade Federation (BFTF), launched in 2010 with public support from the Walloon region and gathering more than twenty FTSEs.

Given the increasing success of FT, a range of initiatives in the domain of "ethical trade" have tried to claim their equivalence or at least their proximity to FT practices and values. Two initiatives were widely covered by the media and by FT stakeholders: the Collibri product range launched by Colruyt, and Efico's Fair and Sustainable Trade label. Fearing confusion among the general public, but also among decision-makers in the context of public procurement, most Belgian FTSEs felt the need for public recognition to protect the FT concept. In 2005, Belgian FTSEs, supported by the TDC, urged for a law that would regulate FT. Such a demand was acknowledged by the three left-wing or center parties: the Socialist Party, the Humanist (Christian-Democrat) Party, and the Ecologists. These three parties each wrote their own law proposal. Slowed down by the political situation from 2007 to 2011, recent attempts have been made to reactivate the process. However, the opposition of right-wing parties and mainstream companies, grouped under the Belgian business federation (FEB)[4], makes the adoption of a law specific to FT highly hypothetical. Indeed, following the evolution of the TDC, the FEB promotes the recognition of a broader and lighter range of ethical practices grouped under the term "sustainable trade."[5]

In 2007, Krier counted nearly 300 worldshops (mainly the Oxfam shops) and 83 full-time equivalents employed by FTSEs. However, Krier's figures are restricted to the four largest FTSEs (the two Oxfam's, Fair Trade Original and MMH). According to the annual reports ordered by the TDC[6], the mean annual growth of FT sales is 15%. While worldshops have seen their sales growing steadily, mainstream sales have grown even faster. In 2007, mainstream sales exceeded sales in the worldshops. From 2005 to 2009, labeled FT sales grew from €15 to 66 million (FLO-I 2010). The number of licensees grew from 48 in 2005 to 112 in 2007 (Poos 2008; Krier 2008). FT bananas reached the highest market share (6% in 2007).

## France[7]

FT was launched in France by several pioneer organizations. Following the call of Abbé Pierre in 1971, Artisans du Monde (hereafter ADM) was initiated in 1974 and incorporated in 1981. Other pioneers include Artisanat SEL, Andines and Ayllu. Until the late 1990s, the French FT sector remained restricted and shared only by a small number of politically engaged organizations. Nevertheless, there was already some tension between ADM, which relied heavily on voluntary work and on worldshops, and Andines, which was opposed to the use of voluntary work and to public subsidies (Diaz Pedregal 2007).

In the 1990s, two major changes occurred. First, after an aborted attempt by ADM to create a French FT label, Max Havelaar France was created in 1992 by several NGOs. It aimed to increase the recognition of FT—which was much less significant at that time in France than in other European countries—and to convince mainstream companies that FT could be worthwhile for them. In 1998, FT-labeled products became available in supermarkets for the first time. While FT became increasingly known by the French public, it was difficult for Max Havelaar and other FTSEs to bring and defend the idea that FT products could be distributed in supermarkets. Indeed, in contrast with other European countries, the opposition to FT mainstreaming has been and still remains strong in France.

In 1997, the Plate-Forme pour le Commerce Equitable (PFCE) was created, grouping together the main FT pioneers and several NGOs. Together, they successfully led campaigns to have FT products distributed in supermarkets. Other activities of the PFCE included organizing the Quinzaine du Commerce Equitable every year, stimulating collaboration among members and promoting FT.

The emergence of new business-oriented FTSEs constituted a second major evolution. In 1999, Alter Eco was founded by Tristan Lecomte. Alter Eco successfully paved the way for business-like FTSEs. It developed a range of quality food products for supermarkets. Owing to the sale of its products in supermarkets, Alter Eco's turnover rapidly grew and exceeded that of most pioneers. The example of Alter Eco was followed by many new small companies, albeit with varying models. Examples include Ethiquable, Ideo, Signaléthique, and so on. Many of these FTSEs distribute their products through both specialized outlets and mainstream shops (Ballet and Carimentrand 2008; Özçağlar-Toulouse et al. 2010). Other companies, however, have been opposed to FT in supermarkets and have joined Andines in the Minga network. The members of Minga are characterized by their strong political agenda and their simultaneous opposition to both ADM (because of its use of volunteers and its NGO-like, nonprofessional functioning) and Max Havelaar (because of its collusion with mainstream companies). Moreover, Minga has been favorable to the extension of FT to local (North-North and South-South) exchanges.

As a result, at least four streams currently characterize the French FT sector. One stream, embodied by ADM and other pioneer FTSEs, relies on worldshops and voluntary work. For them, selling FT products is a way to make the population aware of unfair practices in international trade. Another stream, embodied by Max Havelaar and part of the business-form FTSEs, aims to further penetrate the market with the help of mainstream companies. Their rationale is to increase the FT market share, whatever the distribution channel, so as to create the highest possible volume for producers. The third stream is embodied by Minga and gathers companies combining a strong political profile with a central commercial project, the two being naturally embedded in their businesses. Finally, a lot of FTSEs do not identify themselves in these streams and are characterized by a pragmatic approach (Sarrazin-Biteye 2009). These "independents," often active at a local level, challenge the description of the French landscape based on its national networks (Huybrechts and Sarrazin-Biteye 2008). Therefore, in order to really understand the dynamics and the diversity of the French FT sector, it is useful to observe the local situations, beyond the description of the well-established national actors (e.g., Gateau 2008; Sarrazin-Biteye 2009).

Whereas the different historical streams collaborated through the PFCE platform, the divisions became especially exacerbated when discussing the preparation of a French law on FT. Debates hosted by AFNOR (Agence française de normalisation) brought together PFCE members and FT stakeholders. It is the disagreement on several points—particularly on the participation of mainstream companies and the restriction of FT to North-South exchanges—which led Andines to leave the PFCE and launch its own network (Minga, in 2002). Finally, a law was adopted in 2005 but it only proposed a very general framework describing FT and its distribution strategies. This has not, however, tempered the permanent debates that pervade the French FT sector, with regular criticism both from the inside and from the outside.[8]

According to Krier (2008), there were 165 worldshops in France in 2007, but this number strongly underestimates the number of shops as it only takes ADM shops into account—not those of new FTSEs. The same author counted 85 full-time equivalents in 2005 and in 2008. Still according to Krier, FT sales were generated mainly by mainstream channels: nearly €210 million in sales in 2007 (twice more than in 2005), and €288 million in 2009 (FLO-I 2010), compared with only €20 million in specialized outlets—although the latter is probably also underestimated. FT sales in France are thus characterized by a small market share for specialized shops with regard to that of supermarkets. ADM's turnover, limited to sales in ADM shops, has remained relatively stable over the last years (less than €9 million). It is thus thanks to supermarkets and FTSEs such as Alter Eco and Ethiquable that sales figures have experienced the most dramatic growth in Europe in recent years (nearly doubling every year between 2002 and 2005). As Krier observes, "those organizations which have opted to go for the broadest possible distribution of Fairtrade certified products, such as Malongo, Ethiquable, and AlterEco have seen their turnover skyrocketing, overtaking the pioneering Solidar'Monde and leaving the traditional market leader far behind" (2007, 73). As a parallel, FT recognition in France has grown from only 9% in 2000 to 81% in 2007 (Max Havelaar-Ipsos 2007).

## United Kingdom[9]

The UK is often presented as one of the countries where the FT sector is the most dynamic and the fastest growing (Krier 2005, 2008). Together with the Netherlands, the UK is also one of the first European countries where FT initiatives emerged. Oxfam UK, launched during the First World War, can certainly be considered one of the FT pioneers in Europe. It proposed the idea of selling items from developing countries in charity shops instead of just giving money. The first shop opened in Oxford in 1948 and the concept spread rapidly. However, campaigning has remained Oxfam's main activity: in 2002, it decided to abandon its trading activities and focus on awareness raising and lobbying.

In 1979, Traidcraft was founded as a public limited company specifically devoted to FT. Created with a clear Christian identity[10], Traidcraft first developed its distribution networks through churches and religious groups. Catalog sales and the involvement of numerous volunteers made Traidcraft grow rapidly. A second entity was created in 1986 as a charity named Traidcraft Exchange and focusing on producer support. The two organizations work hand in hand and their actions are ensured homogeneity through the Traidcraft Foundation.

Also in 1979, Equal Exchange was founded as a workers' cooperative by three volunteers involved in development aid. In 1986, given the success of the company, a sister cooperative was created in the US. Many other FTSEs emerged in the 1980s, such as One Village (1980), Siesta (1983), Bishopston Trading (1985), Shared Earth (1986), and Twin (Third World Information Network—1985). Founded by the Greater London Council, Twin is an interesting example of a publicly launched FT initiative. Twin split up its activities: the charity Twin focuses on producer support, while Twin Trading deals with importing the products and designing new supply chains.

Together with Traidcraft, Oxfam UK, and Equal Exchange, Twin was involved in the launch of Cafédirect in 1991. The four FTSEs decided to unite their efforts to launch a commonly owned company focused on one particular product: coffee. Cafédirect was a unique example at that time and became very successful, designing attractive products and distributing them in supermarkets. The success of Cafédirect led Twin to launch other FT companies focused on a particular product: Day Chocolate (later Divine) in 1998, Agrofair (fresh fruit) in 2001, and Liberation (nuts) in 2007. Divine was the first FTSE in which producers (the partner cooperative Kuapa Kokoo) hold shares (45%) and sit on the Board of Directors, an example which would later be followed by other FTSEs.

In 1992, Traidcraft, Oxfam, and three NGOs came together to create the Fairtrade Foundation, which organizes FT labeling in the UK. The first FT labeled products—coffee, chocolate, and tea—were launched in 1994 and were followed by many others, including products branded by supermarkets and food companies in the late 1990s. This led the UK to become a pioneer of FT mainstreaming.[11] Since 1997, the Fairtrade Foundation has been organizing the annual Fairtrade Fortnight, an event aiming to boost FT sales and recognition, especially in supermarkets. Among the supermarket chains, different levels of commitment can be observed (Smith 2010); the Cooperative Group has been the most involved in FT, with a wide range of FT products and a strong commitment to promoting FT.[12]

In the early 1990s, many worldshops were created, often through the impulse of the established pioneers (Traidcraft, Equal Exchange, etc.). These shops joined in 1995 to create the British Association for Fair Trade Shops (BAFTS). BAFTS' mission is to provide support to FT shops and to promote FT at the national level. Members of BAFTS—nearly one hundred in 2008—have to be autonomous (not linked to a particular importer), they must get involved to a certain extent in campaigning and they must seek coherence by applying the FT criteria internally: "The criteria apply equally to how trade is practiced in the North, so shops will be open to customers about business practices, informed about products and treat their own staff well" (BAFTS 2003).

The campaigning efforts of pioneers and of BAFTS led to the adoption of FT products by public entities, including the Parliament, as soon as 1997. Local administrations also started consuming FT products and the title "Fairtrade town" was claimed for the first time in 2001 by a small town called Garstang. Principles for "FT towns" were set and monitored by the

Fairtrade Foundation. They include a strong involvement of public administrations, schools, and local communities who can themselves become Fairtrade. Through imitation of and competition for the "Fairtrade" title, this has led to a very large network of towns, schools, universities, and churches campaigning for FT (Krier 2008).

Many small FTSEs emerged around 2000. Most of these FTSEs focused on a particular product line: jewelry (Silver Chilli, 1999), clothing (People Tree, 2001), olive oil (Zaytoun, 2004), etc. The case of People Tree illustrates the success and the innovation of new FT businesses in the UK. Initially launched by Safia Minney in the early 1990s in Japan, the company met an enormous success by focusing on a previously uncovered area: fashion. Designing fashionable FT clothing allowed People Tree to have its products distributed in mainstream outlets, such as Topshop stores in London. Besides strong commercial dynamics, People Tree has been very involved in campaigning, as a WFTO member: its founder is at the origin of the celebration of the World Fair Trade Day.

The leaders of both pioneer and newcomer FTSEs belonging to WFTO— some of which through BAFTS—meet several times a year to discuss common issues through an informal network called Fair Trade Leaders Forum. Although all British FTSEs are not represented, the Forum can be considered as a major informal network gathering FT importers and distributors in the UK.

In 2002, the Make Poverty History campaign raised enormous enthusiasm among FTSEs and their stakeholders. Many FTSEs got involved in the campaign by selling armbands. This, in turn, had a very positive effect on the sales of FT products. By 2005, 100 British towns had engaged in FT. In 2008, Wales became the first "Fair Trade Nation" in the world thanks to the involvement of Welsh towns, government, and FT supporters (in the first place the association "Fair Trade Wales"). In 2007, UK consumers chose Cafédirect as "the most recommended brand in the UK," among 2000 companies (Krier 2008).

The prospect of the Olympic Games to be held in London in 2012 is now seen as an opportunity for FTSEs and more generally social enterprises. Through the Winning with 2012 campaign, the coalition Social Enterprise London (SEL) aims to put social enterprises, including FTSEs, at the forefront for the delivery of products and services during the games.

According to the Fairtrade Foundation (2011), total labeled FT sales in the UK exceeded £1 billion in 2010, most of which generated in supermarkets. For more than a decade, FT sales have been nearly doubling every year (Krier 2008; FLO-I 2010). According to Krier, sales by FTSEs only reached £100 million in 2008 (63 in 2005). Total sales—labeled and nonlabeled— are much higher than in the three other countries of the study, and growth seems to be continuous. FT awareness reached 97% in 2007 (as opposed to 12% in 2000). In 2007, Krier counted nearly 250 full-time equivalents in British FTSEs.

## Italy[13]

Looking at the figures of labeled sales in Italy would give the impression of a country with a very low development of FT: only €43 million in 2009, i.e., less than €0.6 per capita. As will be examined in this section, this shows that general figures, what's more relating only to one type of product (those which are certified), may hide the "highly distinctive structure" of FT led by FTSEs outside the traditional labeling sphere (Becchetti and Costantino 2010, 182).

The first worldshop was opened in 1981 in Bressanone (South Tirol). But the history of Italian FT is particularly linked to that of CTM Altromercato, the first established FT operator.[14] After few importing and distribution attempts, CTM (Cooperazione Terzo Mondo) was created in 1988. The idea was not only to create an importing organization, from which worldshops could buy their products, but also to foster the development of worldshops and offer them much broader services (training, logistic support, contact with producers, etc.). The cooperative form was chosen by CTM as a vehicle for the participation of the workers. But worldshops were also invited to become members of the cooperative. In the early 1990s, worldshops were created in most cities and towns and some of them joined the CTM cooperative (among which two Roman FTSEs created in 1991). They created the Associazione Bottheghe del Mundo (Assobotteghe) in 1991.

Several importing FTSEs were created in the 1990s, including Equo Mercato (1991), Comercio Alternativo (1992), Equoland (1995), and Roba dell'Altro Mondo (1997). In 1994, the Italian label Transfair Italia (now Fairtrade Italia) was created. The aim was to promote FT in mainstream distribution channels. However, CTM chose not to use the FT label on its products, considering that its brand and identity were sufficient to gain trust from the consumers (Krier 2008). As a result, although other FTSEs (such as Comercio Alternativo) used labeling, sales of labeled FT products remained relatively weak, restricted to only 4000 supermarkets in 2007 (Krier 2008).

In 1998, CTM evolved into a consortium which grouped organizations only (mainly worldshops), not individuals. The consortium form allowed CTM to grow further and integrate up to 120 organizations, representing 350 worldshops (Krier 2008). Also in 1998, the main Italian FTSEs came together to discuss a common standpoint on the definition of and criteria for FT. The final document was published in 1999 under the name Carta Italiana dei Criteri del Commercio Equo e Solidale. Italian FTSEs continue to work together informally on how to implement and monitor the criteria. In 2003, they incorporated their collaboration under the name Assemblea Generale Italiana del Commercio Equo e Solidale (Agices).

Agices created a register of Italian FTSEs respecting its criteria. From the beginning, a central criterion for being on the register was the nonprofit or cooperative status of the organization. Agices recognizes the advantages of having FT products sold in supermarkets, but promotes a clear distinction between mainstream businesses and the network of worldshops. Such a decision reinforced the two-sided nature of FT distribution in Italy (Becchetti and Costantino 2010). The FTSEs' side is very politically involved, particularly the worldshops. AssoBotteghe, grouping only worldshops, is even more radical than Agices, which also includes importers. Certain worldshops left Agices to remain members only of AssoBotteghe. Nevertheless, with its 250 members and its WFTO membership, Agices clearly remains the dominant FT network in Italy (Krier 2008).

Rome became the first Italian FT town in 2005, with the support of Agices. By 2007, 18 towns had received such a title (Krier 2008). Through CTM's Ristorazione Solidale project, schools have become very involved in the consumption and promotion of FT. Such involvement is particularly remarkable and is often given as an example of successful public participation in support of FT. Agices and AssoBotteghe, together with Fairtrade Italia, collaborate for the organization of the annual FT fair called Tuttunaltracosa. More important, the three organizations are the major driving force behind the work towards an Italian law on FT. After recognition and support of FT by several regional authorities, discussions at the national level started in 2006, under the impulse of Italian Parliament Members in favor of FT (grouped in the AIES network[15]). Ideas to be included in the law included special public funding for FTSEs and tax reductions on FT products. The question of who may qualify as an FTSE (only nonprofits and cooperatives, or beyond) is thus crucial in this context. However, while several regions have already passed their law on FT, it has not yet been the case at the national level, where political consensus if obviously more difficult to reach (Becchetti and Costantino 2010).

Italy is characterized by one of the highest numbers of worldshops in Europe, with more than 600 units (Viganò, Glorio, and Villa 2008; Krier 2008). More than half of them are relatively young (created after 2000) and 60% are located in the North of Italy (Viganò, Glorio, and Villa 2008; Krier 2008). Another specific feature that contrasts with other countries is the higher sales by FTSEs compared with supermarkets. However, sales of FT products in supermarkets have grown strongly in recent years, from €25 million in 2004 to €43 million in 2009 (FLO-I 2010; Krier 2008). Despite supermarkets' growing interest, worldshops and importing FTSEs still dominate the Italian FT landscape. Their dynamism, both on the political and economic sides, is characteristic of the Italian FT model (Viganò, Glorio, and Villa 2008; Becchetti and Costantino 2010). In 2007, Krier counted more than 400 full-time equivalents in FTSEs (importers and worldshops), which again constitutes an exceptional number in Europe (Krier 2005, 2008).

## Comparison

Table 2.1 summarizes and compares the main features of FT and FTSEs in the four countries. The focus is laid on the position of pioneers, on their role regarding the mainstream players and the space left for newcomers.

*Table 2.1*    Comparison of the FT Sectors in the Four Countries

|  | Belgium | France | Italy | UK |
|---|---|---|---|---|
| Estimated FT sales (euros)[1] | 75,000,000 | 320,000,000 | 180,000,000 | 1,000,000,000 |
| Sales per capita[2] | 7.09 | 3.94 | 2.54 | 16.43 |
| Highest market share | 6% (banana) | 7% (roasted coffee) | 2% (banana) | 25% (roasted coffee) |
| FT shops | 350 | 300 | 650 | 150 |
| Position of pioneers | Strong | Weak | Very strong | Strong |
| Pioneers' involvement in mainstream[3] | Advanced | Limited | Yes but not through label | Very advanced |
| FT businesses | Recently emerging | Established or still emerging | Still limited | Established, few new ones |

As the table shows, each country has a specific FT configuration. But the strongest resemblances seem to be between Belgium and the UK. In both countries, pioneer FTSEs have been at the basis of the mainstreaming of FT and have been much involved in it. The situation in the UK is more advanced, with a stronger penetration of FT into the mainstream. Italy could be located at the other edge, with a growing but still low level of mainstreaming, part of which is controlled by CTM and bypasses the label. New FTSEs are mainly worldshops: the emergence of specific FT businesses is still very limited. Finally, the situation in France is particular. The pioneers such as ADM, who dominated the landscape until the late 1990s, have been progressively marginalized both by mainstream players encouraged by Max Havelaar, and by FT businesses such as Alter Eco and Ethiquable, which have rapidly grown through mainstream channels (Krier 2008). Moreover, the rise of a new generation of FT businesses hostile to mainstreaming has even challenged the role of ADM as the FT "political reference."

It already appears that the configurations of the national FT landscapes are crucial for understanding FTSEs' organizational models and strategies. The following section details the concrete steps of collection and treatment of the information in the FTSEs.

## METHODOLOGY

### Mixed Methodology

As the first step was to build a typology of organizational models in FT, it was necessary to gather a large number of FTSEs featuring various models,[16]

observe common patterns, and group them into a meaningful taxonomy. Such taxonomy based on a high number of FTSEs from different cultural and socio-economic contexts helped to avoid a number of pitfalls:

- missing a particular type of FTSE because of a too narrow focus on a few cases based on an *a priori* classification
- being attracted only by the famous, well documented cases of FT "success stories"
- generalizing the situation of FTSEs in one particular country to other contexts

However, understanding the meaning and the role of the organizational models also required having a deeper look within individual FTSEs, looking at the logics of the organizational actors who compose them. This was possible though case studies on FTSEs representing particular models in each country. The use of a mixed-methods design enabled "to address more complicated research questions and collect a richer and stronger array of evidence than what can be accomplished by any single method alone" (Yin 2009, 63).

## Interviews

### Process

All FTSEs in each region were contacted by e-mail, with the support of local networks and support structures (see next sections). Face-to-face semi-structured interviews were favored, focusing on the manager/director but also including other organizational actors when possible (managers, employees, volunteers, Board members, etc.). The interviews were prepared by collecting and analyzing data available on the FTSE (website, annual report, studies, information provided by local networks and support structures, etc.).[17]

### The Belgian Study

Before the study, four FTSEs had already extensively been studied thanks to past projects (Huybrechts and Manigart 2003; Huybrechts 2005) and personal contacts. Eleven other FTSEs, both pioneer and newcomers, were added. Their managers were interviewed between June 2007 and November 2008. Besides these fifteen FTSEs, several interviews were made with three NGO representatives and with the coordinators of two major support structures: the Trade for Development Centre and the Belgian Fair Trade Federation. Comprising both pioneer and newcomer FTSEs, BFTF meetings were an excellent avenue to gather insights on the Belgian FT field and its participants.

*The French Study*

After several discussions with representatives of the PFCE in Paris, it was decided to orient the French part of the study to the Rhône-Alpes region.[18] Focusing on a particular region was useful to include smaller and less known FTSEs. Consequently, the study includes many small FT companies often ignored in the research on FT, yet crucial for understanding the diversity of the FTSEs' landscape (Sarrazin-Biteye 2009).

The region of Rhône-Alpes, including major French cities such as Lyon, Grenoble, and Valence, is one of the most dynamic regions in terms of FT. It includes many FTSEs active at different stages of the process (import, transformation, distribution, promotion, etc.). It is no wonder, for instance, that the first European FT Fairs took place in Lyon in 2008 and 2009. The Rhône-Alpes study was largely facilitated by contacts with the Equisol support structure.[19] Equisol is not a network of FTSEs but a platform whose mission is to support the development of the FT sector in Rhône-Alpes and to increase collaboration among the various actors. Equisol's activities include the organization of fairs (among which the 2008 European fair), support for logistic coordination among actors, and education campaigns. Although Equisol is historically close to Max Havelaar France, it progressively opened its scope to other companies involved in FT, belonging to various networks (Minga, ADM, PFCE) or to neither of them. Besides facilitating the contacts with the FTSEs, Equisol provided very interesting feedback to the first findings of this study. Other facilitators for the study were city-level networks and regional structures of national networks. City-level networks include the CLACE[20] in Lyon and Grenoble équitable. The main role of these networks is to organize common FT fairs and to foster knowledge and experience exchanges among the actors.

All the organizations listed on Equisol's website who were totally dedicated to the import and/or the distribution of FT products were contacted. 22 replied positively and led to interviews between September 2007 and May 2008. Besides the FTSEs' managers, other interviewees include representatives from Equisol and the two city-level platforms (Lyon and Grenoble) as well as two NGOs closely linked to FT.

*The British Study*

The selection of the FTSEs was made with the help of British scholars—some of whom were themselves involved in FTSEs. A second source was the BAFTS' website,[21] which lists the FT shops, but also a number of FT importers from which the worldshops can buy FT products. FTSEs (retailers, importers, or both) were contacted in the areas of London and Newcastle, each showing a high concentration of FT actors. Eleven FTSEs participated in the British part of the study (January and February 2008). This is certainly not representative of the total British FT sector, although it seems to reflect the diversity of FTSEs in the UK, from the small importers and worldshops to the large groups.

### The Italian Study

The region of Rome was targeted because the concentration of FTSEs is higher than the national average (Viganò, Glorio, and Villa 2008). As the Roman area mainly counts worldshops, two large importers were included from the North of Italy, the birthplace of Italian FT. Because the Agices network only gathers nonprofit and cooperative FTSEs, and does not include several smaller and more recent initiatives (Viganò, Glorio, and Villa 2008), non-Agices members were also included, some of which members of the AssoBotthega network, others being independent. In Rome, the local network Roma Equa e Solidale (RES), which gathers almost all the Roman FTSEs, was very helpful in making contact with many FTSEs and having an overall view of the local sector. Ten Italian FTSEs were interviewed in May 2008.

## Case Studies

In-depth case studies were conducted with eight individual FTSEs, enabling to take into account the time dimension, the concrete dynamics and power relationships, as well as the viewpoint of several organizational actors (Grenier and Josserand 2007). Multiple cases were chosen to cover a certain extent of organizational diversity and enable some degree of extrapolation (Yin 2009; Blumberg, Cooper, and Schindler 2005). Exemplary and contrasted cases were favored (Eisenhardt and Graebner 2007) and also chosen based on "convenience, access and geographic proximity" (Yin 2009, 93). Hence, the eight FTSEs are not supposed to be representative of the broader study: Belgian FTSEs, as well as larger FTSEs, are over-represented. Nevertheless, deepening the analysis on these few FTSEs appeared useful for understanding the shaping and meaning of the organizational models.

### Citizen Dream (Belgium)

Citizen Dream is a Brussels-based company created in 1998 by a couple of entrepreneurs. The couple had a background in the NGO world, but they nevertheless decided to launch Citizen Dream as a business to avoid what they called "nonprofit inefficiencies" (heavy democratic decision-making process, reluctance for business tools, etc.). Individual shareholders and a partner FTSE were involved in its creation. Citizen Dream started importing from Oxfam-MDM partners in India, but soon after, it developed its own partnerships, mainly with IFAT-WFTO members. In order to gain legitimacy as a FTSE, Citizen Dream became a member of IFAT-WFTO and was thus submitted to an external audit and a self-assessment process. The focus on high-quality products, the communication strategy based on quality and not on FT, and the system of shops owned by franchisees were quite innovative for FT at that time. However, due to internal management problems, rapid growth and the difficulties in trading FT handicraft (SAW-B 2008), the FTSE collapsed in 2008.

### Miel Maya Honing—Maya Fair Trade (Belgium)

MMH was created in 1975 by a group of volunteers who were in contact with honey producers in Central America. It started partnerships with these producer groups and distributed several types of honey, initially through a network of sensitized customers. In 1998, the FTSE was split into a nonprofit entity (MMH) and a cooperative (MFT). Each of these entities specialized in specific functions (respectively, education and producer support; and trading), with separate locations, directors and governance structures. MFT diversified the product range (sweets, gingerbread, cookies, etc.) and distributed them in an increasing number of supermarkets and shops. MMH specialized in education and support to producers as an NGO. Nevertheless, a system of inter-organizational links was established to maintain coherence between the two parts of the group.

### Magasins du Monde-Oxfam (Belgium)

Oxfam-MDM, one of the pioneers of FT in Belgium, started out as a nonprofit, volunteer-based FTSE. When defining the roles of the different Oxfam-named organizations in Belgium, it took the role of importing the handicraft products for the Belgian worldshops. Oxfam-MDM developed a network of nearly one hundred shops in French-speaking Belgium. It was able to gather thousands of volunteers, both to manage the worldshops and to run campaigns. From the beginning, campaigning was a central activity for Oxfam-MDM, allowing it to acquire a high level of recognition together with its Flemish counterpart (see next case). Oxfam-MDM's aim is to build a "movement of citizens," considering the commercialization of FT products as one of the tools to support and concretize its political project and its social mission.

### Oxfam-WW and Oxfam Fairtrade, OWW-OFT (Belgium)

The history of Oxfam-WW is very similar to that of Oxfam-MDM, at least until the mid-1990s. In the Oxfam family, Oxfam-WW is responsible for the import and the distribution of food. This placed Oxfam-WW in a very different position from its French-speaking counterpart. Indeed, it seized the opportunity of selling its food products through mainstream markets. To manage the development and marketing of the products, and to face partnerships with supermarkets and other mainstream businesses, the organization created a specific structure through a cooperative called Oxfam Fairtrade cvba. Oxfam-WW remained a nonprofit organization; in addition to the education and advocacy dimension, it serves as an umbrella for the two hundred worldshops that have acquired juridical independence. In the context of the OWW-OFT group, Oxfam-WW and the worlshops remain the main shareholders of Oxfam-Fairtrade, but part of the shares have become available for individuals and partner institutions (NGOs, etc.).

### Esprit Equo (Italy)

Esprit Equo was created by a Moroccan-Italian couple in 2006. Based on personal relationships with Moroccan producers, they wished to launch a range of quality cosmetics that would provide new market opportunities for these producers. However, Esprit Equo's founders were reluctant to imitate the model of a social cooperative adopted by most Italian FTSEs. They wanted their FTSE to be a business with a clear market orientation, along with a strong attention for the producers' needs. Moreover, they did not want other people to be involved in the venture. Collaboration started with the Italian FTSE Commercio Alternativo for the development of the cosmetics. The intent was to propose these cosmetics through mainstream channels. They also opened their own shop in the center of Rome, to put forward the quality and attractiveness of the products rather than their FT characteristic, along the same lines as FTSEs in other countries, such as Citizen Dream or L'épicerie équitable.

### Pangea-Niente Troppo (Italy)

Pangea was created in 1991 as one of the first worldshops in Rome. Volunteers who were very enthusiastic about the FT project wanted to launch a shop in Rome. Two other shops were opened in the following years. Pangea was soon to join the CTM consortium, and became the intermediate for the distribution of CTM products to supermarkets in the Roman region. Pangea is also a founding member of Agices. In 2004, Pangea united with another worldshop in the area, Niente Troppo, to become Pangea-Niente Troppo (hereafter Pangea-NT).

### Traidcraft (UK)

As previously mentioned, Traidcraft has been a leading FTSE in the British and European FT sector. It evolved into a successful group with a turnover of more than £20 million and influenced the evolution of the whole sector. Traidcraft has played a major role in the launch of Cafédirect and in the constitution of the Fairtrade Foundation. Moreover, owing to its roots in Christian networks, with thousands of volunteers selling its products and relaying its campaigns, Traidcraft remained close to civil society while developing a profitable business. New products were developed in partnership with mainstream businesses and several products with the Traidcraft brand began to be distributed in supermarkets. In the meantime, partnerships were developed with numerous producer groups all over the world. Traidcraft received awards in the UK for the Best Social Account (in 2005) and for Excellence on Stakeholder Dialogue (2006). It also received the Queen's Award for Enterprise (in 2006).

### Saldac (France)

Saldac was created in 2000 by an entrepreneur when returning from an academic field study in Latin America. Having met different groups of Peruvian producers trying to find market opportunities for their products (textile, coffee, cocoa, as well as maca and mate), he decided to progressively import food products from them. Saldac was created as a nonprofit organization but took on a classical business form in 2002. Saldac is an active member of Minga, the French network of politically engaged business-form FTSEs.

### Synthesis

Table 2.2 summarizes some of the core information about the different cases.

*Table 2.2*   The Case Studies

| Name | Country | Legal form | Size | Products |
|---|---|---|---|---|
| Citizen Dream | Belgium | Business | Medium | Handicraft |
| Esprit Equo | Italy | Individual | Small | Cosmetics |
| MMH-MFT | Belgium | Nonprofit + Cooperative | Medium | Food |
| Oxfam-MDM | Belgium | Nonprofit | Large | Handicraft |
| Oxfam-WW | Belgium | Nonprofit + Cooperative | Very large | Food |
| Pangea-Niente Troppo | Italy | Cooperative | Medium | Mixed |
| Saldac | France | Business | Small | Mixed |
| Traidcraft | United Kingdom | Nonprofit + Business | Very large | Mixed |

## CONCLUSION

This chapter has brought to light four different national situations for FT and FTSEs. Italy and the UK are probably the most dissimilar countries. In the former, FTSEs dominate the market through a dense network of world-shops, a strong involvement in education and advocacy, and the control on part of the supermarket distribution at the expense of the Italian label. In the UK, on the contrary, mainstream penetration is advanced and piloted by the label, together with pioneer FTSEs. Worldshop density is low and education and advocacy are delegated to civil society through a network of volunteers mobilized through different Fairtrade institutions (towns, schools, parishes, etc.). The situation of Belgium is closer to that of the UK, with nevertheless a stronger worldshop density and more new business-oriented FTSEs. Finally, the French landscape is rather fragmented, with networks (ADM, Minga, PFCE, etc.) each promoting its own vision of FT and homogenizing its membership accordingly.

In these four contrasted countries, regions with a high density of FTSEs were identified for the study. Interviews with the managers of 57 FTSEs and documentary analyses have provided the data at the sample level. In the meanwhile, 8 FTSEs reflecting different organizational models and cultural/historical backgrounds were selected for in-depth case studies. The data at the sample level will be extensively presented in Chapter 3, while the case study findings will particularly be used in the Chapter 7.

# 3 Categorizing Hybrid Organizational Models

This chapter attempts to structure the diversity of organizational models in the FT field. In the first section, three building blocks forming these models are suggested: the legal form, the architecture, and the governance model. Each of these elements will be examined separately, with a brief theoretical introduction followed by the related findings. Then, in the second section, the findings for the three elements of the organizational model are aggregated to constitute a taxonomy of FTSE's organizational models. Each of the taxonomy's categories is described in terms of core features, internal homogeneity, and possible evolution. Finally, the third section examines to what extent the different models can be discriminated on the basis of a number of variables such as age, size, resources, and goals. More particularly, we try to find out whether the different organizational models can be associated with particular ways of practicing FT.

## ELEMENTS OF ORGANIZATIONAL MODELS

### The Organizational Model as a Construct

In Chapter 1, the study of a range of concepts and movements to which FT can be affiliated suggested specific organizational models for the pursuit of hybrid goals. Core elements of such models were the *legal form* and the *governance model*. Nevertheless, other elements could be used to discriminate between organizations, leading to other boundary lines in the organizational landscape. For instance, if we take a large bureaucratic nonprofit organization, it may have more similarities with other large bureaucratic private or public organizations than with a small nonprofit structure; and the latter may, in turn, be more similar to small entrepreneurial companies than to the large nonprofit in question.

It is suggested here that, more than the size, it is the *architecture* of organizations that deserves attention. Architecture, design, or structure are central notions in organization theory. The perspective adopted here considers the architecture as the result of two main features: how work is divided within the organization (among people, among departments, etc.), and how work is coordinated (Nizet and Pichault 1995; Mintzberg 1980, 1984b,). Concretely, in the case of FTSEs, attention to the architecture may help to understand how the FT activity is organized within the FTSE and concretely translates into functions, units, departments, coordination mechanisms, etc. Such information is not given by the legal form and the governance model—although these different elements of the organizational model are likely to be related to each other.

The remainder of this chapter will describe in more detail how the architecture, legal form, and governance model may be defined and articulated to better capture the diverse and hybrid models in FTSEs.

## The Legal Form

### Introduction

The diversity of legal forms in the FT sector calls for a better understanding of this structural element. In much of the traditional management literature, however, this is not a central issue, since it is implicitly assumed that businesses necessarily take one of the forms suited to them. It seems more an issue for law specialists than for organization theorists. Nevertheless, in economics and sociology, whole streams of literature have emerged and developed exclusively around particular legal forms, specifically around "alternative" legal forms such as nonprofit organizations and cooperatives. In these pieces of literature, the legal form has become a main distinctive characteristic of organizations. As mentioned in the first chapter, the legal form is an important issue in at least two concepts to which FT can be related: cooperatives and the social economy. Yet, it should be noted that several authors working on social enterprise and social entrepreneurship have criticized such a narrow focus and called for a more relaxed view on legal forms (e.g., Battle Anderson and Dees 2006). The legal form is thus only one element of the organizational model.

### Descriptive Findings

The study confirms general observations of the field, which indicate that there is now much more diversity of legal forms than in the early history of the movement (Becchetti and Huybrechts 2008, Huybrechts 2007). Except in Italy, where nearly all FTSEs are social cooperatives, a broad diversity of legal forms is observed in the other regions and countries, as it appears in Table 3.1.

There are different classifications of legal forms according to each national context. Sub-categories may exist, as well as specific features bridging several forms (such as the Société à finalité sociale in Belgium or the Onlus in Italy). The different legal frameworks also include advantages and/or requirements that are very different in each country, as will be examined further.

*Table 3.1*    FTSEs' Legal Forms

| Form<br>Name | Nonprofit | Cooperative | Business | Individual | Group | TOTAL |
|---|---|---|---|---|---|---|
| Belgium | 5 | 2 | 3 | 2 | 3 | 15 |
| Rhône-Alpes | 9 | 1 | 6 | 5 | 1 | 22 |
| England | 1 | 2 | 5 | 0 | 3 | 11 |
| Rome | 1 | 7 | 0 | 1 | 0 | 9 |
| Total | 16 | 12 | 15 | 7 | 7 | 57 |
| Proportion | 28% | 22% | 26% | 12% | 12% | 100% |

# Architecture

## Introduction

As previously mentioned, the architecture, structure, or design of organizations can be decomposed in two elements. First, there is the question of how work is divided among people, units or departments. Second, the question arises of how the different people, units or departments are coordinated. Workers—in the broad sense of the term—may be specialized in one task, or they may master several types of tasks. Horizontal division refers to the number of tasks realized by each operator (the more numerous these tasks, the lower the horizontal division). Vertical division refers to the separation between design and implementation (the more workers are involved at different stages of the work, the lower the vertical division).

Mintzberg (1980) distinguishes six coordination mechanisms among *workers*: mutual adjustment, direct supervision, procedural standardization, results standardization, qualification standardization, and in his later work[1], norms standardization. Nizet and Pichault (1995, 2001) suggest that these six mechanisms can be grouped into three categories: interpersonal mechanisms (mutual adjustment and direct supervision), mechanisms based on work formalization (procedures and results standardization), and mechanisms based on mental representations (qualifications and norms standardization). Division and coordination refer to individual operators. When we consider the level of *departments* (or units), the same categorization of how work is divided and how it is coordinated can be found. Division of work among departments may be based on inputs (e.g., by functions: production, marketing, accounting, etc.) or outputs (e.g., by types of products, clients, markets, etc.). Similar to coordination between operators, interdepartmental coordination may be organized on the basis of three criteria: interpersonal relationships, formalization, and mental representations. One of the main mental representations is ideological mobilization. Ideology can help reduce the divergences among departments and bring them together toward a collectively shared mission. According to Mintzberg (1980), ideology is thus a strong cohesion mechanism that facilitates organizational change.

### Descriptive Findings

If we cross the way in which work is divided and the way in which it is coordinated in the FTSEs, seven categories appear. The percentage of FTSEs is indicated for each category.

- Individual FTSEs (24.5%). No work division and coordination, the entrepreneur is the central figure.
- Polyvalent teams with direct supervision (14%). Coordination is centralized and work division informal. In these FTSEs, the leader manages a small team of employees who perform various tasks.
- Ouput-based FTSEs with direct supervision (5%). This category combines high levels of centralization (in terms of coordination) and formalization (in terms of work division). In these FTSEs, work is organized by outputs (by product, region, type of customer, etc.) and units or departments have been created around these outputs. Coordination is ensured by the entrepreneur, although the mission completes the coordination of the efforts along the same lines.
- Ouput-based FTSEs with standardization of results (9%). While the coordination is less centralized than in the previous categories, work division is more formalized. These FTSEs differ from the previous ones by the fact that they are larger, more formally structured and coordinated by the mission more than by a single entrepreneur. This is likely to entail bureaucratic trends, required both by the division of work—each department has a specific activity or target—and by its coordination.
- Hybrid FTSEs (output and input-based departmentalization) with standardization of results (14%). This situation is similar to the previous category, but with an even more formalized work division. Bureaucratic trends are likely to increase even more for FTSEs that are organized simultaneously by inputs and by outputs. In this case, the FTSE is not dependent upon one founder or entrepreneur, and has a mission and history strong enough to span people and generations.
- Polyvalent teams with mutual adjustment (21%). In this case, coordination is decentralized and work division informal. The most typical case is that of volunteers working together, without strong individual specialization but rather with adhocratic projects. Work division is not as strong and stable as in the case of committees or departments: episodic projects may set the pace of FTSEs' activities.
- Committees with mutual adjustment (12%). In these FTSEs, specialization is more common than in the previous category. Work division is also more formalized. One of the reasons for this is that FTSEs

are larger and thus less likely to remain as teams in which "everyone does everything." Employees and/or volunteers are thus organized in committees. Nevertheless, these committees are less formal than departments, as they may emerge for episodic events and as employees or volunteers may occasionally participate in one or the other. The activities of the FTSE are not clearly defined but may vary according to the episodic projects.

These seven categories are not neatly separated from each other. Nevertheless, when we look at the FTSEs that compose each category, there seems to be a certain resemblance, including in other aspects of the organizational model (see next section).

### *From Architecture to Configuration*

Beyond this static view of architecture, the notion of configuration has emerged to refer not only to "a combination of internally consistent design parameters" such as work division and coordination, but also to the fit of these parameters with the environment (Mintzberg 1980, 323). Combining these different parameters, Mintzberg distinguishes five configurations: the missionary, the bureaucratic, the adhocratic, the entrepreneurial and the professional configuration. In his later writings, he discusses the various possibilities of hybrids combining elements from these different configurations.

In the context of this work, only the configurations corresponding best to the FTSEs' situation will be presented in detail. Among Mintzberg's categories, FTSEs fit best to the missionary configuration, the description of which corresponds well to the philosophy of numerous FTSEs: "The strong system of internal beliefs, built around the organization's mission–whether that be to change society directly in some way, change it indirectly by attracting members and changing them, or merely offering members some pursuit attractive to them–serves to integrate tightly the efforts of insiders." (1984b, 210). These missionary elements nevertheless seem to coexist quite often with those of another configuration, making most FTSEs "hybrids" to a certain extent. The entrepreneurial configuration, particularly, seems widespread among small FTSEs. Larger FTSEs, on the contrary, seem to gradually include bureaucratic trends. And adhocratic trends may be observed particularly in volunteer-based FTSEs.

### *The Missionary Configuration*

The missionary configuration is characterized by a prevalence of mission goals over system goals. Coordination among operators is made through norm standardization. Operators are motivated not by financial rewards—which are generally low—but by norms and values. Vertical and horizontal differentiation is low and operators are highly qualified. The coordination is done through ideological mobilization. Goals are necessarily mission goals, both in the official documents and in the decisions, and are well integrated to each other. The power is in the hands of the strategic core and other organizational actors are involved and loyal to the mission. This configuration seems shared by all FTSEs to a certain extent. But most FTSEs actually combine such configuration with elements from other configurations, corresponding to their age and way of practicing FT.

## *The Entrepreneurial Configuration*

This configuration is characterized by the authority of a leader who is often also the owner and the founder. Vertical work division is strong: operators are under direct hierarchical supervision. Horizontal work division is low: operators are often polyvalent. Departmentalization is done by inputs, but formalization is low. The entrepreneurial configuration is common in young and small organizations with simple technology. The goals in an entrepreneurial configuration are in the first place survival goals, because of the small size of the organization and its dependence on one person. Mission goals may be linked to the entrepreneur's personal values. Power is in the hands of the leader, who gathers the resources, information, and expertise. As there are no (or few) owners other than the leader, there is generally no counter-power.

Many small, young FTSEs have an entrepreneurial configuration. The power is concentrated in the hands of the leader who is also the founder and among the main owners. The mission goals directly depend on his or her vision of FT. The main system goal is survival: in a sector were many small FTSEs collapse, the challenge is to survive in the first years. The employees hired by the leader may have a specific qualification or experience (e.g., accounting, marketing, development, and education), but it is likely that they will perform different tasks. In small FTSEs, it is common for employees to simultaneously sell products, manage stocks, deal with producer organizations, participate in education campaigns, get involved in hiring processes, etc. All the people are under direct supervision of the leader, possibly with an intermediate supervisor (e.g., sales manager). Coordination is in any case interpersonal: there are few formal procedures (or they are not implemented). It is worth noting that entrepreneurial configuration should not be confused with commercial orientation. Nonprofit, volunteer-based FTSEs may be entrepreneurial. Not all the business-form FTSEs are entrepreneurial. Yet, the entrepreneurial configuration seems well suited for a business-focused activity.

When leaders have a forceful character and shape the organization according to their preferences, entrepreneurial configurations may last for some time. But, because of their young age and size and their reliance on a single individual, it is likely that the entrepreneurial configuration will be only temporary: the organization will move to another configuration or disappear. In an unstable environment with few "success stories" to rely on and difficult access to financial resources, the reliance on one or few individuals with a necessarily limited expertise may be a handicap.

In most cases, however, the weaknesses—age, size, and reliance on one individual—kill the configuration instead of the organization (Mintzberg 1984b). This is why entrepreneurial FTSEs might evolve toward a more explicit missionary configuration. Mintzberg explains how, after the departure of the charismatic leader, "there may be a natural tendency for those who remain to consolidate and institutionalize that charisma in the form of 'sagas', norms, and traditions (Clark, 1970, 1972), thereby coalescing around an ideology and so effecting a transition to the missionary" (1984b, 215).

### The Adhocracy

Adhocracy refers to a configuration where people work together in projects. Coordination is made by mutual adjustment and norms standardization. Vertical and horizontal work division is low. Units are grouped by outputs (horizontal differentiation). Linking mechanisms are well developed and mainly based on interpersonal relationships. An adhocratic organization is likely to be young and small. Mission goals prevail and are rarely operational. Operational decisions are decentralized, but strategic decisions remain centralized.

FTSEs with committees or departments organized by projects, i.e., by outputs, tend to function in an adhocratic way. Typically, projects may be launched for particular products or activities (e.g., campaigns). Producer support may also take the form of a range of episodic projects, even when there has been a long-term relationship with the producers. In such a case, the horizontal and vertical differentiation levels are both low. Mission goals clearly prevail. Decision-making is decentralized. In fact, the description of the environment of adhocratic organizations as new, unstable and complex may be seen as the closest to the situation of the FT field.

### Bureaucratic Trends

Bureaucracy is located at the opposite of the entrepreneurial and adhocratic configurations. Whether "machine" or "professional" bureaucracy, work division is high. Units are grouped by inputs (vertical differentiation). This configuration is most likely to develop among large and old organizations. System goals clearly prevail over mission goals, and decisions are decentralized

If we examine the evolution of FT pioneers, a number of bureaucratic evolutions can be identified. Widely commented in the literature is the evolution of partnerships with producer groups, from personalized contacts and flexible arrangements based on mutual trust, to impersonal, standardized relationships based on control (Bisaillon, Gendron, and Turcotte 2005b;

Renard 2003; Diaz Pedregal 2007). The development of standards and certification procedures by FLO is regularly criticized for inducing an increasing formalization and bureaucratization of FTSEs' partnerships with the producers (Lemay 2007; Charlier et al. 2007). In several FTSEs, the leader and the people from the producer support unit regretted that they no longer had the time to visit the producers, that they had lost personal contacts with many of them, and that this was "the other side of the coin" regarding their growth and professionalization. This echoes Mintzberg's comment on why missionaries tend to evolve into bureaucracies: "Time tends to blunt ideology, converting enthusiasm into obligation, traditions into dogmas, norms into rules" (Mintzberg 1984b, 217).

Second, to see the effects of growth, the evolution of worldshops provides interesting illustrations. Several FTSEs gradually hired staff to manage the shop and coach the volunteers, which increased the control over these volunteers. While the teams of volunteers were very mission-driven, "professionalization" was often synonymous with increased bureaucracy (in terms of stock management, accounting, etc.). In several pioneer FTSEs, the commercial development required to hire people from the business world (e.g., in the marketing department). This challenged the initial intent of these FTSEs to keep the difference in salary between the top leader and the lowest positions as low as possible. This is described as follows by Mintzberg: "Status differences thus arise between managers and workers, hierarchy is reinforced, and a transition towards the closed system is encouraged" (1984b, 217).

Nevertheless, it seems that these bureaucratic evolutions are not challenging the mission in such a way that we could speak of bureaucratic configurations. "Pure" machine bureaucracies are not (yet?) to be found in the FT sector. Most FTSEs are too young, too small, too flexible, and too focused on mission goals to become machine bureaucracies. Moreover, even FTSEs that are older and larger than their peers are still far from the model of old and large organizations described by the organization theorists who, following Weber, have explored bureaucracy (Rouleau 2007).

### Hybrid Configurations

In practice, most organizations combine elements of different configurations (e.g., Nizet and Pichault 1995). In the case of FTSEs, it seems reasonable to suggest that there is always at least part of missionary configuration, combined with features of the entrepreneurial, adhocratic or bureaucratic configurations. It may be that an organization is split up in two units, each of which has its own configuration (juxtaposition). Or the whole organization shares two types of configurations (superposition). For Nizet and Pichault (1995), interesting questions to ask are the origin of such hybridization and its consequences in terms of linking among units and power distribution.

Mintzberg (1984a) also analyzes how the different configurations are likely to evolve over time. The organization generally starts with an

*Table 3.2*  Linking Work Division and Coordination with Mintzberg's Configurations

| Work coordination / Work division | Direct supervision | | Standarization of results | | Mutual adjustment | |
|---|---|---|---|---|---|---|
| Individual | 24.5% | Entrepreneurial (and missionary) 44% | / | | / | |
| Polyvalent team | 14% | | / | | 21% | Missionary with adhocratic trends 23% |
| Committees | / | | / | | 12% | |
| Output-based | 5% | | 9% | Missionary with bureautic trends 23% | / | |
| Hybrid | / | | 14% | | / | |

entrepreneurial configuration. Then, with the growth of the organization, the founder is likely to retire and the organization to move on to a missionary, a bureaucratic or an adhocratic configuration. Finally, in order not to decline, organizations may try revitalization or restructuring processes. This is referred to as the "organizational lifecycle," which will be applied to FTSEs at the end of this chapter.

Table 3.2 locates the observed configurations in the table crossing work division and coordination and mentions the percentage of FTSEs that seem closest to each configuration.

## Governance

### Introduction

Governance is a notion that can be used with very different meanings and on different levels of analysis (Cornforth 2003). While issues of "corporate governance" have increasingly been discussed, the academic research on organizational governance in a wider context than that of the large, quoted corporation is still limited. According to Cornforth (2003, 2), "[t]here appears to have been an implicit assumption that what matters in organizations is the way they are managed" [rather than the way they are governed].

The focus here is on the governance structures such as the General Assembly (GA) and the Board of Directors (Board), although these are only the most formal channels through which organizations are governed (Charreaux 1997; Saidel 1998). Reviewing the literature on Boards in different types of organizational forms, Cornforth (2003) identifies a number of questions that may be grouped into two major issues: the role of the Board (the functions it performs and its relationships with the management) and its composition. These two issues can be extended to the other governance bodies. Both the role and the composition of the governance structures depend much on the paradigm through which governance—and more generally the organization—is examined. Cornforth identifies six paradigms or perspectives for examining governance structures:

### Agency Theory: A Compliance Model

Agency theory considers that the main function of the governance structures is to control management, and to ensure compliance of managers with the shareholders' interests. Several authors suggest that agency theory is difficult to apply in all types of organizations, particularly in "non-investor-owned" forms such as nonprofits, because of the ambiguity over who the principals or owners are (Cornforth 2003). Yet, in any type of organizational form, even in nonprofits (Labie 2005), an agency perspective may be useful when we look at the governance structures as "guardians" of the organizational missions. Members of these structures should thus represent the "principals" (owners, members, society, etc.) and be able to control that the managers effectively pursue these missions.

### Stewardship Theory: A Partnership Model

Stewardship theory has an opposite, nonopportunistic view on managers, who are seen as the "stewards" of the organization's resources. The manager(s) and the governance structures are thus viewed as partners. The main function of governance is to increase organizational performance. The Board has a strategic function of implementing the mission. Its members should thus be selected on the basis of their expertise.

### Resource Dependence Theory: A Co-optation Model

In a resource dependence perspective, the governance structures are located at the interface between the organization and its environment. They thus constitute a means to reduce uncertainty by establishing linkages with other organizations and stakeholders so as to capture and secure resources (role of "boundary-spanning"). Members of the governance structures should be selected on the basis of their links with constituencies able to provide valuable resources.

### A Democratic Perspective

From such a perspective, governance structures should be elected by and represent the organization's membership. Board members should thus be appointed less because of their expertise than based on how well they represent the broader community of members.

### A Stakeholder Perspective

According to the stakeholder perspective, organizations have a responsibility toward various stakeholders concerned by their activity. The governance structures may thus be a place through which stakeholders are represented and have an influence on organizations. "By incorporating different stakeholders on boards, it is expected that organizations will be more likely to respond to broader social interests than the narrow interests of one group. This leads to a political role for boards negotiating and resolving the potential conflicting interests of different stakeholder groups in order to determine the objectives of the organization and set policy" (Cornforth 2003, 9). According to Cornforth, the practice of stakeholder involvement is more common and less controversial in nonprofit and cooperative organizations than in traditional businesses.

### Managerial Hegemony Theory: A "Rubber Stamp" Model

Managerial hegemony theory is based on the thesis of Berle and Means (1932), who state that control is no longer exerted by the owners but rather by the managers. In this perspective, governance structures, particularly the Board, may be seen as "rubber stamps" for managers, providing legitimacy to their actions. Such a vision of governance is likely to be the most adequate when managers are in a powerful situation (typically when they have been holding their function for a long time), while members of the governance structures have only limited time and access to information.

Cornforth calls for a multi-paradigm approach, in which each paradigm brings a particular insight to the understanding of governance. This is convergent with the blending of different approaches proposed in this book. According to Cornforth, such theoretical blending may help to highlight the paradoxes and tensions in governance. For instance, in terms of roles of governance, a typical source of tension lies between conformance (agency) and performance (stewardship). Another source of tension is that between representative (democracy, stakeholder-based) and professional (stewardship, agency) governance.

Compared with much work on governance that focuses on the members of governance structures as the main source of information, the methodology used in this study took the standpoint of the managers, following Mole (2003). The case studies, however, enabled an extended vision combining the perspectives from managers, staff, Board members and various stakeholders. Questions on governance in the general study concerned both the composition and the roles (as perceived by the managers) of the different governance bodies, including the General Assembly, the Board, and Advisory Boards where applicable.

## Descriptive Findings

### Roles: General Assembly (GA)

When asked what was the role of the GA in their FTSE, 63% of the managers mentioned "representation," although it seemed to take on different meanings in terms of who should be represented (volunteers, sharehold ers, producers, etc.). It is in FTSEs involving volunteers that representation seemed most central, in line with the "democratic" paradigm. "Control" was the other function that was often cited (52%): such an "agency view" was mostly perceived by managers of larger FTSEs.

In smaller FTSEs centered around one or several founders/managers, the latter mainly viewed a formal role for the GA. The GA existed only "on paper," to fulfill the legal requirements. In these cases, the GA was either composed only of the founders/managers, or included friends or family with no intent of taking real decision-making power. This may be assimi- lated to the "rubber stamp" model of managerial hegemony. Few managers considered the GA as a pool of expertise for decision-making, in accor- dance with the stewardship model. Other roles (e.g., boundary-spanning) were rarely mentioned.

### Board of Directors

Answers about the role of the Board were more diverse and also more complete. "Representation" and "control" were again the most frequently- cited functions, but in the reverse order (64% for the first and 79% for the second). Provision of expertise to guide decision-making followed closely with 61%, particularly in more business-oriented FTSEs. Certain manag- ers explicitly mentioned the type of expertise available within their Board. Other managers rather insisted on the Board as an audience to expose par- ticular problems and obtain advice thanks to collective thinking (manage- rial hegemony model).

Only 20% of the interviewed managers mentioned the role of giving access to resources and legitimacy. 26% of the managers mentioned the Board as a tool to exchange information with stakeholder groups involved in the FTSE (typically volunteers, but also employees and partners).

### Advisory Board (AB)

While the main role of the ABs was to give advice, the content of such advice varied much. Advice on economic issues was mentioned by 34% of the managers of FTSEs having at least one AB. Advice on producer sup- port was mentioned by 44% of the managers in question. 24% mentioned advice on political issues. Most of the ABs focused on only one of these three functions.

*Composition: General Assembly and Board of Directors*

The first interesting observation is that managers rarely distinguished the GA and the Board when mentioning the types of people and stakeholders represented. This is why these two structures will be considered jointly in this section. The identical composition of these two structures may seem logical, since the Board is elected by the GA. Board members might, however, be co-opted, thus not originate from the GA (Campi, Defourny, and Grégoire 2006). The differences between Board and GA seemed, nevertheless, very slight. Based on the composition of both governance structures, three categories could be distinguished.

### FTSEs Dominated by Founders/managers and "investors" (32%)

In small entrepreneurial FTSEs, it often happened that the founders were either in sufficient number to compose the GA and the Board (generally the legal minimum was three), or were supported by a few investors, yet without real decision-making power. In these cases, the founders wished to manage the FTSE on their own and thus did not need or want to involve other people, beyond a small number of investors who were often friends or family members. The size of the Board was thus quite small (three to five members).

In this model, governance and management are in the same hands, which contrasts with the agency model. As previously mentioned, this leads governance to be exerted by the managers themselves. The governance structures exist either only on paper or are, at best, rubber stamps that may give legitimacy and in some cases expertise to support the managers' action (managerial hegemony model and, to a lesser extent, stewardship model). Several managers mentioned a dilemma with regard to expertise: they could either take total freedom, ignoring the governance structures, but also the available expertise, or ask for more expertise but then with more (perceived) constraints on their action. For some of these managers, a solution was to capture expertise through an advisory—thus nonconstraining—board. The stewardship model seemed stronger in two cases of "mother FTSEs" having founded a new FTSE. The mother FTSE's managers were represented on the daughter FTSE's Board to ensure that performance and coherence with the formers' strategy. This case may thus be seen as a mix between an agency view (control) and a stewardship model, with managers of the mother and the daughter FTSE working together to increase the global performance.

### FTSEs Dominated by Volunteers (38%)

Volunteers are people who work voluntarily and regularly for the FTSE (in a worldshop, a warehouse, for education or lobbying campaigns, for administrative tasks, etc.). Most nonprofit FTSEs' governance structures were mainly composed of volunteers. Others involved stakeholders such as employees but only to a certain extent, with volunteers remaining dominant.[2] Volunteer-based FTSEs put much emphasis on representation, in compliance with the democratic model widely observed in nonprofit and cooperative organizations (Spear 2004). In the context of FT, internal democracy may be seen as part of the political side of the FT project, coherently to what is required for the producers in the South (Develtere and Pollet 2005). In several worldshop-based FTSEs, the shops of each region elected their representatives on the Board. This led volunteer-based Boards to a medium or large size (6 to 20 members) compared with other FTSEs.

Representation also allowed volunteers to control the FTSE, acting as guardians of the organizational missions. Managers of volunteer-based FTSEs reported that the control by volunteers particularly aimed at the socio-political missions. Attention to the economic performance increased very much in times of crisis, confirming the ability of volunteer-based Boards to increase control, policy-making, and activity in these periods (Miller-Millesen 2003).

Third, volunteers were also involved in governance because of their expertise (either in a control or in a partnership perspective), because of their access to resources and/or because of their boundary-spanning role. These alternative roles for volunteers seemed stronger for "co-opted" Board members. These members typically originated from other NGOs, from the academia or from the business world and were involved because of their specific expertise or networking role. This could lead to tensions between the democratic model of the Board and the performance model, as observed by Cornforth (2003).

### Multi-stakeholder FTSEs (30%)

A number of FTSEs had different types of stakeholders involved in their governance structures, without one exclusive dominant group. The presence of various stakeholders led to larger Boards than in the two other models (large to very large, from 10 to 20 members).

Some of these FTSEs were initially single-stakeholder (typically, volunteer-based) and progressively included other stakeholders in the governance structures. These stakeholders then acquired increasing decision-making power. Other FTSEs immediately started with a multi-stakeholder model, for instance, when this was required by law (SCIC model in France). In both cases, the presence of multiple stakeholders makes the resource-access and the boundary-spanning roles of governance much more important and effective than in the other models of governance.

If we take the example of Soli'gren, the representation of public authorities (the city of Grenoble), NGOs, local producers, volunteers, employees, and customers was perceived as an extremely valuable asset in maintaining and improving the relationships with all these stakeholders (stakeholder perspective) and to secure resources from them (resource dependence

*Table 3.3*   The Three Governance Models

| | Founder/manager-investor dominated | Volunteer-based | Multi-stakeholder |
|---|---|---|---|
| Average size of Board | Small (3–5) | Medium to very large (6–20) | Large to very large (10–20) |
| Main functions | Rubber stamp and expertise | Representation, expertise and control | Representation, expertise, control, boundary-spanning and access to resources |
| Paradigms | Managerial hegemony and stewardship | Democracy, stewardship and agency | Various |
| Tensions | Total managerial freedom versus expertise | Representation and control versus expertise | Various |

perspective). These resources included subsidies, facilities given by the municipality (for instance, a low rent location for the shop and the offices), support and legitimacy from other NGOs, customers' loyalty, and so on. However, the heterogeneity of interests could lead to tensions. The constitution of the product range required negotiations between the local producers trying to increase the proportion for their products, and development NGOs preferring products from the South.

Focusing on Boards, we obtain the following synthesis table, including the average size of the Boards, the functions they perform, the paradigms that best describe them and the possible tensions between the different functions.

It is striking to observe that the three models range from a very basic role of governance, with much power to the manager, to much more complex models that provide a range of assets (expertise, resources, etc.), but also of tensions among the different functions. FTSEs thus face the challenge of finding an adequate balance between assets and complexity. The analytical chapters, and particularly the seventh chapter, will provide propositions on how to deal with such a challenge.

### Advisory Boards (AB)

In 42% of the FTSEs, advisory boards (ABs) were set up to give advice on a particular issue. The names varied: advisory committee, advisory group, specific committee, etc. While ABs are not much commented in the governance literature, they play a crucial role, performing tasks neglected by the Board and linking the organization to key stakeholders in the environment (Saidel 1998).

Three types of ABs were identified, corresponding to the three dimensions of FT:

- Economic AB: a group of people with entrepreneurial experience and skills invited to play the role of consultants on economic decision-making
- Producer support AB: a group of people whose mission is to help the FTSE select the producers, follow up on them, and increase the impact on their communities
- Political AB: a group of people interested in the political mission of the FTSE and contributing to its design and diffusion

Economic ABs seem to be set up when it appears that the existing governance bodies (typically the Board) lack skills and experience to advise the staff about the trading activity. It may be that the Board is composed of volunteers because the FTSE is volunteer-based. In such a case, the election of the Board members is likely to lead to representation (democratic model) rather than expertise (stewardship model). This is typically what occurred in one of the "group" FTSEs. When the original nonprofit FTSE created a second, commercial company, volunteers wished to keep the control over the latter through a majority of shares and a Board predominantly made up of volunteers. It quickly became apparent, however, that the volunteers on the Board were facing difficulties in taking commercial decisions (strategic contribution), and in controlling the commercial strategy and the financial situation. Under the impulse of the marketing director, an AB was set up for this purpose, instead of changing the Board and challenging its role of democratic representation. The AB had no decision-making power but its advice was seriously taken into account by the Board. At this stage, the AB can be seen as a solution to bring expertise without challenging the democratic perspective to which many volunteers are quite attached. Another type of economic AB was when an individual FT entrepreneur required economic advice. Several entrepreneurs mentioned that they had built a network of relationships in the business world to collect commercial and financial advice. This enabled them to benefit from advice without having to share the control of their venture.

Second, producer support ABs (often called "partnership" or "producers" commissions) were mainly found in volunteer-based FTSEs. The intent was to give the volunteers a control over the "core business" of the FTSE: the partnerships with the producers. Volunteers did not want the decisions regarding producers to be taken only by the staff, which might induce technical, procedural, and opaque decision-making. The idea was also to submit the delicate questions around partnerships with producers to a broader assembly. In several cases, NGOs and people with experience in development cooperation were invited to join the partnership commission.

Third, political ABs were also found in a number of volunteer-based FTSEs. However, political ABs were often also political *action* groups. In the study, FTSEs with political ABs expected advice (besides action) not only on the political project of FT but, more broadly, on related topics. Examples include Oxfam, ADM teams, and Italian FTSEs such as Il Fiore, Pangea-NT, and Mondo Solidale. In two of these examples, the political AB was at the origin of a political reflection on how to bring the FTSE closer to sustainable development, for instance, by introducing local products in the assortment.

In conclusion, it seems that ABs were set up to compensate for a "weakness" in the governance structures (economic ABs) or to reinforce the decision-making in an area where the FTSE required broader thinking (producer support and political ABs).

## TOWARDS A TAXONOMY OF ORGANIZATIONAL MODELS

The three elements presented here—legal form, architecture, and governance—were combined thanks to cluster analysis.[3] Five categories emerged that seemed internally consistent while sufficiently distinct from each other. This section reviews these categories, starting with the simplest and gradually adding complexity.

### Type 1: Individual FTSEs

The first category is composed of thirteen *individual or quasi-individual FTSEs*. These FTSEs are very simple and often small (in terms of both people and turnover). Individual FTSEs are quite specific because they are not exactly "organizations"—they may at best be considered as "potential organizations." Their number, and their growth, especially in France and in Belgium, made them a key category to fully capture the current scope of organizational diversity in FT. In all the individual FTSEs of the study, the entrepreneurs are polyvalent people having a specific expertise in terms of products (e.g., Satya-Pure Elements and Vino Mundo) and/or distribution strategies (e.g., Esprit Equo). It may be people converting an existing business to FT (e.g., Vino Mundo, Il Fiore, D'ici et de là-bas) or FT ventures created from scratch.

The most natural evolution for individual FTSEs is to grow, hire employees, obtain additional capital, and thus move to the next, type 2 category. We can find such an evolution in the cases of Siesta and Karawan (which became businesses with several shareholders and employees). Another possible—but seemingly more exceptional—evolution is toward involving noninvestors and to associate them collectively into ownership (e.g., by setting up a nonprofit or a cooperative). A third and more widespread evolution is toward expanding the venture while remaining as a single entrepreneur: the interviews suggest that this was more often due to a choice of the entrepreneur, reluctant to lose the control of the venture, than to the inability to find associates.

## Type 2: Entrepreneurial, Business-form FTSEs

In the second category, we find thirteen *business-form, entrepreneurial, and manager-owned FTSEs* that include a few associates[4] or sometimes also other stakeholders. These FTSEs are either organized as polyvalent teams or departmentalized by outputs. Their size is, logically, larger than in the first category.

This category is more homogeneous than the previous one. The core is made of manager-owned, entrepreneurial, business-form FTSEs, although there are a number of exceptions, in terms of legal form (e.g., the nonprofit Fair Trade Original and the cooperative Emile) and governance (multi-stakeholder schemes in Citizen Dream and Cafédirect).

Entrepreneurial businesses may grow, to a certain extent, without changing their configuration. But as described by Mintzberg (1980), continued growth and/or departure of the founder will inevitably push the organization from an entrepreneurial to a more missionary—and probably more bureaucratic—configuration. We could call such a configuration, in which the mission embodied by the founder has been translated to the organizational level, "missionary businesses." People Tree offers a good example of such an evolution. Another possible evolution is toward the "group" structure (type 5).

## Type 3: Volunteer-based FTSEs

The third category is composed of sixteen *volunteer-based*, missionary-adhocratic nonprofit or cooperative FTSEs. FTSEs in this category are generally older than in the previous category, although several volunteer-based nonprofit FTSEs were recently created (e.g., ADM shops or Roman worldshops). The size is medium or large in terms of the number of people involved (employees and volunteers), but relatively small in terms of turnover, at least compared to the number of people involved.

Central in this category is the volunteer-based governance and functioning, more than the legal form (nonprofit or cooperative, according to the context). The configuration of these FTSEs is often explicitly missionary-adhocratic. Indeed, while the mission is a powerful coordination mode, it often expresses itself through adhocratic decision modes, especially in smaller nonprofits or cooperatives: leaders may emerge, strong personalities may coexist, but equality of statuses is favored in the context of a drive for democracy and participation. The drive for equality also concerns employees, with a salary differentiation meant to be as low as possible. The larger the FTSE, however, the more difficult it is to maintain such equality.[5] Nevertheless, despite the differences between small, adhocratic, and large, bureaucratic volunteer-based FTSEs, the dominance of volunteers at the governance and the operational level makes these FTSEs relatively homogeneous.

Several larger and older volunteer-based FTSEs evolved into group structures (type 5). The subsequent chapters will offer rich interpretations to understand this phenomenon. Another possible evolution is to the "multistakeholder cooperative" form, with possible inclusion of stakeholders other than volunteers in the governance structures. Several Italian FT pioneers have evolved in this way, taking benefit of the change toward the newly created social cooperative framework to open their governance structures to a wider array of stakeholders. Finally, Saldac provides an example of the possible evolution from a volunteer-based nonprofit form to a professionalized business form, when founders wish to show that they are a "true" business, albeit with social and political aims.

## Type 4: Multi-stakeholder Cooperatives

The fourth category is composed of seven FTSEs, the distinctive features of which are easy to identify: they are all multi-stakeholder cooperatives. These two attributes, nevertheless, are not automatically linked to each other. Indeed, as we have seen, multi-stakeholder FTSEs are not necessarily cooperatives: they can be businesses, nonprofits or group structures. And cooperative FTSEs are not necessarily multi-stakeholder organizations. But there seems to be a strong congruence between the cooperative form and the multistakeholder configuration. The reason might be that the cooperative form offers an alternative to and intermediate solution between volunteer-based nonprofits and manager-owned businesses. For instance, when a group of managers or employees is at the origin of the FTSE and values the cooperative ideal, the worker cooperative form is interesting—e.g., Just Fair Trade and Ethiquable. And in the context of FT, workers seem to be keen to include other stakeholders such as volunteers (if any), donors, partner NGOs, investors, etc. While many FTSEs include several stakeholders in their governance structures, the multi-stakeholder nature is particularly strong in cooperatives such as Soli'gren and Pangea-NT. In terms of architecture, many solutions are available depending upon the size and the activities of the FTSE. But the architecture is likely to be modeled according to the strong missionary ideal of multi-stakeholder FTSEs, with little differentiation among the employees and coordination through mutual adjustment.

Multi-stakeholder cooperatives are less likely than volunteer-based FTSEs to evolve into groups, probably because the cooperative form seems already perceived as an organizational model that enables to pursue hybrid goals. Moreover, the cooperative form still enables volunteers to be involved without necessarily bringing capital. This is especially the case in the new cooperative forms specifically designed for combining economic activity, social mission, and advocacy (e.g., the Italian social cooperatives, the solidarity cooperatives in France, and the CIC in the UK). Hence, unlike nonprofit FTSEs, multi-stakeholder FT cooperatives enjoyed much latitude in dealing with hybrid goals and activities.

## Type 5: Group Structures

Finally, the fifth category is that of the older and larger hybrid, slightly bureaucratic, and multi-stakeholder FTSEs, typically group structures (MMH-MFT, Traidcraft, etc.—eight FTSEs). While FTSEs organized as groups all distinguish the economic and the socio-political functions of FT, the legal forms adopted for each of the entities may vary. The nonprofit form is often privileged for the socio-political entity, while the commercial entity may take a cooperative or a business form. The governance of these FTSEs is generally multi-stakeholder. The governance and architecture of groups seems more complex than in other FTSEs. This is why bureaucratic trends are almost inevitable, with the mission formalized into charters and procedures. Traidcraft provides, again, an interesting example, with a "Deed of mutual covenant" "which enshrines Traidcraft's foundation principles and sets out the basis for mutual co-operation"[6]. Moreover, a foundation was set up specifically as a guardian of the overall mission of the group.

It is difficult to predict how groups might evolve in terms of their organizational model. Together with age and size, complexity is likely to increase, with a formalization of the linkages between the entities (criteria for dividing the economic value generated, procedures for selecting producer groups and ensuring their follow-up, etc.). However, the two entities might also, in the absence of coordination, specialize to such an extent that they would follow separate ways and become totally distinct organizations. In such a scenario, the nonprofit entity, disconnected from the economic activity, would become very similar to other development and/or advocacy NGOs. Conversely, the business entity would lose its connection with the socio-political dimensions and become similar to other businesses. When asked about the added value of the group structure, however, the interviewees seemed keen to keep strong links between the entities to avoid such an "isomorphic" scenario, as will be explained further.

## Outliers and Missing Categories

Certain FTSEs do not fall neatly into one of the categories and combine characteristics of two categories. Typically, Cafédirect is a unique example in that it combines features of the types 4 and 5 categories (because of the multi-stakeholder governance and the missionary-bureaucratic nature) and the type 2 category (because of the business legal form and functioning as well as the 100% market resources). Cafédirect can be considered as a particularly interesting and pioneer example of an original organizational model. More generally, the taxonomy does not pretend to exhaust all the organizational avenues when launching a FT activity. Indeed, the capacity of social—including organizational—innovation of FTSEs implies the possibility of multiple other organizational combinations. Nevertheless, this taxonomy seems broad enough to include the different models observed in the four regions. Based on the literature on FTSEs in other countries, it seems reasonable to assume that the categories do reflect common patterns that can be observed at this date among FTSEs in the North and, more globally, among social enterprises.

## Organizational Trajectories

On the basis of the observations of how certain FTSEs have evolved from one category to another, it is possible to perceive a number of common patterns. This may be linked to the notion of "organizational life cycle," which has been developed by configuration theorists (Mintzberg 1984a). The specific contribution here is to include the legal form and the governance model in the structural analysis. Obviously, the study is far from sufficient to claim validity and extrapolation to all FTSEs, let alone all social enterprises. It is thus important to highlight the hypothetical nature of this exercise. Indeed, while certain organizational changes are well documented (for instance, the emergence of group structures), most others are illustrated only by one or two examples in the study. Nevertheless, there are some hints about how FTSEs in each category are *likely* to evolve. The different trajectories are depicted in the following figure. While all categories are also exposed to failure, it seems that young and thus small FTSEs are even more fragile.

The different categories have been depicted horizontally according to Mintzberg's configurations. While the missionary configuration is common to all FTSEs, the three other trends that coexist with such a missionary

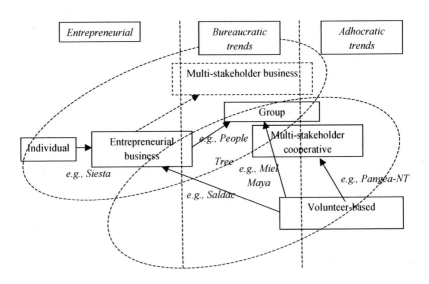

*Figure 3.1*   Possible organizational trajectories.

configuration are positioned from left to right. It is worth noting that the left and right columns—respectively, the entrepreneurial and the adhocratic trends—seem to correspond to FTSEs' configurations at the time of their creation, while the middle column—the bureaucratic trends–seems to consist of much older and larger FTSEs. It is thus logical that most arrows depicting changes in organizational models go from the extreme sides to the middle.

Indeed, FTSEs are not likely to immediately start off as multi-stakeholder groups or cooperatives: the only example in the study is that of Soli'gren, in which the multi-stakeholder governance was directly linked to the SCIC form imposed by the city of Grenoble. Except this case, these two types of large and complex multi-stakeholder FTSEs generally originated from volunteer-based nonprofit or cooperative FTSEs. The multi-stakeholder nature is thus, in most cases, a feature that is acquired gradually. For instance, in Pangea-NT, the founding members were all originally volunteers, but they later specialized into more specific and diversified functions: some became employed by the FTSE, others got involved in NGOs that later became associated in the governance of the FTSE, and others simply supported the FTSE through buying shares and FT products. The number of members also increased dramatically (to over 500 people) and reinforced the multi-stakeholder orientation. The same evolution occurred, for instance, in MMH-MFT, whose volunteer-based membership was progressively diversified to adapt to the distinct missions of the two organizational entities.

Our description up to this point concerns FTSEs with an originally voluntary basis. This is represented by the oval on the right. While there may be entrepreneurial dynamics in volunteer-based FTSEs, most of these FTSEs are characterized by strong missionary-adhocratic dynamics, which are likely to evolve into a stronger bureaucratization with the growth of the FTSE. Bureaucratization may occur even when the FTSE retains a nonprofit and voluntary-dominated form, as the case of Oxfam-MDM illustrates.

The common feature of FTSEs in the left oval is their entrepreneurial dynamics, which contrasts with the voluntary basis observed in the FTSEs in the other oval. The entrepreneurial dynamics, however, may evolve toward more adhocracy and/or bureaucracy, if the founding entrepreneur(s) is (are) replaced by a more collective management. There is no sufficient empirical evidence of this possible evolution, simply because the rather entrepreneurial FTSEs are often very young and are still led by their founding entrepreneur(s).

It is worth noting that certain FTSEs are located at the intersection between the two ovals. Indeed, entrepreneurial FTSEs that include multiple, including "nonbusiness" stakeholders (e.g., Citizen Dream) may become increasingly similar to FTSEs having moved from a voluntary basis to entrepreneurial dynamics (e.g., Saldac). In this intersection, we may also locate multi-stakeholder group structures as well as FTSEs such as Cafédirect, which were created by volunteer-based pioneer FTSEs—and thus have a strong link with the right oval—but with a business form and dynamics that resemble FTSEs from the upper left oval, although often with a larger size.

## LINKS WITH OTHER KEY VARIABLES

In this section, a range of variables that might be linked to the FTSEs' organizational models are examined. Three types of variables are examined: descriptive organizational variables (region, age and size); variables often commented in the FT literature (economic function in the supply chain and products); and variables relating to the "profile" regarding the three dimensions of FT (resources, leaders' profiles, goals, and activities). The links highlighted in this section constitute a data pool at the sample level which will be interpreted throughout the following chapters.

## Region

It is in Italy that the FTSEs' organizational models seem most homogeneous. Except Esprit Equo, all the Italian FTSEs in the study are social cooperatives. Half of them can be categorized as volunteer-based, while the other half evolved to a more multi-stakeholder configuration. In France (Rhône-Alpes), we find mainly the first three types of FTSEs—individual, business, and volunteer-based. More complex, multi-stakeholder forms are less common than in the other regions. All types of FTSEs are represented in the British part of the study and, to a lesser extent, in Belgium (where the "group" category is more represented among the larger FTSEs). Much of the subsequent analyses will be devoted to understanding which factors lead to such different landscapes.

## Age

It is striking to observe that more than 50% of the FTSEs in the study were created after 2000. While the average age is twelve years, the median age is only seven years.

The wide majority of individual FTSEs (type 1) are very recent. Entrepreneurial business-form FTSEs (type 2) are also relatively recent but part of them are older. This finding contrasts with what could have been expected from typical descriptions of the pioneers of the movement (see Chapter 1). A number of pioneer FTSEs indeed started, for instance, as small family businesses (e.g., Siesta and One Village in the UK). Although many volunteer-based nonprofit or cooperative FTSEs (type 3) were created before 1990, recently-created FTSEs also followed that model. This is typically the case in worldshop networks such as ADM in France, in which new members are required to adopt such a model. It is also worth noting that several volunteer-based FTSEs evolved into multi-stakeholder structures such as cooperatives

(Italy) and groups (Belgium). Multi-stakeholder cooperative FTSEs mainly emerged in Italy in the 1990s and early 2000s, and more recently in France (e.g., Soli'gren) and in the UK (e.g., Zaytoun). Finally, group structures are mainly widespread among old pioneer FTSEs that started as volunteer-based organizations (Oxfam-Wereldwinkels, MMH-MFT, etc.).

To examine the influence of the period in which the FTSEs were created, it may also be interesting to look at the initial legal form chosen. Indeed, this may help to understand how certain forms appeared suitable at the creation of the FTSEs, but less afterwards. The nonprofit form, for instance, was rarely maintained over time. The number of newly created nonprofit FTSEs globally decreased, while individual FTSEs emerged after 2000. Cooperative and business-form FTSEs, which emerged in significant proportions in the 1990s, have been relatively stable over time. Finally, it is in the last period that the legal forms adopted by newly created FTSEs have been the most diversified—although the nonprofit one seems less an option for new FTSEs. To summarize, certain links can be observed between the age of FTSEs and their organizational models. There are not clear-cut differences, however, among the different generations of FTSEs, and diversity, although increased with time, was already observed, although to a lesser extent, in the early decades. The influence of age might also be linked to the size of FTSEs: a complex structure such as the multi-stakeholder cooperative or group requires a large size—at least in terms of staff—whereas a simple structure such as the entrepreneurial form or the small team of volunteers is unlikely to remain unchanged with the growth of the FTSE.

## Size

Several indicators were available from the interviews: turnover (sales and subsidies, donations, etc.), sales, capital, and number of full-time equivalents.

If we look at the total annual turnover, figures range from €15,000 to 28 million, with an average of €2 million but a median of only €200,000. This confirms that there are many very small FTSEs and that the average turnover is increased by a small number of very large FTSEs. Indeed, more than 60% have a turnover under €250,000, and only 10% exceed €3 million. Furthermore, converging with other studies on FTSEs (Viganò, Glorio, and Villa 2008; Krier 2008), importing FTSEs have a higher turnover than worldshops.

In terms of the number of employees, more than 50% of the FTSEs are very small, with less than 2 full-time equivalents. While the median is 2, the average is 5.5. This is somewhat lower than in other studies (e.g., 7 average in Viganò, Glorio, and Villa 2008). In any case, as observed by Moore et al. (2009), FTSEs are far under the limit size of SMEs (250 employees according to the European Commission). Most of them can be considered as micro-businesses (less than 10 employees).

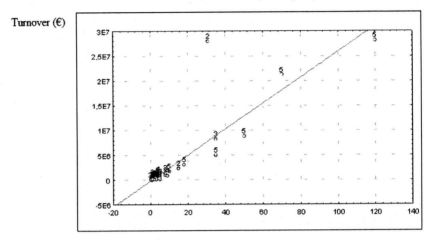

*Figure 3.2*    Turnover and staff (2007 figures).


Illustrating the correlation between turnover and staff size (full-time equivalents), the different types of FTSEs appear relatively heterogeneous in terms of size.

The first observation is that, on average, each full-time equivalent "brings" approximately €250,000 to the FTSE (in terms of sales, subsidies or donations). This amount seemed lower in volunteer-based FTSEs (type 3) and higher in type 2 and type 5 FTSEs. The FTSEs in the "type 5" category, i.e., the group structures, were clearly larger than the other types of FTSEs. Among the other models, multi-stakeholder cooperatives (type 4) and business-form FTSEs (type 2) were globally larger than individual (type 1) and volunteer-based (type 3) FTSEs. Individual FTSEs had very small turnovers (often below €100,000) and, by definition, very low employment. Volunteer-based FTSEs are also quite small (rarely over €1 million turnover and 5 full-time equivalents), with only a few exceptions (such as Oxfam-MDM). Multi-stakeholder cooperatives were all medium-sized (between €500,000 and 1,500,000 and between 2 and 9 full-time equivalents). Business-form FTSEs were generally medium-sized to large, with a few very large ones.[7]


## Economic Function

Following the FT literature, FTSEs can also be discriminated based on their role in the FT supply chain. The involvement in import, transformation, wholesale or retail may influence the type of organizational model adopted. Import means that the FTSE has a direct relationship with one or several producer groups in the South from which it imports regularly. Transformation implies that the FTSE has a unit where the product is transformed in some way (for instance, cocoa transformed into chocolate or cotton used to manufacture garments). Wholesale means that the FTSE has at least a partial function of selling FT products to other companies or institutional buyers (schools, government, etc.). Finally, the retail function implies having one or several shops where individual customers can buy FT products.

A rapid glance at the FT sector might highlight importers on the one hand, and retailers such as worldshops on the other. However, many FTSEs combine different functions or add a function to the primary activity (for instance, worldshops that start direct import). Most FTSEs (81% of the study) have a retailing function. This is an important element because it means that most FTSEs in the study are in direct contact with the final customer. Second, a large part of the FTSEs (58%) have an import function, which means that they are engaged in partnerships with the producers. Finally, the transformation and wholesale functions are developed only by a minority of FTSEs (respectively, 26% and 32%).

Surprisingly, there did not seem to be significant correlations between the economic function and the organizational model. Indeed, the various types of FTSEs were present at all the stages of the supply chain in the North. Identical models were thus adopted by FTSEs with different economic functions; whether they imported and/or distributed FT products thus seemed to matter less than where they put the emphasis in terms of combining the hybrid dimensions of FT.

## Products

The two traditional product categories of FT are food and handicraft products. Food products include drinks (coffee, cocoa, tea, fruit juices, wine, beer, etc.), fruits (bananas, pineapples, etc.), honey, rice and other cereals (quinoa, etc.), biscuits, spices, and many other products. Most of these products are already or potentially labeled by Fairtrade International (together with a few nonfood products such as cotton and roses). Handicraft also covers a wide range of products, from textiles to ceramics, from home furnishings to musical instruments. The scope of FT products has, however, increased tremendously in the last years. A whole range of "nonfood" products has been developed besides handicrafts, particularly clothing and cosmetics. The scope of FT products is likely to still increase in the near future. In the study, most FTSEs propose food or handicraft products (or both). While the proportion of labeled products has generally increased, several FTSEs also sell nonlabeled FT food. Following the example of Cafédirect, the newer FTSEs focus much more than the pioneers on one particular product or product range (coffee, wine, chocolate, garments, jewelry, etc.).

As much of the FT literature emphasize the differences between the various products and supply chains, the types of products dealt with by FTSEs and their distribution strategy (specialized or mainstream) might be expected to have an important influence on FTSEs' organizational models. Typically, a focus on food products, involving mainstream distribution and higher volumes, might lead to more business-oriented models. While some FTSEs verified this expectation (Cafédirect, Oxfam Fairtrade, etc.), there were also business-oriented handicraft FTSEs (e.g., Citizen Dream, Signaléthique) and volunteer-based FTSEs focused on food products (several Italian and Belgian FTSEs). More generally, the study did not show a clear link between the types of products traded by the FTSEs and their organizational model.

## Leaders' Profiles

Organizational models might also depend to a certain extent on the managers' profile, experience and education. Based on the interviews, three profile categories were distinguished. These categories must be considered as ideal types that are likely to coexist to varying extents in the profile of each leader. The description is thus rather caricatural. The percentages refer to the proportion of leaders for which each type of profile seemed dominant.

### Activists (Dominant for 39% of the FTSEs' Leaders)

Although there may be several meanings for the term "activist," in the case of FTSEs' leaders it means that their initial investment in the FTSE had a political motive. Activists did not become involved in the FTSE primarily to run a business, but rather to participate in its political project. For them, FTSEs are a channel through which education, regulation, and advocacy can be led with the goal of transforming the rules of international trade. Producer support is important insofar as it concretizes the broader political project.

Most founders of the pioneer FTSEs had activist profiles. With the economic evolution of the sector, however, an exclusively activist profile was often considered as insufficient to run an FTSE. Some of the initial activists added other elements, typically business training, and succeeded in maintaining their leadership; others were replaced by people with more complete profiles. This last situation was observed in several pioneer FTSEs whose growth required managers with more business expertise.

### Developers (Dominant for 30%)

The second type of profile could be located closer to the "social" dimension. Developers have a background of development cooperation and are motivated primarily by the mission of producer support. Often, before creating or becoming involved in an FTSE, they met producer groups during travels or missions in the South, thus becoming familiar with their situation, and willing to help them find market opportunities in the North. Some of them may thus see FT as a development project (Poncelet, Defourny, and De Pelsmacker 2005). The economic and political activities are rather seen as means to achieve the final goal of helping the producers' communities to develop. Most FTSEs' leaders partially appeared as "developers," with some experience with producer groups. Nevertheless, such experience alone seemed insufficient to run the FTSE. This was even truer since the emergence of certification, which took over the monitoring of producer groups. Indeed, as certifiers regularly visited the producer organizations and check their conformity with the FT criteria, it became less crucial (although still useful) for FTSEs to send their own staff to visit the producers in the South. Nevertheless, the "developer" skills remain useful for managing an FTSE, especially when there is a direct import from the producers.

### Business People (31%)

The third profile seemed increasingly present among FTSEs' leaders. People with previous experience in the business world who want to engage in an activity with more ethical values became more and more involved in FTSEs. Some of them founded new FTSEs with a stronger commercial vision–albeit with social purposes. Others got involved in FTSEs looking for people with business experience for the managerial functions. Finally, several leaders freshly graduated from business schools and preferred to create their own ethical business than to join a "mainstream" corporation.

Whatever their background, most "business people" tried to also include "developer" and, to a lesser extent, "activist" skills to their business profile. In the interviews with these types of managers, it appeared that many of them, after having started the job in the FTSE, traveled to meet established or potential partner producer groups. Furthermore, most "activists" and "developers" reported the need for more business skills to properly run their FTSE and to have more legitimacy in their function. Several managers participated in training sessions for that purpose, and two managers even obtained degrees from business schools while working in their organization.

To try to gather multidimensional expertise at the management level, FTSEs have various choices. They can look for the person combining these different dimensions. For instance, someone from the business world with high ideals and some experience in development cooperation (the typical profile of new FTSEs' leaders). Or, when there are different departments (e.g., marketing, producer support, and advocacy), they may prefer to have two or three different leaders working together. Finally, the different types of profiles can also be applied to FTSEs' employees and workers. In the early history of FT pioneers, most FTSEs were composed mainly of activists (volunteers and employees). Then, with the commercial development of the sector, people with a business background were increasingly hired, confirming trends observed in Fair Trade (Davies, Doherty, and Knox 2010) and in social enterprises in other fields. Therefore, it is common to have staff with different backgrounds according to the role they play in the FTSE (or the department they belong to in the case of larger FTSEs).

Leaders with a predominantly "activist" profile, who were previously active in advocacy NGOs or within the same FTSE (as volunteers or campaigners for instance), were logically much more present in volunteer-based FTSEs and multi-stakeholder nonprofit and cooperative FTSEs (types 2 and 3). Larger nonprofit pioneers, however, started hiring managers with a more business-oriented profile.

On the other hand, there were also leaders with activist profiles in business-form FTSEs. Examples include One Village and Equomondo (as well as other members of the Minga network).

Leaders with a predominantly "developer" profile, i.e., people who were previously active in development NGOs or working on social issues as expatriates in the South, were found in all types of FTSEs, particularly in individual and business-form FTSEs.

Finally, leaders with an education in business or previous experience in the business world were found primarily in business-form and individual FTSEs, but also in other FTSEs. They remained absent from "pure" nonprofits. Nevertheless, they may be leading groups including a nonprofit entity (e.g., OWW-OFT and Max Havelaar). A French FTSE active in selling T-shirts illustrates the link between business school education and the creation of FTSEs with a business form. Three friends launched the project in 2006 after their studies in management. They rapidly structured themselves as a business-form FTSE.

> *The only other possible form was the SCOP [workers' cooperative], but it looked too complex. Moreover, we wanted a simple business form, you know, we're a business. And a business form is more serious in front of commercial partners and customers. After two years, we're happy to have organized ourselves as a business. It corresponds to what we are and what we want to do. But our [FT] standards remain high.*

The last sentence is typical and was heard in many interviews with more business-oriented FTSEs. The interviewees seemed to feel the need to reassure the audience: we are a business *but* our ethical standards are high.

In the cases of small FTSEs led by the people who founded them, the leader had an important influence on the choice of the organizational model (Spence and Rutherfoord 2001). In older and larger FTSEs that hired new leaders, however, the relationship is likely to be reversed: the FTSE, according to its mission and its form, chooses the leader whose profile best fits its expectations.

## Resources

FTSEs have access to several types of financial resources: sales, public subsidies, gifts, etc. Contrarily to certain images, the study clearly showed that FTSEs mainly rely on commercial incomes, through the sales of their products. The average percentage of commercial incomes was 95.7% of the total resources. Public subsidies and gifts were limited, never exceeding 35% of the incomes, even for pioneer nonprofit FTSEs. The vast majority of these FTSEs with noncommercial incomes reported a decrease, not in the actual amounts generated from these two sources of income, but in their proportions in relation to the total income because of the increase in sales. This is consistent with the "commercialization" trend observed among nonprofit organizations (Weisbrod 1998) and social enterprises (Dart 2004), especially in the so-called "social enterprise" school of thought (Battle Anderson and Dees 2006; Dart 2004). Several FTSEs, however, still diversified their income sources, being closer to the model described by the EMES and social innovation streams. Noncommercial incomes varied according to the regions: they were mainly subsidies in Belgium and in Italy and gifts in the UK.

Categories 1, 2, and 4 nearly exclusively relied on commercial incomes. Volunteer-based FTSEs and group structures had a lower proportion of commercial incomes (as groups include a volunteer-based entity). It should be noted that voluntary work can be considered as a specific and tangible resource. However, it is difficult to determine its value, as the time spent by volunteers is not fixed and because their "production" is often untangible. It can nevertheless be assumed that such value is high, especially in worldshops where having volunteers enables sparing on the costs of hiring professional sellers.

## Goals

Goals or missions are key elements, especially in the study of social enterprises (Defourny and Nyssens 2006). Indeed, social enterprises are depicted as particularly suited to the pursuit of multiple economic and social goals (Bacchiega and Borzaga 2001; Mair and Marti 2006). As organizational models are designed to enable the achievement of particular goals, it is useful to precisely define what should be understood through the term "goals." The first question is probably: whose goals? Much of the conventional economic and managerial literature speaks about "organizational goals" (Hatch 1999). This expression, however, is increasingly rejected by social scientists and particularly organization theorists. For McAuley *et al.* for instance, "to talk of social collectivities such as organizations as having goals, as if they were an individual person, can be misleading because it creates an image of agreement amongst members regarding the purposes of an organization that might not exist" (2007, 13). By viewing organizations in such a way, "we may accidentally exclude and subjugate the priorities of the vast majority of organization members and those in the wider community who are not members but who are simultaneously affected by the organization's operation" (14).

In small organizations consisting only of an entrepreneur or a few other people, it is not too problematic to speak of "organizational goals" as a synonym for "leader's goals" (Spence and Rutherfoord 2001). In larger structures, however, such an association would indeed ignore the vast majority of organization members. Mintzberg (1983; 1986) and other authors subscribing to a "political" perspective consider that it is rather individuals and social groups who carry particular goals. If these individuals and groups reach a sufficient level of power, their goals may become organizational goals, thereby increasing their legitimacy and their power (Nizet and Pichault 2001). If several groups try to influence organizational goals, it is likely that organizations will pursue multiple goals (Mintzberg 1986).

Organizations have not only multiple goals linked to their different constituents, but also different types of goals. A classical distinction is the one made between official goals, which are very general, and operational goals, which guide concrete actions. Conventional approaches consider that the managers determine the official goals, which are then translated at the operational level by their subordinates (Hatch 1999). Political approaches, by contrast, insist on the conflicts that inevitably appear among the goals carried by different actors in and outside the organization.

A second distinction can be made between "system goals" and "mission goals." Pichault and Nizet (1995) expand upon this distinction introduced by Mintzberg (2002):

- Mission goals: the goals linked to the products, services or clients of the organization
- System goals: the goals linked to the organization and its members, independently from the products and services of the organization. Such goals include survival, efficiency, control of the environment, and growth.

How are the different goals of FTSEs associated with the hybrid dimensions of FT? The following table provides a nonexhaustive list of goals related to the three dimensions.

It is worth noting that most of the goals suggested in the grid are "mission goals." They are specific to FT, i.e., to the products and services of FTSEs viewed in a broad sense. "Social goals" are the closest to the description of mission goals, as they express what FTSEs normally seek to ultimately achieve. Certain "political goals" are also close to mission goals, especially as means to contribute to the social goals. However, political activities also contribute to such system goals as gaining legitimacy and controlling the

*Table 3.4* Organizational Goals for FTSEs

| Dimension | Possible goal |
|---|---|
| Social | To support small-scale and/or marginalised producer groups |
| | To empower producer groups and increase their capacities |
| | To reach the wider community behind producers |
| Economic | To gain market shares |
| | To increase consumer satisfaction |
| | To generate profits |
| Political | To influence international trading rules in a way that is more favourable to the producers in the South |
| | To watch and denounce unethical practices by corporations |
| | To encourage consumers toward more ethical buying behavior |

environment. A goal such as "encouraging consumers towards more ethical buying behavior" may be ambiguous. On the one hand, it may be seen as a mission goal on its own, or at least as a contribution to the social mission. But on the other hand, it may also be seen as a tool to increase sales and/or legitimacy, thereby being closer to a system goal. Finally, system goals seem more present in the category of "economic goals": "making profit" and "gaining market shares" can be directly linked to considerations of survival, efficiency, and growth. However, these goals are often presented by FTSEs as means or at least intermediate goals, the achievement of which is necessary to pursue the social goals (Davies and Crane 2003). In this study, goals were captured in a twofold way: through the official mission statements and through asking the managers how they describe the goals of their organization.

## Activities

Beyond the goals, it is useful to understand what FTSEs concretely do. Capturing FTSEs' activities implies determining to what extent FTSEs are involved in trading, in producer support, and in education, regulation, and advocacy. Different indicators can be mobilized, for instance, the stated activities (what does the FTSE announce that it does?), the number of employees involved in the activities or the percentage of the expenses devoted to the activity. The different answers were categorized into three common patterns or "levels of involvement" in each activity. These levels of involvement are based on several elements such as: level of strategic attention; resources specific to the activity; training for employees and volunteers; etc. While these elements are supported by empirical evidence, their aggregation is necessarily subjective. To avoid size effects, the priority given to each of the activities rather than the absolute amount of activities was examined.

The three categories of involvement for the *economic activity* were based on the characterization of the market orientation of social enterprises, including risk-taking, cost recovery, efficient deployment of resources, strategic operations, etc. (Nicholls and Cho 2006). Many FTSEs in the "low" category were volunteer-based and unable to understand and/or answer questions on turnover, margins, and market environment. At the other extreme, "high" category FTSEs had explicit tools for collecting these data and reacting in an "efficient" way, even in very small FTSEs.

Similar categories could be distinguished for the *political activity* (education, regulation, and advocacy). Finally, for the *social* activity (producer support), FTSEs having only a retailing function were distinguished from those importing directly from producers, so as not to bias the categories on the basis of incomparable indicators (e.g., frequency of visits to producers).

Obviously, discrepancies may exist between the stated levels of involvement and the concrete situation. Moreover, as suggested by Nicholls and Cho (2006), the evaluation of the social mission is laden with normative values, with "best practices" varying greatly depending upon the interviewee. For most FTSEs, regular visits to producers and personal contacts were a sign of high social involvement. For other FTSEs though, such an attitude was considered as paternalistic and as having less impact on producers than an indirect, more formal relationship (for instance, through the interface of a labeling organization). The same goes for long-term relationships with producers. While most FTSEs valued them in any situation, others were much more cautious and pointed out the risk of putting producers in a "dependence trap" (Poncelet, Defourny, and De Pelsmacker 2005). The definition of these different attitudes from "low" to "high" would inevitably entail a normative judgment.

Discourses and activities around the social dimension vary with age and size (the bigger and older the FTSE, the more institutionalized the producer support). There is much diversity in terms of the types of producer groups supported (size, legal form, etc.); of pre-financing given to the producers (frequency and amount); of the number of producer groups; of the number of visits per year etc. But none of these features seemed to vary significantly with the organizational model.

It is rather on the economic and political dimensions that more striking differences could be observed. Regarding economic involvement, organizational models did not offer similar patterns. Business-form and individual FTSEs had medium or high levels of economic activity (rather high in businesses and medium among individuals). Groups also predominantly had a high level of economic involvement, which may be explained by the fact that they include one business-oriented entity. Multi-stakeholder cooperatives had heterogeneous levels of involvement, centered on the "medium" dimension. Finally, volunteer-based FTSEs had a predominantly "low" or "medium" level of economic involvement. Only a minority had a "high" level of involvement.

Regarding political involvement, FTSEs distinguished themselves even more sharply through their organizational model. Groups and volunteer-based FTSEs had higher levels of political involvement than other types of FTSEs. Most multi-stakeholder cooperatives also had a high level of political involvement, but a minority had a low level. Business-form and individual FTSEs fell within the margins of medium-level involvement, with minorities with a low or high level of involvement.

In fact, we can summarize the behaviors in terms of economic and political activities in three broad patterns:

- Predominance of political over economic activities: type 3 FTSEs
- Predominance of economic over political activities: most types 1 & 2, part of type 4 FTSEs
- High importance for both types of activities: type 5, most type 4, part of type 2 FTSEs

### *Illustrations*

It may be useful to illustrate the general links presented here with some examples confirming these links as well as a few exceptions.

An example of a nonprofit FTSE very involved politically is Oxfam-MDM. A large part of the employees were active either in campaigning and education, or in training the volunteers who themselves diffused the campaigns locally. The legal form has remained unchanged since its creation. It is put forward to emphasize Oxfam's primary goal of being a citizens' movement, which differentiates Oxfam from other Belgian FTSEs who evolved toward a more business-oriented form. The recent strategic reflection led by the Board[8] confirmed the importance of explicitly stating the non-profit-seeking (*"sans but lucratif"*) mission. But the economic dimension was not neglected. For instance, new rules were established to increase the level of economic responsibility of the worldshops, leading to the closure of some of the poorly performing shops. This and other factors such as hiring practices revealed a gradual reinforcement of the economic dimension, even if it remained submitted to the social and political goals.

Volunteer-based cooperatives such as Il Fiore were also very involved politically while having a low degree of economic focus. Il Fiore presented itself as a crossing point where people can exchange their ideas about how to make trade—and the whole world—fairer. The FTSE rejected products labeled by Transfair because of their presence in supermarkets and the absence of a guarantee regarding a personal relationship with the producers. The FTSE also participated in boycotting campaigns, for instance, against Coca-Cola.

In the groups, the hybrid structure seemed to clearly reflect respective foci on the economic and on the socio-political dimensions. The nonprofit entities of OWW-OFT, MMH, People Tree, Traidcraft, or Soli'gren all specifically targeted social and political action. In these groups, the cooperative or business entities had a much stronger economic orientation, as they leave the political and social dimensions to their nonprofit sister organizations. Nevertheless, their commercial activity generally remained under a certain control by the latter, through a majority of shares reserved to the nonprofit (e.g., Oxfam-WW, MMH) or through the presence of volunteers, among other stakeholders, in the governance structures (e.g., Pangea-NT).

Most multi-stakeholder cooperatives, for instance, the social cooperatives in Italy, combined a high level of political involvement with a medium or high level of economic activity. A good example is Pangea-NT, which ran education and lobbying campaigns on a regular basis, together with other CTM members. Simultaneously, Pangea received the exclusive right to negotiate the distribution of CTM products in Roman supermarkets, thereby developing expertise in the commercial activity.

Concerning FTSEs with a classical business form, their economic involvement was logically higher than other types of FTSEs. However, while the political focus is generally lower if not absent, there are some interesting exceptions. One of them is Saldac, which was created in 2000 as a nonprofit organization ("association") and changed in 2002 to a business form ("société anonyme"). While maintaining a radical political message, Saldac reinforced its economic focus simultaneously with its change in legal form.

Finally, individual FTSEs in the study were generally more focused more on the economic than on the political side. This does not mean that they did not subscribe to the political project of FT and to (some of) the actions of other FTSEs. An entrepreneur confirmed:

> *The first thing we have to keep in mind is to earn sufficiently to be able to live. Contrarily to other FTSEs' managers, I have no certainty about how much I'll have at the end of the month, if anything, and generally it's much lower than any worker or employee, let alone manager! Of course, I'm interested in the political goals of FT. I try to participate at my level, in my shop. But I couldn't spend resources or too much time on this. The same goes for producers: I'd like to go there [to Latin America] and learn more about them. But in the current situation I can't.*

The economic focus on entrepreneurial FTSEs thus appeared a matter of constraint (efficiency) rather than a lack of interest in the social and political dimensions of FT. This observation will be further interpreted in the next chapter.

## Synthesis: Synergies and Tensions

The organizational variables such as activities, goals, resources, and leaders' profiles can all be decomposed into economic, social, and political components. In other words, the combination of these elements within the organizational model locates the FTSEs in the FT landscape. This section examines how the five types of models integrate these different elements.

The individual and manager-owned businesses (types 1 and 2) seem located quite close to each other. They are also close to a 100% sales-based resource mix, to the "business" and—more surprisingly—"developer" leaders' profiles, and to the predominance of economic activities. However, while all these FTSEs use market resources and mechanisms, it does not mean that their goals and activities are restricted to the economic sphere. As the previous section has shown, there is even a minority of businesses that is very involved in the political project of FT.

The volunteer-based FTSEs (type 3) are quite different from this model. They partly rely on noncommercial resources, they are led by people with rather activist profiles, and their goals and activities are predominantly socio-political. This does not mean that the economic activity is not developed, but rather that it is a side dimension compared to the socio-political one.

Multi-stakeholder cooperatives (type 4) seem located in between these two positions. While, as we have seen, their resources are exclusively commercial, the profiles of their leaders are mixed, as well as their goals and activities. This suggests that commercial resources are used for hybrid goals (social and political purposes). The resource mix is different in group structures, in which each entity has its own specific incomes. Despite this difference, type 4 and type 5 FTSEs seem to go furthest in the integration of hybrid goals and activities, thus appearing in the middle of the continuum between the two previous groups (commercial and volunteer-based FTSEs).

This analysis has remained quite static and does not show the organizational trajectories. We should thus view these three broad families as distinct backgrounds of FTSEs against which the latter may evolve, and not as distinct categories that include homogeneous FTSEs.

A common view is that the activities, goals and resources mobilized in the context of FT necessarily converge with each other. As we have seen, the synergy between economic, social, and political foci is in fact at the basis of the FT idea. The promoters of FT mainstreaming are in line with this view when they claim that selling more FT products (economic activity) automatically benefits the producers (social goal). More politically involved FT operators also rely on the assumption that campaigning and lobbying (political activity) is a tool for obtaining better opportunities for small-scale producers. In both types of FTSEs, the social aim was used to justify economic or political dynamics, confirming Davies and Crane's (2003) observation of the social mission as the overarching motive for decision-making in the case of Divine Chocolate. Reverse relationships, although rarely claimed explicitly, were observed as well. In many cases, the social aim was a stimulator for the economic development of the FT operator—either mainstream businesses or FTSEs. Similarly, the partnership with producers could be "used" to drive a political cause. Even without instrumental intent, the social dimension is rarely the only final end: it coexists with economic and political goals.

The common view considers that FT allows its operators to contribute to the different goals simultaneously, even when specialising in one of them. This is in line with much of the literature on social enterprise, underlining the complementarities between the social mission and the economic activity. For instance, Austin *et al.* (2006) suggest that "[t]he social dimensions and the business dimensions [ . . . ] must be aligned with each other. The closer the alignment, the greater the potential for joint value creation" (177). Alter (2006) sees FTSEs as being embedded, program-based social enterprises in which "high compatibility between business and social mission exists," with the possibility of "accomplishing mission goals while simultaneously increasing financial self-sufficiency" (207). This is even truer since the emergence of FT labeling: labels are supposed to ensure that the sale of FT products automatically benefits the producers. More generally, the different trends in the FT movement, from the more business-minded to the more political, are often presented as complementary (Nicholls 2010).

The multiple goals of FT entail elements that may, however, contradict each other so that it is impossible to combine them in a synergetic way (Diaz Pedregal 2007). There may be tensions, for instance, between the goal of reaching marginalized producers and certain economic imperatives (access of producers to export capacities, high-quality products, etc.). The economic imperative of selling FT products may contradict certain political aims, for instance, in the case of an FTSEs reluctant to criticize unethical practices by a corporation with whom it has a commercial partnership. And the exclusive aim of supporting specific producers may be pursued at the expense of other social groups (other producers in the region, producers in the North, workers involved along the supply chain, etc.). While many authors mention tensions throughout the movement (e.g., Schümperli Younossian 2006), few have examined how these tensions are also potentially present within each FTSE. Such tensions will be examined as a transversal concern in the following chapters.

## CONCLUSION

First, this chapter has highlighted different types of legal forms, architectures and governance models. Based on commonly observed combinations of these three elements, a taxonomy including five categories has been built: individual ventures, entrepreneurial businesses, volunteer-based FTSEs, multi-stakeholder cooperatives, and group structures. These categories have been analyzed in depth and illustrated with exemplary cases as well as "outlier" and hybrid cases. Then, the different models have been contrasted with each other regarding other variables such as region, age, size, resources, goals, and leaders' profiles. While important differences have been highlighted in terms of region, age, and size, the most fundamental differences relate to the positioning with regard to the FT practice. Taking resources, goals, activities, and leaders' profiles globally, major differences have been observed. Volunteer-based FTSEs are more activist-based, include noncommercial resources, and predominantly focus on the socio-political dimension of FT. Individual and business-form FTSEs, on the contrary, rely only on sales, involve business expertise, and, despite a number of exceptions, mainly focus on the economic dimension of FT. Multi-stakeholder cooperatives and groups, although they do not constitute homogeneous categories, seem to have an intermediate position, involving various profiles and simultaneously combining high levels of involvement in the economic and political dimensions of FT.

# Part II
# Theoretical Perspectives

# 4  Theoretical Framework

To understand how and why FTSEs adopt diverse models, various theoretical approaches within the framework of organization studies are available. Among these, the (new) institutional approaches in economics and sociology seem particularly adequate. The following section describes the origins and main features of each approach. Then, these approaches are compared with each other both on their key assumptions and on their contribution to the study of FTSEs' diverse models.

## OVERVIEW OF THEORETICAL APPROACHES

### From "One Best Way" to Organizational Diversity

From the late 1800s to the 1970s, several approaches set the basis of organization theory. Before the Second World War, the classical approaches such as the Scientific Management school (Taylor, Fayol) and the Human Relations movement (Barnard, Mayo, etc.) tried to determine how businesses and the individuals who compose them should best achieve harmony and efficiency ("one best way"). After the Second World War, sociologists rediscovered the work of Max Weber and examined bureaucracy in organizations, questioning these "one best way" approaches. During the same period, psychologists and economists became interested in issues concerning decision-making, replacing the view of "full rationality" hypothesized by classical economic theory with a more realistic "bounded rationality" (Simon, March, Cyert, Olsen, etc.).

In the 1950s and 1960s, contingency theory and especially "structural contingency" examined the influence of the environment on the structure of organizations (Lawrence and Lorsch 1967). Because each organization is surrounded by a specific environment, it will adopt the organizational form that best suits the technical and economic features of this environment. For instance, the more stable an environment, i.e., the more changes can be anticipated, the more "mechanical" the structure—strong work division, formalization, and departmentalization. In an unstable environment, structures are more likely to be "organic"—more flat, with mutual adjustment and departmentalization by outputs (Burns and Stalker 1961 and Mintzberg 1982 and 1986, cited in Nizet and Pichault 1995). These propositions were developed in the context of the "configuration" approach (Mintzberg 1980; Miller 1986), which can be viewed as a direct extension of the structural contingency approach (Nizet and Pichault 1995; Rouleau 2007).

From the late 1970s, a renewal was observed in the theoretical propositions on organizations. These renewed approaches mainly arose in sociology and economics.[1]

## Sociology

The first body of theories arose in sociology and extended the work of structural contingency. One of the main approaches was new institutionalism. New institutionalism or (neo-)institutional theory built on the propositions of the "old" institutionalism (see Selznick 1996 for a review), rejecting traditional rationalist models and developing the view of organizational choices as heavily constrained by their culture and environment. The founding articles of neo-institutional theory are generally located in the late 1970s. In 1977 more precisely, Meyer and Rowan wrote "Institutionalized Organizations: Formal Structure as Myth and Ceremony" (1977). DiMaggio and Powell's famous "The Iron Cage Revisited: Institutional Isomorphism and Collective Rationality in Organizational Fields" followed in 1983, as well as several others (Scott and Meyer 1983, Zucker 1985—for a compilation, see Powell and DiMaggio 1991). Neo-institutional authors distinguish themselves from structural contingency in that they perceive the environment in a much broader way: not only through its technical and economic features, but also through symbolic and cultural dimensions. Second, the organizational structure is also seen in a symbolic way, as reflecting the characteristics of the environment more than efficiency concerns. As stated by Powell and DiMaggio (1991, 13), new institutionalism "locates irrationality in the formal structure itself, attributing the diffusion of certain departments and operating procedures to interorganizational influences, conformity, and the persuasiveness of cultural accounts, rather than to the functions they are intended to perform" (Powell and DiMaggio 1991, 13).

Neo-institutional theory has been used by so many academics that it is in fact hybridizing elements from various theoretical fields, sometimes leading to paradoxical arguments (Tolbert and Zucker 1996). Reacting to the criticism toward the deterministic nature of this theory, Powell, Zucker, Hardy and other authors reconsider the role of agency, i.e., the capacity of actors to make choices despite institutional pressures, and their capacity to influence and even create institutions.

Building on the notion of "institutional entrepreneurship" introduced by DiMaggio (1988), several authors try to understand how and by whom institutions are shaped. They examine how organizations and other actors interact to create new fields of practice and develop the norms which will prevail for newcomers (e.g., Maguire, Hardy, and Lawrence 2004 studying the structuration of HIV treatment advocacy in Canada). These authors try to establish links with the literature on entrepreneurship, following Schumpeter's conception of entrepreneurship that concerns not only individuals but also organizations and institutions. Moreover, entrepreneurship is not understood so much in the sense of the creation of particular organizations, but rather as the "generation of new organizational models and policies that change the direction and flow of organizational activity" (Hwang and Powell 2005, 180).

Subsequent developments have extended the idea of institutional entrepreneurship to the broader concept of "institutional work," referring to the actors' strategies not only in shaping but also in maintaining and disrupting institutions (Lawrence and Suddaby 2006). Through the central place of agency, it may be suggested that the institutional work approach is distinct from the abovementioned institutional writings and reconnects to a certain extent with Selznick's pioneering work. However, the (re) introduction of agency in a basically deterministic and structural framework may be paradoxical. This is referred to as the "embedded agency" paradox, as summarized in the following question: "how can organizations or individuals innovate if their beliefs and actions are determined by the institutional environment they wish to change?" (Leca, Battilana, and Boxenbaum 2008, 4).

To overcome this paradox and provide "a link between institutions and action," or, in other words, "between the macro, structural perspectives of Meyer and Rowan (1977) and DiMaggio and Powell (1983) and Zucker's more micro, process approaches" (Thornton and Ocasio 2008, 100), the notion of "institutional logic" has been developed by Jackall (1988) and Friedland and Alford (1991). Drawing on their work, Thornton and Ocasio (1999, 804) have defined institutional logics as "the socially constructed, historical patterns of material practices, assumptions, values, beliefs, and rules by which individuals produce and reproduce their material subsistence, organize time and space, and provide meaning to their social reality." This work will explore both the structural and agency-based sides of institutional theory to investigate organizational diversity in FT, thereby hoping to overcome the apparent "embedded agency" paradox.

## Economics

Both classical and neo-classical economics, as developed in the nineteenth and twentieth centuries, paid little attention to the structure and functioning of organizations. "Firms" offer products on the market with the goal of maximizing their profit. "Consumers" buy these products and maximize their utility according to their preferences. Supply (by firms) and demand (by consumers) are coordinated naturally by market forces. Although the "test of reality" pushed neo-classical economists to add complexity to the initial model (by including market imperfections, externalities, and other economic agents such as the State), firms remained, in their view, a "black box" that does not need to be opened (Slitter and Spencer 2000; Williamson 1979; Coase 1937, 1998).

The first attempt to open this black box was made by Ronald Coase in 1937. In "The nature of the firm," Coase examined the following question: why are certain transactions operated through organizations instead of simply through the market? Coase introduced the notion of "transaction cost" to explain the existence of firms: in some cases, it is less costly (in terms of information, negotiation, etc.) to coordinate the transactions of economic agents through firms than it would be through the market. The firm and the market are thus two distinct institutions. The analysis of Coase is based on the notion of contracts between agents (short-term contracts on the market versus long-term contracts through firms). Such a "contractual" view, although sharing common assumptions with the neo-classical tradition (Slitter and Spencer 2000), led to a stronger complexity in micro-economic analysis and to a much stronger attention to organizations (Coase 1998).

Since the 1970s, numerous economists were inspired by the contractual view and claimed their affiliation to Coase (Barney and Hesterly 1996; Coase 1998). However, they diverged much in their interpretation of the notions of contract and transaction cost, which led the contractual approach to be divided into two schools of thought (Foss 1993, 130).

The first school of thought, led by Akerlof (1970), Alchian and Demsetz (1972) and Jensen and Meckling (1976), examines markets and firms in terms of contractual relationships and incentive problems. The authors of this school of thought, while referring to Coase's work, follow a perspective that does not fundamentally challenge the assumptions of the orthodox neo-classical approach (Foss 1993). Indeed, only the assumption of perfect information is questioned through the analysis of "information asymmetries." As Akerlof demonstrated in the market of second-hand cars ("lemons"), information asymmetries about the quality of the products may lead to opportunistic behaviors that may disable the functioning of markets and thus require the rise of new institutional arrangements. Contracts are thus viewed as tools to limit opportunism and correct the institutional failure—"market failure" or "contract failure"—induced by information asymmetries. To locate these asymmetries, it is thus crucial to understand the characteristics of the types of goods produced, as will be explained further.

Much of the analysis explores incentive problems: which contracts are likely to ensure that agents will conform to what is expected of them? The most famous illustration of contracts as incentive tools is the agency theory (Jensen and Meckling 1976). Agency theory explores the relationships between "principals" and "agents," typically between shareholders and managers, trying to determine how the actions of the agents can best be aligned with the expectations of their principals. Authors of the agency theory conclude that incentive issues and agency problems are best handled through the classical capitalist firm model. However, the firm itself is viewed as a "legal fiction" (Jensen and Meckling 1976): it is only a formal expression of a nexus of contracts (Fama and Jensen 1983). The vision of the firm as an institution made of a complex set of contracts is so strong that the notions of "the entrepreneur" and "the firm" have been abandoned (Foss 1993; Bacchiega and Borzaga 2001; Lemaître 2009). Another application of this first contractual view is the property rights theory developed by Grossman, Hart, and Moore.

The second school of thought drawing on Coase was led by Williamson (1979, 1985, 1995, 2002b, 2002a). Williamson and other authors re-actualized Coase's notion of "transaction costs" and built a "transaction cost theory." Transaction cost theory aims to understand, more than in the previous school of thought, under what conditions coordination of agents through the market is substituted by coordination through the hierarchy of a firm or organization (Williamson 1979). The firm is depicted in a more complex way than as a simple "nexus of contracts." Contracts are unable to rule all possible situations. As contracts are incomplete, agents may act opportunistically by using such incompleteness to their advantage (Williamson 1985, 2002b).

Beyond contract incompleteness, a major feature of this second school of thought is the use of Herbert Simon's (1955) concept of "bounded rationality."[2] The study of the organization as a coordination mechanism, and not simply a nexus of contracts, also leads to a stronger focus on its internal functioning. Organizations have the choice among several institutional arrangements or "governance structures" to ensure an efficient implementation of contracts and avoid opportunism. Such institutional choices will depend on the minimization of the transaction costs that confront organizations according to the types of goods they produce and the configuration of the market.

The view of organizational structures—typically the investor-owned corporation—as institutions was also developed, at a wider and more historical level, by authors such as North (North 1990, 1991; Davis and North 1971). The work of Williamson, North, and other authors has in common reference to the early "institutional" school in economics, led by Veblen, Commons, and Mitchell (Williamson 2000; Arrow 1987; Coase 1998). By qualifying transaction cost theory and other related contractual approaches as "new institutional economics," Williamson, North, and other authors simultaneously affiliated their work to the historical perspective of the institutional school, and underlined their specific contribution through a stronger and more theoretically founded micro-economic analysis (Coase 1998).

As will be developed in the next chapter, whole streams of literature have used the economic neo-institutional approach(es) to explain the emergence of alternative types of private organizations such as nonprofits (Hansmann 1980; Krashinsky 1986), cooperatives (Hansmann 1999; Platteau 1987; Ben-Ner and Gui 2000), and other social enterprises, many of which adopt one of these two forms (Bacchiega and Borzaga 2001).

## Synthesis and Comparison

The explanations of why particular organizational models are adopted, as well as the level of discretion given to organizational decision-makers, differ a lot depending on the approach. In the economic neo-institutional approach[3], it is the configuration of transactions that determines the less costly institutional arrangement and thus the organizational form (Williamson 1979). For early neo-institutional sociologists, however, organizations follow "scripts" provided by the environment, with little discretion power (Tolbert and Zucker 1996). These scripts tend to push organizations in a same field to resemble each other, thereby reducing the initial organizational diversity (DiMaggio and Powell 1983). In later institutional developments, however, organizational actors are granted a much higher level of discretion and are able to engage in strategic manoeuvres to shape their environment. This partly converges with "resource dependence theory" (see Chapter 3), in which organizations secure access to resources and thus reduce their dependence on that environment (Pfeffer and Salancik 1978). In fact, the different approaches make the shaping of the organizational model dependent on factors that are themselves diverse: respectively, the costs of transactions, and the institutional logics (either imposed on or strategically appropriated by the organizations). The diversity of modalities for these variables opens the door, in each approach, for diversity in organizational models.

It is worth noting that economic and sociological neo-institutionalism have been the two major theoretical frameworks used to investigate the emergence of social enterprise. From an economic perspective, social enterprise is viewed as a new institution capable of exceeding the failures of previous models—particularly the traditional nonprofit organization—by "strengthening the fiduciary relationship within and around the organization" (Bacchiega and Borzaga 2001, 273). The strengthening of "trust signals" is achieved through a number of organizational characteristics—social mission, economic democracy, involvement of multiple stakeholders, etc.—which go beyond the mere prohibition of profit distribution (Bacchiega and Borzaga 2001; Petrella 2003). From a sociological neo-institutional perspective, social enterprise has been presented as the result of the increasing power of entrepreneurial logics and language in the area of social action (Dart 2004; Grenier 2006). Social enterprise has also emerged as a new model better able to deal with certain societal challenges than traditional models of social action. Such diagnosis of the extant failures and the theorization of new arrangements by social entrepreneurs can be seen as a typical illustration of institutional work dynamics (Mair and Marti 2006; Nicholls 2010). The present multi-theoretical approach follows Nicholls and Cho's (2006) call for a stronger social science theoretical basis to apprehend social enterprise.

Barney and Hesterly (1996) suggest that the different institutional approaches resemble each other through their common focus on how organizations are structured and how they seek to survive. Schneiberg (2005), on his turn, highlights the strength of combining the different new institutional approaches. This is why, to avoid confusion, it may be useful to compare the different theoretical approaches to each other.

Economic and sociological new institutionalisms rely on different assumptions and have developed in different directions, with few citations among the authors of both approaches. The respective founding authors, however, more easily analyze the place of their approach within the broader institutionalist tradition (e.g., Coase 1998; Williamson 2000; Powell 1991). Comparisons can also be found in articles drawing on both approaches (e.g., Schneiberg 2005) or in books on organization theory (e.g., Clegg and Hardy 1999). Among the different authors of new institutional economics, those of the "historical stream" (North 1991; Davis and North 1971; North 1990) seem to be the closest to sociological new institutionalism (Powell and DiMaggio 1991). Powell, in the introduction of his 1991 book, acknowledged such cross-feeding and common institutional background, while also insisting on the differences between the two approaches, which he located at three levels:

- The meaning of an "institution." Neo-institutional economists view them as governance structures designed to minimize transaction costs. The sociological tradition, however, views institutions as social and historical constructions that have progressively rendered certain behaviors as taken for granted.
- The origins of institutions. In the economic approach, institutional arrangements result from "adaptive solutions to problems of opportunism, imperfect or asymmetric information, and costly monitoring" (9). The sociological approach, by contrast, considers that choices and behaviors are constrained by collective constructions and past experiences that define standards of appropriateness.
- The rigidity of institutions. For neo-institutional economists, institutions are "provisional, temporary resting places on the way to an efficient equilibrium solution" (10). In the sociological view, institutions are much slower to change. Accordingly, organizational change is often "episodical and dramatic, responding to institutional change at the macro-level, rather than incremental and smooth" (11).

One way of explaining these differences is to consider, following Williamson (2000), that sociological and economic new institutionalism do not

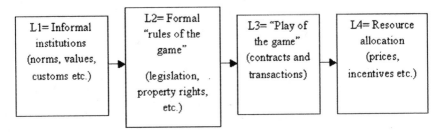

*Figure 4.1*   Williamson's four institutional levels.

refer to the same *level* of institutions. Williamson distinguishes four institutional levels, from the most global to the narrowest, each level imposing constraints on the following one.

Williamson locates sociological new institutionalism in L1, property rights theory in L2, transaction cost theory in L3, and neo-classical economics in L4. In fact, while economic new institutionalism analyses both L2 and L3, sociological new institutionalism deals with both informal (L1) and formal (L2) institutional levels. In any case, Williamson's hierarchization of the levels is interesting because it admits that the "rules" and the "play" of the game (the core of his analysis) are constrained by the broader institutional environment described by the sociological authors. This explains some of the divergences described by Powell (1991), for instance, the fact that informal institutions at society's level are much slower to change than institutional arrangements at the organizational level.

More fundamentally, the two approaches also differ in the way they view the social actor (Tolbert and Zucker 1996). In the economic approach, individuals and organizations are capable of choosing the most efficient institutional arrangements in any given situation, albeit with a bounded rationality. In the sociological approach, "'oversocialized' individuals are assumed to accept and follow social norms unquestioningly, without any reflection or behavioral resistance based on their own particular, personal interests" (170). Tolbert and Zucker suggest that these general models "should be treated not as oppositional but rather as representing two ends of a continuum of decision-making processes and behaviors" (170). While certain authors follow Tolbert and Zucker by calling for a combination of or at least a dialogue between the two approaches (Schneiberg 2005; Immergut 1998), little work has followed this perspective.

When we look at later institutional developments, it is interesting to note the shift away from the deterministic arguments from both economic and sociological new institutionalism. According to Tolbert and Zucker (1996), many authors claiming affiliation to the neo-institutional approach started using arguments that are closer to resource dependence theory. In their view, this stems from the discomfort of these authors regarding the static and passive depiction of organizations in the early neo-institutional work. As a result, they suggest that the frontiers between the two approaches are currently blurring; the latest developments in "institutional entrepreneurship" or "institutional work" may be seen as the result of cross-pollination between the early institutional perspective and the strategic arguments developed in resource dependence theory. Much convergence can be found between institutional work and resource dependence theory. In both cases, the focus is not so much on how organizations are constrained by the environment, but rather on how they will react to it and try to alter it. "Noting that an organization's environment is enacted, or created by attentional processes, tends to shift the focus from characteristics of the objective environment to characteristics of the decision process" in organizations (Pfeffer and Salancik 1978, 74). However, institutional work includes field-level analysis (not just taking the standpoint of one focal organization) and extends the analysis not just to organizations but also to individuals, coalitions of organizations or other actors.

Several authors have graphically illustrated how different approaches in organization theory can be located on axes representing particular dimensions or paradigms (see, e.g., Scott 2003). In order to locate the different approaches of this work, two axes seem particularly adequate. The vertical axis considers the level of rationality left to organizational actors by the different theoretical approaches. The horizontal axis depicts whether organizational behavior rather results from factors that are exterior and anterior to the organization (deterministic view), or from a process that occurs simultaneously in the organization itself (agency view).[4] Considering institutional work as a distinct perspective, the three institutional approaches can be located on these two axes, as depicted in the following figure.

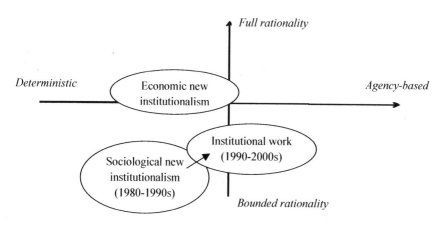

*Figure 4.2*   Graphical comparison of the theoretical approaches.

Sociological new institutionalism is the easiest to locate: it considers that organizational actors are influenced by institutional processes that are totally out of their reach (they thus have a very bounded rationality) and that are clearly external and anterior to the organization (located at a much higher level of society and culture). Organizations are totally constrained by the institutions that surround them; they are not only unable to influence these institutions (determination), but they are also largely unaware of how these institutions affect them (low rationality). By contrast, economic new institutionalism depicts organizations as much more rational—although their rationality is described as bounded compared to that considered in mainstream economic theory—and influenced by elements that are mainly external and anterior to them. Even if some strategic choices are acknowledged, there is a strong determinism in the sense that, in the long term, only the most efficient "governance structures" (in the broad sense) will survive.

The institutional work approach assumes a higher level of agency (and, to a lesser extent, rationality) than the early institutionalist writings. It looks at how organizational actors—often in the context of coalitions of actors—may participate in shaping institutions. As previously mentioned, the introduction of agency in a basically deterministic framework may lead to the "embedded agency" paradox (e.g., Leca, Battilana, and Boxenbaum 2008; Battilana and D'Aunno 2009) resulting from the partial overlap with deterministic arguments, as depicted in the figure.

Such distinction between the deterministic and agency-based ways introduces different ways of seeing the shaping of organizational models and interpreting organizational diversity. As a result, the three following chapters will be articulated around these different views: economic, institutional-deterministic, and institutional-strategic.

# 5  Fair Trade Social Enterprises as Efficient Institutional Arrangements

This chapter uses economic new institutionalism to interpret the taxonomy and the distinctive features of each organizational model. The first section recalls the usefulness of economic new institutionalism to analyze FTSEs' models. Then, the next section distinguishes how the hybrid nature of FT can be expressed in terms of economic goods. The following sections are based on the FTSEs' legal forms and governance structures. They seek to interpret the observed relationships between goals and activities, as well as resources, and the organizational model. The arguments stem from two types of "transaction costs": the costs of market contracting and the costs of ownership. Finally, special attention is devoted to the inclusion of customers and producers as an innovative governance practice.

## THEORETICAL BACKGROUND

The economic (new) institutional approach offers a first possible explanation of the diversity of FTSEs' organizational models. From an economic perspective, organizational forms are primarily seen as ownership arrangements.[1] Organizational economics have thus mainly developed around the arrangements or forms enabling the reduction of transaction costs induced by opportunism in a context of incomplete contracts and bounded rationality (Milgrom and Roberts 1992; Barney and Hesterly 1996).[2]

As mentioned in Chapter 4, risks of opportunism greatly depend on the information asymmetries inherent in the production of certain types of goods. In the economic literature, a "good" is understood in a broad sense. It refers to the type of economic production in which the organization is involved. A good is private when it can be consumed as an individual and isolated unit, with individual payment by the purchaser (e.g., Milgrom and Roberts 1992). Most of the classical consumption goods (food, clothing, etc.) are private. Other types of goods are the public goods. This means that it is not possible to exclude people from the consumption of the good—"nonexcludable" characteristic—and that the consumption of one unit does not reduce the availability of the good for other people—"nonrival" characteristic (Samuelson 1954). Air and public defense are examples of public goods. Nevertheless, certain goods are excludable but nonrival ("club goods," e.g., a theater representation), or nonexcludable but rival ("merit goods," e.g., fish from the ocean). Both types of goods are also called quasi-public goods (e.g., Minasian 1964). The production of nonexcludable goods induces "free rider" problems (Olson 1965). Indeed, as no one can be excluded from the consumption of the good, the provider is unable to charge individual prices that cover the production costs. Consumers will thus be able to not pay without being detected, or consumers will pay less than what they would be prepared to pay for the service. Their unwillingness to reveal how much they would be ready to pay induces an information asymmetry at the expense of the provider (Olson 1965).

Trust goods are another source of information asymmetry. The quality of trust goods cannot easily be observed *ex-ante* or even *ex-post* by the buyer, and the latter needs to trust the provider about the stated level of quality. When is this situation observed? First, when the good is a service difficult to evaluate *ex-ante* (e.g., a surgical operation or a car repair). Second, when the buyer is different from the beneficiary and when the latter is unable to inform the former about the quality of the good. This may occur, for instance, because of the age of the beneficiaries (e.g., little children in a nursery or elderly persons in a hospital), their situation (e.g., people with a mental disease or handicap in a specialized institution) or their geographical distance from the buyer. This last situation finds a good illustration in the case of development cooperation. A good example is a development NGO that announces, for example, the construction of a school in an African village. Individuals will give money to the NGO if they trust that the NGO will effectively use their donation—at least partly—to build the school. They will not be able to personally check whether this is the case and whether the beneficiaries in the African village are satisfied, unless at a very high cost (traveling to observe the NGO's achievements and ask for feedback). There is thus a strong information asymmetry between the provider (the NGO) and the "buyer" (the donor).

For neo-institutional economists, the existence of information asymmetries and the free-rider problem causes certain markets to fail, opening the space for "alternative" institutions (e.g., Williamson 1985). Typically, the inability of the market—in the sense of classical corporate firms—to overcome the free-rider problem obliges the state to produce certain public or quasi-public goods. Nevertheless, certain goods were made excludable thanks to technical solutions, thus allowing for-profit firms to produce goods that were previously reserved to the state—e.g., highway roads, bridges, cable television, etc. (e.g., Minasian 1964). For other goods, excludability is a matter of political choice (e.g., health and education are public goods in some countries but not in others). The state, however, may also "fail," because of limited resources, the inability to detect consumers' demand, or, as will be explained further, because of the "median voter problem" (Black

1948). Hence, alternative institutional arrangements may emerge that allow service providers to simultaneously overcome the failures of the market and of the state. Nonprofit and cooperative organizations are examples of such arrangements, as will be explained further in this chapter.

Specific organizational forms emerge because they entail assets that allow them to produce certain goods more efficiently than other forms (e.g., Barney and Hesterly 1996). Noncapitalist forms will be particularly cost-minimizing solutions in the case of trust and public good production (Krashinsky 1986). As each organizational form is a specific answer to the production challenges of a good (Williamson 2000), the diverse possible combinations of goods open the way for organizational diversity (Handy 1997).

A major contribution to the comparison of diverse organizational forms is Hansmann's book *The Ownership of Enterprise* (1996). Hansmann's analysis is particularly useful because it bridges several contributions to neo-institutional economics (transaction cost theory, agency theory, property rights theory). Hansmann summarizes the links between transaction costs and ownership arrangements as follows. Firms have contractual relationships with a number of stakeholders such as customers, suppliers, employees, etc. The main question is: why and how will ownership be "given" to one particular category over another? The answer lies in the notion of *cost of market contracting*: assigning ownership to a particular category of patrons allows to reduce the costs that would be endured through a traditional market relationship with that stakeholder. These costs are a consequence of market imperfections ("contract failures"). However, assigning ownership also entails costs that are often underestimated in classical transaction cost theory (Barney and Hesterly 1996). Such *costs of ownership* include agency costs and costs of collective decision-making. Agency costs are the result of the need to control managers and of the inefficiencies inevitably caused by the managers, over whom control is necessarily incomplete. The costs of collective decision-making result from the difficulty of owners in making common decisions. There is thus no universal "best way," but there are a set of efficient (i.e., cost-minimizing) solutions. Thus, according to Hansmann, the most efficient assignment of ownership is the one that minimizes the sum, over all the patrons of the firm, of the costs of market contracting and the costs of ownership.

The different types of organizational forms are as many institutional arrangements that allow for sparing on costs that would have been endured through a market solution, while simultaneously avoiding too high ownership costs. In other words, the organizational form should represent an efficient balance between the internalization of operations that would be too costly to conduct through the market, and the costs of managing such internalization through ownership "given" to particular stakeholders.

FT is an interesting case of a complex, multidimensional activity, which implies the production of various types of economic *goods*. Certain of these goods induce information asymmetries and thus open the door to opportunistic behavior—both ex-ante (adverse selection) and ex-post (moral hazard) (Williamson 1985; Akerlof 1970). FTSEs will thus need to adopt organizational devices which protect them from opportunism at the lowest possible cost.

## FT DECOMPOSED INTO THREE TYPES OF GOODS

Much in the way that the FT concept has been decomposed in Chapter 1, it is possible to decompose the FT product from an economic point of view, seeing it as a "bundle of characteristics" similarly to the analyses of Delaval (2003), Becchetti and Rosati (2005), or Balineau and Dufeu (2010).

Take a FT product (a banana, a bottle of wine, a piece of handicraft, etc.). The first thing people see in a FT product is not the fact that the good has been produced under "fair" conditions: we first see a banana, a bottle of wine, or a piece of handicraft. This constitutes the "physical," "material," or "observable" part of the FT good. Without a label, brand, or explanation, a FT good cannot be distinguished from any other type of good. Not taking into account the conditions of production is in fact characteristic for the vast majority of goods traded in mainstream channels. Thus, we can assume that, if we had to ignore the conditions of production and exchange under the FT criteria, we would fall back into the logic of pure economic trading. The material characteristic of the FT product can thus be considered as a classical *private good*. Similarly to any consumption item, the product in its physical dimension is produced by growers or craftsmen—it is because we first think of the material good that we call them "producers"—in the South, and financed and consumed by consumers in the North—who consume the product for which they have paid.

Particular to FT, however, is the fact that the conditions under which the good has been produced matter quite a lot. The consumers do not only buy a banana: they also "buy" the guarantee that the producer has received a fair deal, including a fair price and other advantages (pre-financing, long-term relationship, etc.). Nevertheless, such a guarantee is only the word of the organization: the consumer cannot verify, or at least not at a reasonable cost, whether the organization selling the product has really implemented what it claims. There is thus an important information asymmetry requiring trust between the agents. If we had to isolate only the promise of giving a fairer deal to producers in the South, we could thus easily define it as a *trust good*. A trust good is characterized by an information asymmetry between the buyer and the provider, which disables the buyer from assessing the quality of the good (Milgrom and Roberts 1992). The FT market gives a striking illustration of such information asymmetry, much as has been described in the case of donors toward a development NGO. Indeed, the beneficiaries of the trust dimension of producer support (the producers in the South) are located far from the ones who finance it (the consumers in the North).[3] Hence, even in the case of regular purchase,[4] the FT consumers are unable to directly verify whether their purchase will benefit the producers as claimed by the seller—the FTSE.

Producer support, however, is not the only immaterial element that consumers may find when buying FT products. Through their purchase, consumers may also support the project of making global international trade fairer (De Pelsmacker, Driesen, and Rayp 2005; Özçağlar-Toulouse, Shiu, and Shaw 2006). Indeed, it is often not only about buying a particular product and thereby supporting the particular producers who stand behind it. Initial FT experiences have scaled up and formalized producer support through a broader regulatory framework. This framework can be seen as a "product" in itself, which is not intended only to rule over the trading exchanges in FT, but also to serve as an example toward mainstream trading practices. Therefore, the activities of lobbying governments and mainstream multinationals, as well as educating consumers to include ethical considerations in their general buying behavior, are also part of the "FT bundle" bought by the consumer (Becchetti and Rosati 2005). Of course, this third, political aspect of the FT good may be more or less present according to the type of provider and consumer involved in the buying process. For an activist consumer buying in a worldshop, the issues of regulation, education, and advocacy are probably much more present than for an ethically minded consumer in a supermarket (Becchetti and Huybrechts 2008).

The dimensions of regulation, education, and lobbying can be described as a *(quasi-) public or collective good*. As previously mentioned, a public good is defined as nonrival—the consumption by an agent does not diminish the available quantities for other agents—and nonexcludable—it is impossible to exclude an agent from the consumption of the good (Samuelson 1954). Public awareness toward more sustainable consumer habits and the setting up of new rules for commercial exchange are two elements that cannot be divided into separate consumption units (nonexcludability) and for which it is impossible to exclude consumers by charging high prices (nonrivalry).

In brief, a FT product is thus a complex bundle composed of private, public, and trust goods. Other authors who have tried to characterize the nature of FT goods tend to suggest a similar conclusion (see, e.g., Balineau and Dufeu 2010). More generally, Bacchiega and Borzaga (2001) highlight the ability of social enterprises to produce multiple types of goods, which translates into a wide range of legal forms. Table 5.1 summarizes the producers, the beneficiaries, and the financers of the three types of goods that can be identified as composing the FT concept.

The assumption of the economic institutional approach is that the nature of the produced goods and the resources required for such production constitute a major explanation for the differences in organizational forms (Handy 1997; Ben-Ner 2002; Ben-Ner and Van Hoomissen 1991; Anheier 2005). This enables us to interpret the links highlighted in Chapter 3 between, on the one hand, the organizational form, and, on the other

*Table 5.1*  Economic Goods Inherent in FT

| Dimension | In the FT bundle | Producers | Main beneficiaries | Nature |
|---|---|---|---|---|
| Economic— Trade | Material good | Producers (South) | Consumers (North) | **Private good** |
| Social— Producer support | "Fair" characteristic | North and South organizations | Producers (South) | **Trust good** |
| Political— Education | Political project | FTSEs (North) Labelers Producers (South) Stakeholders | Consumers, producers, community | **Public good** |
| Political— Regulation | | | | |

hand, a range of variables linked to the "transactional situation" of FTSEs: goals, activities, resources, etc. To sharpen the analysis, the arguments respectively applying to the legal form and to the governance models are examined separately.

## EXPLAINING THE DIFFERENT LEGAL FORMS

For neo-institutional economists, who tend to view the firm as a "nexus of contracts,"[5] the legal form corresponds to the legal expression of ownership configuration and as the matrix in which contracts can be bounded (Alchian and Demsetz 1972; Coase 1937; Williamson 1979). To explain the different legal forms of FTSEs, the argumentation will be structured through a number of questions based on the field observation, particularly on the successive emergence/adoption of legal forms in relation to particular combinations of economic, social, and political activities (see also Huybrechts 2007).

### Why Did Most Pioneer FTSEs Emerge As Nonprofits with a High Level of Socio-political Involvement?

Nonprofit organizations are characterized by the "nondistribution constraint," i.e., the prohibition to distribute net earnings (after taxes and expenses) to any "residual claimant"[6] (Hansmann 1980). The people in charge of the organization, who sit on the Board, have the residual control right (the ultimate decision-making power) but cannot sell this right nor claim any right on the assets of the organization (Glaeser 2003; Hansmann 1980). Thus, there is no owner with complete property rights (both the rights on control and on residual income).

The arguments of this section are inspired by a rich theoretical body around nonprofit organizations. The emergence factors of nonprofit organizations have been studied on two different sides: the demand-side and the supply-side (Ben-Ner and Gui 2000; Steinberg 2006). In fact, the arguments on the demand side can be linked to the notion of "costs of market contracting" (Hansmann 1996). In brief, as we will see, the emergence of the nonprofit form is explained through its ability to overcome the failures of both the market and the state to produce trust and collective goods—such as those included in the FT bundle   at a low cost. The arguments on the supply-side consider the profiles and the motivations behind the creation of nonprofit organizations, which may include, at least partly, arguments in terms of costs of ownership.

### Costs of Market Contracting

First, in the presence of trust goods, the adoption of the nonprofit form makes it possible to overcome the market failures such as information asymmetry. FT offers an example of information asymmetry because the beneficiary of the trust good (the producer in the South) is different from the purchaser of that good (the consumer in the North) and because the former is unable to systematically inform the latter about the effectiveness and the quality of the support provided by the FTSE—in the first place the FTSEs' compliance with the FT criteria.

Such an asymmetry could easily be exploited if the firm had a profit-maximizing goal: the firm would then simply reduce the quality of the good and increase its profit. Witnessing such a reduction of quality, consumers would cease to buy the products and the market would collapse, as Akerlof (1970) described for second-hand cars. This is why economists interested in nonprofit organizations justify the existence of such organizations by suggesting that their nondistribution constraint strongly reduces their likelihood of exploiting the information asymmetry. The nondistribution constraint would thus act as a trust signal toward the purchaser. As Hansmann (1980: 844) states: "the advantage of a nonprofit producer is that [in case of a contract failure] the discipline of the market is supplemented by an additional protection given to the consumer by another, broader 'contract', the organization's commitment to devote its entire earnings to the production of services."

This argument finds a good illustration in the case of the FT purchase: given that the consumers in the North cannot immediately verify whether the principles claimed by the FT operator are fully enforced, they will ask for guarantees from the firm when purchasing the product. The nondistribution constraint can precisely fulfill the role of a trust signal, at least ensuring the consumers that the additional price they pay for a good of FT quality will not explicitly be appropriated in the form of profit for shareholders.

One could object that the nonprofit organization might still act in an opportunistic way, for example by using the FT price differential for raising the salaries of the managers. This phenomenon is called "implicit distribution," as opposed to explicit distribution of the surplus to the share-holders (e.g., Gui 1991). This is why nonprofits generally add other trust guarantees in order to secure their social mission. One of these guarantees is the involvement of different trust-giving stakeholders (e.g., donors and volunteers) in the governance structures, as will be examined further in this chapter.

Moreover, the assumption that nonprofit organizations are necessarily more trustworthy may also be criticized. For instance, this assumption supposes that the customers or funders of these organizations are aware of and sensitive to the legal form, which is probably not always the case in practice. Moreover, the trust-giving character of the nondistribution constraint may be reduced when other trust signals are proposed, such as public recognition or a label.

In the absence of such signals, however, the nonprofit form is the most efficient to produce trust goods. This explains why the nonprofit form was chosen by most FTSEs created in the 1970s and 1980s (before the creation of the label) adopted a nonprofit form. As the findings show, it is particularly after the early 1990s—which corresponds to the emergence of labeling—that organizational diversity among FTSEs increased. The emergence of labeling, nevertheless, did not suppress the assets of the nonprofit form. Indeed, while labeling appeared as an efficient solution for entrepreneurs or businesses (discussed later in this chapter), it represented an additional cost for nonprofit FTSEs. This was clearly confirmed in the field study. Several leaders of pioneer FTSEs mentioned that the label was not absolutely necessary, even in mainstream channels (e.g., concerning Oxfam in Belgium, the brand of which is still more famous than the Max Havelaar label). In such a case, having a label on the products was rather a way to promote the global FT movement and to maintain good relationships with Max Havelaar, not so much a condition for convincing the consumers.

But it is not only for the trust dimension of FT that the adoption—and maintaining—of the nonprofit form is a cost-minimizing solution. Indeed, a large part of the justification of this form derives from its adequacy in the production of public goods. Institutional economists consider that these goods cannot be provided by for-profit companies due to the problem of free-riding. Indeed, as already mentioned, due to the nonexcludable nature of public goods, consumers can benefit from them without paying for it or only at a lower rate than what they would be prepared to pay. Therefore, a for-profit firm will not be able to cover its costs and will thus be reluctant to produce such goods. As a result, the demand will not be met (problem of "sub-optimal provision").

This is why it is traditionally the government that produces public goods (e.g., defense and education). However, governmental action is constrained due to the "median voter" problem. According to the public choice school (e.g., Boyne 1998), when defining the optimal quantity of public good produced, the state chooses the quantity preferred by the median voter. Thus, two categories of people necessarily remain unsatisfied: those who would prefer less public good and those who would prefer more. For the latter, the additional quantity of desired public good can be obtained through a non-profit organization (Weisbrod 1975). Nonprofit organizations are assumed to be better able to overcome the free-riding problem because consumers are more likely to reveal their preferences to a firm with a lesser likelihood of opportunism. Moreover, nonprofit organizations are able to raise specific, noncommercial resources that allow them to cover the costs of producing public goods, e.g., donations, public grants, and voluntary work (Weisbrod 1975; Kingma 1997).

The political dimension of FT, corresponding to the production of a public good, fits well to this explanation. It can be assumed that the public authorities—in a broad sense, i.e., supranational authorities such as the European Union and the World Trade Organization—have chosen a medium level of regulation for international trade that leaves a whole portion of the population unsatisfied. A certain number of citizens would indeed prefer more regulation, for instance, concerning the prices paid to small-scale producers in the South. One of the solutions for these consumers may be to support a nonprofit that proposes a stronger regulation framework. Such support may take the form of gifts or, more interestingly, as FT allows, through the purchase of a product traded under such a stronger regulatory framework.

The latter example of unsatisfied consumers shows that the supply of goods through a nonprofit structure may come from the demand-side itself. Indeed, when there are demanding stakeholders who do not find an existing provider for the good they expect, an interesting solution is to become themselves involved in the creation of a nonprofit organization (Ben-Ner and Van Hoomissen 1991). The interviews with a number of pioneer FT entrepreneurs confirm that they were precisely the ones who were initially interested, as consumers, in buying fairly traded goods, but could not have their demand satisfied either by the state (because of the median voter problem) or by for-profit companies (because of the risks of opportunism). Following such an approach, we can consider that the creation of a nonprofit organization allowed these potential consumers to satisfy their demand while keeping the control of the fair nature of the demanded good. This is another reason for the adoption of the nonprofit form by pioneers involved in the creation of a new regulatory framework. But the assets in terms of public goods production also explain why, in the presence of other forms of FTSEs, nonprofits seem to specialize even more in regulation, education, and advocacy. An extreme example is that of Oxfam UK, which totally ceased the trading activity to focus on education and advocacy. It seems clear that the current proportion of nonprofit FTSEs, albeit decreasing, is due to their ability to "boost" the political agenda of FT.

It must be noted, though, that nonprofits are not unable to provide private goods. This is important because the sole institutional assets of nonprofits in terms of trust and public dimensions would not have been sufficient to engage in the FT activity. Indeed, the mainly nonprofit pioneer FTSEs managed to organize supply and distribution chains, to gain customers, and to organize a "niche" with such a success that they revealed an economic potential and attracted mainstream companies and new businesses. This is why nonprofit FTSEs can easily be considered as social enterprises that have demonstrated innovation and risk-taking. From an economic institutional standpoint, this is also an example of the strength of nonprofits as incumbents of newly created markets in which the private good production is one among other elements (Hansmann 1996, 1988; Bacchiega and Borzaga 2001).

While we find a number of nonprofit FTSEs that have been successful in their commercial development (e.g., Fair Trade Original in Belgium), it is a fact that most of them, as it appeared in Chapter 3, have a limited turnover, even when including subsidies and donations. There seems to be a threshold which most nonprofits cannot overcome without changing their organizational form. Such economic obstacles are part of what Salamon (1987) describes as "voluntary failures." One of them is the inability to raise capital. On the one hand, the fact that nonprofits do not need to raise capital is a central reason for which groups of people wishing to create an FTSE but lacking financial means have preferred the nonprofit form. This may explain why the nonprofit form is only adopted by a minority of new FTSEs. However, what appeared as a less costly solution at the time of creation has often presented disadvantages with the growth of FTSEs. Indeed, limited capital often did not allow wide-scale commercial expansion. The relationship between legal form and types of goods produced can thus be read in two directions: FTSEs chose the nonprofit form as the most suited to produce the trust and public elements of the FT bundle, but in the meantime the nonprofit form precisely disabled them from giving a central place to the economic activity. Nonprofit FTSEs suffer in fact from high costs of market contracting concerning their financial inputs (bank loans with high interest rates). This is why, in the case of a desire for commercial expansion, nonprofit FTSEs have a strong incentive in "giving" ownership to stakeholders who have access to capital. This is a fundamental reason behind the evolution of most "successful" pioneer nonprofit FTSEs toward forms with explicit ownership (such as cooperatives or group structures).

## Costs of Ownership

People create nonprofit organizations not only because of the opportunity to meet demands that are not met either by the market or by the state, but also to satisfy their own preference for the nonprofit form. This is why several authors suggest that nonprofits are often created by idealistic entrepreneurs (Rose-Ackerman 1987; James 1990). However, the creation and the management of a nonprofit organization also entail costs. These costs are likely to be high because there are, by definition, several founders, and because these founders are not the owners in the full sense of the term: they may have the ultimate decision-making rights but they have no right on the assets of the organization, which reduces their incentives in monitoring the efficiency of its management and functioning. As there are no true owners, nonprofits represent the "ultimate" in terms of separation between ownership and control (Hansmann 1996, 238). This might induce high agency costs. Hansmann suggests, however, that the "value congruence" among people on the Board and in the management make that such costs are not necessarily higher than in other types of organizations, thereby easing the adoption of the nonprofit form. Moreover, the costs of agency across the organization are likely to be even lower if we consider that the employees are more motivated to contribute to the social mission, as certain authors have suggested for nonprofit FTSEs (Diaz Pedregal 2006), and, more generally, social enterprises (Bacchiega and Borzaga 2001).

Costs of collective decision-making are assumed to increase with the heterogeneity of the decision-makers. Certain authors have thus suggested that the nonprofit form allowed the reduction of these costs by increasing homogeneity, through a common ideal and a "strong belief about the proper way to provide a particular service" (Rose-Ackerman 1996, 719). Nonprofits are thus more likely to appear in contexts in which the founders are mobilized around a common ideal (Rose-Ackerman 1987; James 1990). In the case of FT, when we look at the history of the nonprofit pioneers, it clearly appears that the common goal of helping small-scale producers in the South was so predominant that the founders did not imagine adopting an organizational form that would have allowed, even theoretically, the generation of profits for themselves. Moreover, the ideal was often embedded in a broader ideology or religion favorable to the selfless promotion and concretization of FT (see, e.g., the Christian roots of Traidcraft and ADM). Finally, the nonprofit form served as a guarantee to all the supporters (customers, volunteers, donors, etc.) that the social mission was really the primary goal pursued (Rose-Ackerman 1987).

## Conclusion

In conclusion, the emergence of pioneer FTSEs as nonprofit organizations highly involved in the socio-political dimensions can be explained by (1) their ability to produce trust and public goods at a much lower cost than for-profit companies and public authorities, and by (2) the reasonable costs of ownership due to the absence of requirements in terms of capital provision, and the often observed common ideal among the founders, supposed to reduce heterogeneity and thus ease decision-making. But the analysis should be qualified, as all pioneer FTSEs and all politically involved FTSEs are not necessarily nonprofits. Moreover, the evolution of several pioneer nonprofits into more commercial models indicates that the nonprofit form is rarely suited in the case of important commercial expansion.

## Why Was the Cooperative Form Preferred
## for a Higher Economic Focus?

As discussed in Chapter 1, there are many convergences between FT and the cooperative movement; it is thus logical that the cooperative form was adopted by several FTSEs (Develtere and Pollet 2005; Crowell and Reed 2009). It can be FTSEs which have the cooperative form from the beginning, or nonprofits that have evolved as cooperatives (or groups including a cooperative entity). The latter two organizational changes were particularly observed in Italy (from nonprofit to social cooperative) and in Belgium (from nonprofit to group structure). As the study findings show, cooperative FTSEs seemed more balanced than nonprofits in terms of involvement in the economic and political dimensions of FT, with certain cooperatives combining high levels of involvement in both dimensions. Moreover, cooperative FTSEs have higher proportions of commercial resources than nonprofit FTSEs. Which economic neo-institutional arguments could explain the growing interest of FTSEs in the cooperative model?

### Costs of Market Contracting

The most common economic reason for the existence of cooperatives is market configuration (Hansmann 1996, 1999). For instance, in agricultural markets characterized by a monopsonistic situation, that is, a high number of providers for a low number of purchasers, farmers have an interest in constituting a cooperative that will buy their production at a higher price than market purchasers. Such rationale is very useful for understanding why FT producers in the South have grouped themselves into cooperatives (Nicholls and Opal 2005; Becchetti and Huybrechts 2008; Hayes 2006).

If, on the contrary, the market is characterized by a monopoly, that is, a high number of purchasers for a low number of sellers, consumers may be attracted by the cooperative form in order to obtain lower prices through joint purchases. Consumer cooperatives in Europe emerged for that reason. In the case of FTSEs, however, it is exactly the opposite: consumers want to pay higher prices than market standards in order to contribute to the development of producers in the South. Thus, the factors influencing the emergence of FT cooperatives in the North seem quite different from those of traditional cooperatives. In contrast to traditional cooperatives, cooperative FTSEs aim at providing an advantage much more to an external stakeholder group (producers in the South) than to themselves. FT cooperatives can thus be qualified as "general interest" organizations, illustrating a growing trend in the cooperative world to evolve away from the exclusively "mutual interest" tradition (Develtere and Pollet 2005; Tadros and Malo 2002; Monnier and Thiry 1997).

If not market configuration, what could be the FTSEs' reasons for adopting (or evolving to) the cooperative form? Institutional economists point at legal and fiscal reasons such as tax exemptions (Hansmann 1996). But, in the study, FTSEs organized as cooperatives do not seem to benefit from fiscal or other legal preferences (see Chapter 6). As a matter of fact, the adoption of the cooperative form by FTSEs can be interpreted through many of the arguments used to explain the adoption of the nonprofit form. Indeed, certain authors have suggested that the contractual assets of nonprofit organizations are shared to a certain extent by cooperatives that are driven by the "cooperative ideal" (i.e., the ideological principles of the cooperative movement, as promoted by the International Cooperative Alliance). Such an ideal, combined with the limited distribution of profits and the democratic decision-making process, would provide signals against opportunistic behavior and would thus allow for the production of trust goods. Certain authors consider that the trust signals of cooperatives may be as strong as those enjoyed by nonprofits (Spear 2000; Mertens 2005).

The "general interest" orientation of cooperative FTSEs is likely to be stronger than in other cooperatives because of the very principles of FT. These principles, on their turn, may be reinforced by the trustworthiness of the cooperative form. Such a trust signal may be even stronger in FT cooperatives because they are generally not owned by a single category of people who have economic transactions with the organization, but by one or several "selfless"[7] stakeholders such as volunteers, donors, NGOs etc. Moreover, cooperative FTSEs seem both able and interested in investing in public goods such as education, advocacy, and regulation—although, as the findings showed, to a lesser extent than nonprofits. For that purpose, general interest cooperatives may also rely, insofar as the legal framework allows, on noncommercial resources such as gifts, voluntary work, or public subsidies (Spear 2000). This was observed especially in Italy and, to a lesser extent, in the UK.

So far, we have discussed why the cooperative institutional arrangement does not seem to suffer from handicaps in relation to the nonprofit arrangement for the production of trust and collective goods. But we need to go further to explain why the cooperative arrangement was *preferred* to the nonprofit one, either by newly created FTSEs, or by existing ones shifting from the latter to the former in countries such as Italy and Belgium. The explanation may lie in the third type of good present in the "FT bundle": the private good production. The previous section showed that nonprofits were not unable to produce it—otherwise they would not have been able to initiate and expand the market—but that they rapidly met obstacles in expanding such a production. Besides the previously discussed limited access to capital, we could also mention the weak incentives to economic performance, as profit is not distributed, at least not explicitly. While the nonprofit form appeared as an efficient arrangement to overcome the combined failures of the state and particularly of the market in developing a fair trading system, it appeared less efficient when it came to expand that system beyond the niche, i.e., to invest in private good production, especially from the moment the two other—political and social—dimensions were already "established" (respectively, through public awareness and the establishment of rules for trading partnerships, and through the implementation of these rules and their control by labels and certification schemes).

The study showed that cooperative FTSEs were more focused on the economic activity than nonprofit ones. As we will see in Chapter 6, a first reason for this is that the legal framework—for instance, in Italy—may put less restriction on the commercial activity for cooperatives than it does for nonprofits. Furthermore, cooperatives have easier access to capital since they are able to remunerate that capital (Levi 2005; Hansmann 1999). The interviews at several FTSEs having evolved from a nonprofit to a cooperative model confirmed that they strongly increased their financial means when evolving from the nonprofit to the cooperative form. Indeed, through certain—albeit limited—remuneration of the capital, the people already involved in the nonprofit FTSE (volunteers, employees, supporters, etc.) had incentives to bring in capital. But in the three previously mentioned cases, the evolution to the cooperative form, either exclusively as a cooperative or in the context of a group structure, was coupled with a new wave of individuals and institutions who financially participated in these FTSEs. This reinforced the multi-stakeholder nature of these FTSEs, which may partly explain why cooperative and group FTSEs are more multi-stakeholder than nonprofit ones. Although most of the owners do not expect high financial returns, in many cases a minimal retribution covering the inflation rate is welcome—this was confirmed in interviews with several shareholders in the context of the case studies. The economic argument explaining that ownership by people who invest money reduces the costs of market contracting that would have been endured through borrowing money through the market (typically from a bank) is thus further illustrated since the owners do not expect high returns and thus lend their money at a very low cost.

But the people and institutions investing in cooperative FTSEs are rarely only "investors." Indeed, most of them at least have sympathy for the FT project, and are often involved in it much beyond financial investment. This provides another advantage to cooperative FTSEs in terms of incentives (Levi 2005; Hansmann 1999). For instance, in a workers' cooperative, the literature suggests that workers will be more motivated to give their working power to an organization they own. They will thus be less inclined to behave opportunistically, for instance, by working less efficiently, because it would ultimately reduce the value of their company as well as the value for the producers, which would be contrary to their ideal. The manager of a French workers' coop confirmed the employees' commitment to developing new distribution strategies (e.g., by opening a new shop) in order to increase the economic performance. Another case is that of FTSEs whose members are the worldshops. When the worldshops own the cooperative umbrella which is responsible for the import and development of products, they gain a twofold motivation in contributing to the cooperative's success:

they receive a financial return based on these perforamances, and they are dependent on its survival to remain as a shop enjoying the coop's name and product sourcing. In contrast, the worldshops having no such autonomy and incentives seemed less performing, with losses sometimes remaining undetected or tolerated. The participation of shops in the importer's owner-ship is not meant to be *the* solution to increase their economic performance, but it may be a device that strengthens their economic focus.

### Costs of Ownership

While enabling the cost-reduction of market contracting, ownership by certain stakeholders entails costs. Costs of ownership theoretically differ according to the stakeholder group that owns the cooperative (Hansmann 1996). In workers' cooperatives, agency costs are very low (because the managers are the owners), but costs of collective decision-making can be high, for instance, if employees have different statuses and salaries. In con-sumers' cooperatives, it is just the opposite: agency costs are similar to those of traditional businesses (because managers may act contrarily to the owners' interest), but costs of collective decision-making are likely to be low (because all consumers/owners have the same interest, i.e., lowering the prices).

As previously mentioned, while certain cooperative FTSEs are owned by their workers (e.g., Ethiquable and Tout l'or du monde) and/or by workers and volunteers (e.g., Just Fair Trade and Equo%), most are multi-stake-holder, also including supporters, shops, NGOs etc. In all these cases, the involvement of the stakeholders in management decreases agency costs. Costs of collective decision-making may, however, be particularly high when stakeholders' interests are divergent. From the interviews, it appears that the costs of having heterogeneous stakeholders as owners are at least partly counterbalanced by the advantages they bring (see the section on governance) and by the ideological homogeneity concerning the FT project. Indeed, while there may be disagreements, for instance, between work-ers who desire higher salaries and volunteers who prefer that the value be transferred totally to producers—as reported in Pangea NT—there is at least a basic consensus on the fact that producers should be the main ben-eficiaries of the activity.

## Why Moving To "Business" Forms?

A first problem in this section is in naming the FTSEs that are neither nonprofits, nor cooperatives. The literature on nonprofit organizations calls them, in contrast with nonprofits, "for-profit" organizations. But this term assumes that profit-making is necessarily the main objective of these organizations—which may be questioned in general, and particularly in the case of FT.[8] In his 1996 book focusing on ownership configurations,

Hansmann simply refers to "investor-owned firms." But FT businesses are not necessarily owned—or not only—by investors, as discussed in Chapter 3. In this section, "business forms," although not a very rigorous expression, will be preferred to other terms.[9]

### Costs of Market Contracting

Basically, the literature states that business-form companies are particularly suited to producing purely private goods, where no—or little—market failure applies. This reason, added to the fact that internalizing capital supply strongly reduces the costs of market contracting,[10] explains why business forms are the most widespread model in our economies (Hansmann 1996). But what can explain the adoption of business forms in the FT sector, in which private good production is only part of the FT bundle?

From an economic institutional perspective, business companies can theoretically not overcome free-riding problems and thus cannot provide a sufficient quantity of public goods to meet the demand left unsatisfied by the state (Weisbrod 1975). Concretely, in the case of FT, business firms should not be interested in providing education and regulation services. Indeed, business firms would have problems obtaining payment from all the beneficiaries of such services and determining their willingness to pay. Hence, unless they have another, nonfinancial advantage in return, business firms should not be, economically speaking, interested in engaging in activities linked to education, advocacy, and regulation.

Concerning trust goods, contractual authors consider that the suspicion of opportunistic behavior (by potential consumers or funders) could undermine business firms' trustworthiness regarding the stated level of quality. In the case of FT, FTSEs with a business form would have difficulties convincing the consumer about the effectiveness of producer support. Indeed, it is reasonable to assume that if a business firm (e.g., a supermarket chain) had been the first to come up with the idea of Fair Trade, it would have received skepticism (LeClair 2002). This may be one of the reasons why business forms remained relatively absent of the FT sector until the mid-1990s.[11] Thus, which factors favored the adoption of business forms over the last decades? We can underpin four complementary elements.

First, the FT sector gradually evolved from a small-scale charitable initiative conducted by volunteers with low-quality products to a well organized and increasingly professional niche. By doing so, pioneer nonprofit FTSEs revealed an existing demand and organized a credible response, thereby confirming the ability of nonprofit organizations to detect unsatisfied demands (Ben-Ner and Van Hoomissen 1991; Gui 1987). Of course, the emergence of business-form FTSEs, and, more broadly, the development of mainstreaming, further developed the scale and the professionalism of FT. But it is thanks to the initial efforts of pioneer FTSEs that structured supply chains, set rules, and campaigned to increase consumers' interest that existing businesses were able to and interested in embracing FT, and that entrepreneurs were encouraged to create FTSEs under a "business" form.

Second, the emergence of certification implied a growing dissociation between the commercial provision of the goods and the certification of their "fair quality." Whereas, previously, the fair quality of a good was linked to the institutional assets of the FT providers (i.e., the trust signals of nonprofits and cooperatives), the development of a label made it possible to gather these quality signals into a "package" that can be available for any type of organization. As a result, it is no longer the company in itself that must demonstrate compliance with the FT criteria, but it is the label directly affixed on the goods. Certification can thus be seen as a cost-reducing device that allowed FTSEs to choose the business form without being suspected of lower ethical standards. But, while this reason is crucial in explaining why mainstream businesses entered the sector of FT food, it is not sufficient for explaining the adoption of the business form by FTSEs, especially among those dealing with nonlabeled products (handicraft, cosmetics, nonlabeled food etc.).

In fact, a third observed reason is that business-form FTSEs do not seem to be suffering from handicaps relating to the trust signals for producer support, even when their products are not labeled. Contrarily to the theoretical predictions, business-form FTSEs seem able to give sufficient trust to the customers and to convince them that they are actually doing what they claim—i.e., supporting the producers through fair partnerships. When asked generally why they had chosen the legal form, and specifically if that choice had been made with the intention of instilling trust in the customers' eyes, only a small minority of interviewed managers considered the trust-giving force of the legal form to be an important factor. Such an observation is consistent with recent theoretical advances that nuance the link between the legal form (particularly the nonprofit form) and the ability to give trust. Indeed, many other signals exist besides the legal form, such as reputation (Ortmann and Schlesinger 1997; Radbourne 2003) and governance (Austin 1998; Cornforth and Simpson 2002; Middleton 1987). Reputation and recognition by well established stakeholders (e.g., NGOs) and by other FTSEs were often mentioned in the interviews, sometimes with more weight than labeling.

Finally, as observed in Chapter 4, business-form FTSEs are not necessarily unable to engage in education, regulation, and advocacy. Despite the "nonrival" and "nonexcludable" nature of these goods, FTSEs may choose to produce them while adopting a business legal form. The case of several members of Minga in Rhône-Alpes, as well as that of One Village in the UK, suggests that education, regulation, and advocacy activities may be central in business-form FTSEs. While, in most other FT businesses, political involvement was lower and expressed more implicitly, it was present for instance through the blog of the manager, through collective participation in campaigns of FT networks, etc. The exceptions to the rule already show the limitations of the contractual arguments and call for taking into account other types of factors.

### Costs of Ownership

In business firms, the costs of collective decision-making are supposed to be lower than in nonprofit and cooperative organizations, because of the convergence of interests among owners to maximize profits. If we replace profit maximization by value maximization through economic development, then we may find the same convergence among business FTSEs' owners. Agency costs should theoretically be as high as in cooperatives. However, most business-form FTSEs are owned partly by the managers themselves, with a number of investors who are often closely related to the manager. While managers may be weakly controlled, leading to inefficient decisions, the likelihood of managerial opportunism is much lower when the managers are themselves owners of the FTSE. Moreover, if these managers make decisions with only little involvement of the other investors, then the costs of collective decision-making—but also the control by these other investors—may be particularly low, as will be discussed in the section on governance.

## What Are the Assets of Individual Entrepreneurs?

Individual companies are a particular organizational form that is little treated explicitly in the economic institutional literature. A contractual analysis would probably consider that the individual company is the first stage of organizational development. This is consistent with Hansmann's (1996) presentation of entrepreneurs as "brokers" who conceive potential organizations and then sell them to the most appropriate category of stakeholders. But the field observations also show that certain entrepreneurs choose to remain alone and do not necessarily desire organizational growth and complexity.

### Costs of Market Contracting

The study has shown that individual FTSEs behave more or less similarly in terms of product mixes, confirming the identical organizational assets compared to business-form FTSEs. The main difference between the two forms is that individual FTSEs do not enjoy the low-cost access to capital through investors' ownership. Another difference is that, in individual companies, the product mix depends primarily on the manager's interests and preferences. If the manager is willing to spend time on campaigning or advocacy, it is possible even in the absence of specific resources. Such an investment, however, may not be stable in time as it depends on the willingness of one individual. Moreover, one might object that, as the entrepreneurs have to live from the activity, their interests will be protected before any other consideration. There are many examples, however, in which individuals committed to FT seem to capture only very little financial benefit from their venture. Other "altruistic" motivations, including "warm-glow" effects (Andreoni 1990), are thus also operating in this category of FTSEs.

### Costs of Ownership

An individual company may be seen as a very basic nexus of contracts, in which the entrepreneur embodies a range of functions that can be performed internally, while externalizing the other functions. The advantages are very clear: the costs of ownership are particularly low. As the founder, the "governant" and the manager are one single person, there are no agency costs. Costs of collective decision-making are also nonexistent.

The problem, however, is that all the transactions must be undertaken through the market: capital and product supply, logistics, sales etc. From a contractual standpoint, this solution is likely to be interesting when these transactions are relatively simple to handle and when personal relationships can instill the trust necessary to avoid opportunism. The interviews with individual FT entrepreneurs confirm the importance of personal relationships at different levels: financial supply (loans by family and friends), product supply (partnerships with one or two producer groups), distribution (deals with "friend" shops), and so on. Because the costs of ownership are very low but the costs of market contracting are very high, following Hansmann, ownership should be "given" to a particular stakeholder category, most probably investors when the need for capital grows. Only time will tell whether this is also likely to happen to individual FTSEs.

## Synthesis: Why Do Several Legal Forms Coexist?

Table 5.2 summarizes, in terms of costs of market contracting and costs of ownership, the contractual assets and weaknesses of the different legal forms in the context of the FT activity, both from a theoretical standpoint and as observed through the interviews.

From an economic institutional perspective, each FTSE will adopt the legal form that gives it the most suited assets in relation to the types of goods it produces as well as its potential owners. Organizational change, in this context, can typically be understood as the consequence of a shift in the types of goods produced. The diversity of legal forms in a given sector has led to growing literature on so-called "mixed-form markets" (e.g., Marwell and McInerney 2005). Such literature mainly highlights the complementary features, typically between nonprofit and businesses, and the opportunities for collaboration (O'Regan and Oster 2000; Austin 2000; Galaskiewicz and Colman 2006). FT is an example of such a market (Becchetti and Huybrechts 2008). In this context, there may be a distribution of roles among providers according to the nature of the goods that

*Table 5.2*   Institutional Assets of the Different Legal Forms in the FT Context

| | | *Nonprofit* | *Cooperative* | *Business* | *Individual* |
|---|---|---|---|---|---|
| Costs of private good production | *Theoretically* | High (limited capital, limited incentives) | Low | | |
| | *Observed* | Medium | Low | | |
| Costs of trust good production | *Theoretically* | Low (nondistribution constraint) | Medium | Low | |
| | *Observed* | Insufficient alone (other devices needed) | Low (similarly to nonprofits) | Other devices: label, reputation, networking, etc. | |
| Costs of public good production | *Theoretically* | Low (willingness to pay & specific resources) | Medium | Very high | Very high |
| | *Observed* | Low | Variable | Possible (directly or not) in various ways | |
| Agency costs | *Theoretically* | High | Medium | Medium | Very low |
| | *Observed* | Very low (value congruence) | Low (value congruence and managers' ownership) | Low (managers' ownership) | Very low |
| Costs of collective decision-making | *Theoretically* | Low | High | Low | Very low |
| | *Observed* | Low | Medium (multi-stakeholdership) | Low | Very low |

they produce. Handy (1997), for instance, suggests that business firms will focus on the production of private goods with an observable quality, while nonprofit organizations will be preferred for the production of less easily observable goods such as trust and public goods. This argument does not seem to be entirely confirmed in the FT sector: indeed, the study shows that all nonprofit FTSEs produce private goods and that several business-form

FTSEs produce trust goods (typically when their products are not labeled) and, to a lesser extent, public goods. Such a distribution, however, might be increasingly observed if FTSEs were to focus on one particular dimension of FT. A current illustration of Handy's argument may already be found through the case of group structures.

### Group Structures

Groups consist of the combination of two legal forms, such as nonprofit and cooperative or nonprofit and business. To follow Handy's (1997) argument, such groups can be described by the complementary assets of two legal forms. Each of these forms will be suited for the production of particular goods, typically a cooperative or business form for the economic dimension (private good production) and a nonprofit form for the social and political dimensions (trust and public goods). The observations and interviews clearly confirmed such a distribution of roles. But other arguments in terms of transaction costs may explain the development of groups as advanced multidivisional structures. Consider the situation of large polyvalent FTSEs simultaneously involved in import and distribution, product development, producer support, and advocacy. The diffusion of information from the operational level to the top management is made difficult, not only because of the size of the FTSE, but most importantly because the diverse operational units have different "jargon." People in the top management, but also people in support functions—for instance, the communication unit— are supposed to equally understand sales figures, development projects for producer groups, and advocacy campaigns. And people from the top management are supposed to give instructions and objectives to these different units using their jargon. As summarized by Barney and Hesterly (1996, 114), "the complexity of the enterprise overwhelms the information processing capacity—or, in [transaction cost] terms, the bounded rationality—of top managers."

The issue of incentives may then be raised. How is it possible to motivate, for instance, people in sales and marketing, when the sales figures are diluted in the total turnover of the organization, including subsidies and donations? And how is it possible to control the performance of each unit? The economic approach suggests that a strong departmentalization of the organization offers a cost-minimizing solution when a certain level of size and complexity is reached. "Dividing the firm into quasi-autonomous divisions facilitates clearer performance goals at lower levels of the organization" (Barney and Hesterly 1996, 114).

But it is reasonable to suggest that the hybrid nature of FT has lowered the threshold from which it is more "efficient" to departmentalize. The interviews in OWW-OFT, MFT and Traidcraft illustrated some of the information and incentive issues even on relatively small scales compared to mainstream businesses. The creation of specific organizational entities in the context of groups also shows that the large FTSEs[12] push their departmentalization very far. The opportunities to capture specific subsidies or gifts through the isolation of noneconomic functions are not sufficient to explain such an advanced specialization. It appears that large FTSEs have created groups in order to clarify their activities and to assign specific goals, as well as a specific identity and culture, to each of the entities.

## The Blurring Frontiers of Social Enterprise

Beyond showing that different forms coexist in the FT sector, the study findings also seem to show that they resemble each other more than what could have been expected from the economic literature. First, despite some nuances between nonprofit and cooperative FTSEs—with the latter generally focused less on the political and more on the economic dimension than the former—these two forms seem to enjoy more or less the same assets in the context of FT. This echoes several authors' observations of blurring boundaries between nonprofits and cooperatives, considered by many as two legal expressions of a common type of organization.[13] The convergence seemed particularly striking between nonprofits that have evolved toward a stronger commercial activity and cooperatives that have included "public interest" goals. As we have seen, the approaches of "social economy" or "third sector," and of "social enterprise," both include nonprofit and cooperative organizations. Certain authors consider that the increasing commercial or productive orientation of nonprofits, combined with the increasing general interest profile of cooperatives, has gradually blurred the differences between these two legal forms (Borzaga and Spear 2004; Defourny 2001). The EMES social enterprise approach particularly insists on the similarities between the two legal forms, considering that the adoption of one or another legal form—influenced by many factors such as national legislation—is less important than the common philosophy of these organizations that run a commercial activity with an explicit goal of pursuing social missions and serving the community rather than making profit (Defourny 2001; Defourny and Nyssens 2006).

But the findings show that this philosophy—and practice—seems also shared to a certain extent by the entrepreneurial "business-form" and individual FTSEs. As we will see in the next section, the stronger focus of these FTSEs on the economic activity does not seem to compromise their social mission nor the ability, for some of them, to "serve the community" through their political involvement. The common rationale in FT is precisely that a higher economic activity increases the social impact. The social nature of business-form FTSEs might be an argument in favor of larger conceptions of social enterprise that extend beyond the traditional borders of the social economy. This converges with the idea of "blurring boundaries," considering that social enterprises may be found within any type of legal form (Austin, Stevenson, and Wei-Skillern 2006; Battle Anderson and Dees 2006). We will come back on these convergences in the next chapters.

The case of FTSEs also shows that social enterprise models may be considered as innovative institutional arrangements which overcome not only market and state failures, but also "nonprofit failures." As the study shows, market failures in the production of trust and collective goods are overcome, not—or not only—by the nondistribution constraint, but also by the primacy of the social mission and the possible involvement of trust-giving stakeholders. And the failure of traditional nonprofits to develop and grow an innovative market-based solution to social issues is overcome by the ability of FT social enterprises—including nonprofits—to raise entrepreneurial skills, market resources, and financial means. FTSEs show that, through the multiple assets allowing to pursue a diversity of goals, social enterprises may be seen as new institutional arrangements that exceed the reliance on one particular legal form (Bacchiega and Borzaga 2001; Nicholls and Cho 2006).

## Conclusion

The economic neo-institutional approach is useful for understanding why initial pioneer FTSEs have adopted the nonprofit form and why these FTSEs still have a stronger political involvement than FTSEs with other legal forms. It also explains why FTSEs progressively adopted (or evolved into) cooperative and "business" forms that enable a stronger focus on the economic dimension while maintaining opportunities to pursue the socio-political dimensions of FT. The emergence of business forms was also (partly) explained using economic institutional arguments. Individual FTSEs were depicted as an embryonic stage of business-form FTSEs (which still needs to be demonstrated). And group structures were analyzed not only as combinations of forms suited for the production of specific goods, but also as efficient solutions in terms of information processing and incentives.

At the end of this analysis of FTSEs' legal forms, several questions remain unanswered by the contractual approach, such as:

- Why do certain FTSEs with a similar legal form have different behaviors in terms of goals and activities?
- Why do certain business-form FTSEs get involved in political activities, even without specific resources and assets?
- Why are the theoretical differences between nonprofits and cooperatives not really confirmed in the FT sector?

The exceptions to the theoretical propositions are numerous. A major teaching from the empirical observations is that business-form and individual FTSEs seem quite different from the "investor-owned" model as depicted by economic new institutionalism. Indeed, as most FT businesses do not have profit-making as their primary aim, arguments in terms of inability to instill trust seem inadequate. While business-form FTSEs seem indeed more centered on the economic dimension of FT, there is no reason to consider that the social mission is necessarily less important than in other FTSEs, and there may be some political involvement in a number of cases. Moreover, business-form FTSEs are not necessarily better equipped, for instance, to raise capital. Indeed, the creation of an FTSE can hardly be considered as an investment with good profitability prospects. It may happen that some shareholders expect some minimal return so as to ensure that the FTSE runs its business properly. But, again, this is very far from the traditional figure of the shareholders putting pressure on the company to obtain a high return on investment. Therefore, as previously mentioned, business-form FTSEs can be considered as social enterprises that are closer to the nonprofit and cooperative FTSEs than to for-profit companies. They could be described as "companies with a self-imposed restriction on profit distribution." Although the possibility exists of seeing a business-form FTSE seeking to maximize profits above other considerations, it has not been observed in the study.

Finally, the general nuance is that the legal form alone is insufficient for providing assets for the production of private, public, and trust goods. Other elements of organizational form, as well as strategies such as the personal involvement of the leader, reputation, networking, partnerships, or labeling, provide "cost-minimizing solutions" that may be more efficient than the legal form. Moreover, the legal form is also the result of the costs of ownership. The example of individual FTSEs shows that, when there is only one or few individual(s) involved in the FTSE, the argumentation in terms of types of goods produced is likely to be outweighed by the "zero ownership costs" that these FTSEs enjoy. Ownership and governance is thus also an element that deserves further analysis using economic institutionalism.

## GOVERNANCE

This section mainly examines the functions and composition of the governance bodies such as the General Assembly and the Board of Directors. It aims to interpret why the different governance models imply different goals, activities and resources (see also Huybrechts 2010c). First, the three main governance models will be examined under the perspective of the control over the goods produced, expanding the agency view to a broader conception of "control" (not just financial). The particular case of consumer and producer ownership will then be analyzed from a transaction cost standpoint.

### Governance as a Control Device

From an economic institutional perspective, the GA and particularly the Board are typically seen as tools for the owners to control the management of their organization. Much attention is therefore given to the control and information issues linked to the relationships between owners and managers—"agency" issues (Jensen and Meckling 1976; Fama and Jensen 1983). Such an agency view of governance is dominant in the contractual approach, not only for the study of corporations, but also in the context of nonprofit and cooperative organizations (Ezzamel and Watson 1983; Miller-Millesen 2003; Labie 2005).

In the context of FT, however, attention to the controlling function of the Board implies determining the object of such a control. Is it the economic performance? Is it the impact on producers? Is it the success of campaigns? Second, control will depend on who is the principal: while, in investor-owned companies, the question is straightforward; it is more difficult in alternative types of organizations (Cornforth 2003): is it the volunteers, the other stakeholders, society in general (Oliver 1992)? These two questions (nature of control and principals) will guide the analysis for the three types of governance models identified in Chapter 3.

### Manager and/or investor-owned FTSEs (Types 1 and 2)

FTSEs with medium or high levels of involvement in the economic dimension are governed by managers and/or shareholders, possibly associated with experts and other stakeholders. This can be explained by the fact that these stakeholders are likely to care about the economic viability of their organization. If we consider investors alone, then this link reflects a classical principal-agent relationship in which the investors monitor the managers on how the latter maximize the former's financial contribution.

Nevertheless, the presence of investors on FTSEs' Boards brings to light two fundamental nuances. First, in all the FTSEs corresponding to this governance model, the managers are among the owners. Collusion between ownership and management is thus important, contradicting the model of separation between ownership and control (Jensen and Meckling 1976; Fama and Jensen 1983). The monitoring role of the investors is thus likely to be neglected, especially if these "investors" are relatives or friends of the managers. On the other hand, the entrepreneurs, being themselves investors-owners, have an additional incentive not to compromise the financial performance of the FTSE.

The second nuance to the link between managers and investors on the Board and economic focus is that these stakeholders, in the context of FT, often also pay attention to the other dimensions of the FT activity. As financial involvement in a small new FTSE is not likely to yield high profitability, it seems clear that the investors have other motivations. One motivation may be, simply, the personal relationship with the manager. But, more broadly, the interviews with shareholders in the context of the case studies suggested that investors were interested as much in how the livelihoods of producers were improved as in the economic performance of the organization. Or, more exactly, they required a level of performance that would safeguard their investment and allow for producer support, but not one that would be made at the expense of the producers. We are thus in a situation in which investors accept to reduce their return on investment or at least to let it be constrained by other considerations. The study clearly showed that investors, and managers themselves, had an interest in not allowing the social and political dimensions to be overlooked.

The expertise necessary to control the noneconomic dimensions may, however, be problematic. Investors and managers may be specialized in monitoring the commercial and financial performance only. Control must thus in somes cases be brought in from another actor, for instance, the labeling organization—whose control, however, is only partial—or simply other FTSEs, typically in the context of a network. Several managers partly explained their involvement in networks (particularly in France and in Belgium) as a way to compensate for the weak internal control of their social mission (let alone their political involvement). As a conclusion, it is not because the governance structures are composed of managers and investors who are *theoretically* concerned about the economic performance of the organization, and because the economic focus is stronger, that these organizations will pay attention *only* to this dimension.

### Volunteer-based FTSEs (Type 3)

The field analysis has shown that volunteer-based FTSEs are particularly active in education, regulation, and advocacy. In an agency perspective, we could see governance structures as a tool for volunteers to control the level and nature of the public good production. Indeed, as customers do not pay individually for the "consumption" of education, regulation, and advocacy, there is no incentive for the organization to produce as much of this public good as what is announced. Contractual work on nonprofit organizations suggests that these organizations are able to mobilize other resources (subsidies, gifts, etc.) that allow them to produce public goods even when customers cannot be required to pay proportionally to their consumption. Moreover, their trustworthiness makes customers keener to reveal their willingness to pay. But even a nonprofit organization could use subsidies or gifts for other purposes and provide a sub-optimal quantity of public good.

The "principals" for such production, however, are not—or at least not only—the volunteers themselves, but, more broadly, the recipients of education, regulation, and advocacy, i.e., citizens and the society in general. Harrow and Palmer (2003) speak of such a control as "public ownership." Indeed, citizens are numerous, heterogeneous and not organized collectively. When volunteers participate in public good production, they may thus be assumed to represent the citizens to a certain extent, or at least to constitute a link between the FTSE and the broader society. This dynamics finds an illustration in several volunteer-based FTSEs. For instance, in Oxfam-MDM, volunteers on the Board each represent a larger group of volunteers in a particular region. This group is the most visible part of an even larger community of supporters and customers who are interested in Oxfam's socio-political agenda.

Concerning the specific social mission of producer support, a similar reasoning may be applied. The governance structures of FTSEs are supposed to control that managers, and organizational actors in general, do not act opportunistically at the expense of the producers' welfare. Initial economic theories on nonprofit organizations claimed that the nondistribution constraint of these organizations eliminated the incentives for opportunistic behavior. But more recent work suggests that the trust-giving nature of the nondistribution constraint is limited and that other devices such as governance are necessary to complete it (Ortmann and Schlesinger 1997). Again, volunteers are not the only principals who wish to see the FTSE fulfil its social mission, but they are the ones that exert the control on behalf of the larger community—even when no concrete "mandate" has been given.

Moreover, in a context in which consumers, who should be particularly concerned about the completion of the social mission, are poorly represented on FTSEs' Boards (see next section), volunteers' control may be seen as a less costly solution for FTSEs than customers' direct involvement. Indeed, volunteers are already active in the FTSE and are able to instill trust in customers and other stakeholders requiring trust guarantees. The rationale is the following: if volunteers, who are close to the organization, are ready to give time (or money if we apply the same analysis to donors) "for free" while they closely witness how the organization functions, then it must mean that the organization does not act opportunistically (Enjolras 2000; Ben-Ner and Gui 2000). This argument assumes that if these stakeholders detected opportunism, they would withdraw their support.

Control by volunteers over the social and political dimensions confirms the role of volunteers as "guardians" of the mission (Harrow and Palmer 2003). Such a guardian role, however, may also apply to the financial and economic dimensions of FTSEs' activities. Indeed, as Harrow and Palmer (2003) observe, volunteers on the Board are increasingly accountable for the financial situation of the organization. As volunteer-based FTSEs experience increased pressure for financial control, this leads to selecting Board members with financial expertise. Several volunteer-based Boards also strongly increased their monitoring in times of crisis, not only on the FTSE's accountancy, but on the whole economic activity. Although the findings show that such an activity is not as central in volunteer-based FTSEs as it is in other FTSEs, it should not be concluded that the economic dimension is out of reach of volunteers' control.

### Multi-stakeholder FTSEs (Types 4 and 5)

Multi-stakeholder FTSEs seemed to combine high levels of economic, social and political activity. But is there a causal effect between multi-stakeholdership—i.e., the presence of diverse stakeholders in the governance structures—and the pursuit of diverse 'missions? This is suggested—yet not formally demonstrated—by recent work in other fields of social enterprise, such as work integration (Campi, Defourny, and Grégoire 2006; Defourny and Nyssens 2006). The study shows that multi-stakeholder FTSEs, particularly group structures, combined the hybrid dimensions of FT in a more complete and explicit way. The multi-stakeholder configuration can thus be seen as a device that *secures* the simultaneous pursuit of the three dimensions. Indeed, extending the previous analyses of volunteer-based and manager-investor-dominated Boards, and assuming that partner NGOs and financial institutions behave similarly, respectively, to the first and the second stakeholder type, then it is logical that the combination of all these stakeholders contributes to bringing multidimensional control and expertise.

This was confirmed, for instance, by the manager of a labeling FTSE, who explained that gathering diverse expertise and controlling capabilities from stakeholders such as investors, partner NGOs, financial institutions, and volunteers, provided expertise and insight on virtually any issue in the organization. This shows that the agency view is insufficient to capture the specific features of multi-stakeholder Boards: other perspectives such as the stewardship vision (Board members as partners), and the resource dependence view (Board members as "boundary-spanners") seem particularly useful.

In terms of ownership costs, the heterogeneity of stakeholders' interests, but also the large size of multi-stakeholder Boards, greatly increase the costs of collective decision-making compared to single-stakeholder FTSEs. This is why multi-stakeholder Boards were generally found in larger FTSEs able to bear these costs and enjoy the advantages of control and expertise on the missions that are clearly more multidimensional than in smaller, single-stakeholder FTSEs.

The next section examines two types of stakeholders for which the involvement is rare because costly: customers and producers.

## Customer and Producer Ownership

Customers and producers seemed little involved in the governance of FTSEs, even in the multi-stakeholder models. This section examines the arguments explaining such a situation and examines the exceptions to the rule, which might indicate future trends.

### Customers

Only two FTSEs in the study organized the formal involvement of customers.[14] In the case of Soli'gren, such an involvement was due to the legal requirements of the SCIC form (which will be described in Chapter 6). Nonetheless, according to Soli'gren's managers, such requirements allowed the FTSE to understand customers' expectations and to have feedback, not only on Soli'gren's commercial offer, but also on its various education and public awareness activities. Moreover, customers' involvement seemed to increase their loyalty, along the lines of Hansmann's (1996) description of the advantages of customers' ownership. However, the fact that such a solution would not have been set up without legal requirement, and the fact that few other FTSEs have a similar system, illustrates the high transaction costs linked to identifying motivated customers and organizing their representation. One way to reduce these costs is to give incentives for customers to identify themselves. Cafédirect provided an interesting example, with the possibility of subscribing to "Friends of Cafédirect" via the website and gaining a number of advantages.[15] The "Friends" then elect their representative on Cafédirect's Board. In fact, such a system of organizing customers seems useful when (1) there is no system of volunteering that allows enthusiastic customers to get involved, and (2) the FTSE is large enough and has resources to devote to it.

## Producers

Producer involvement, while probably responding to a normative trend (see Chapter 6), may also be examined as a cost-reducing device. Many FTSEs complain that ensuring the quality of the products is very costly. "Quality" may refer to the material aspects as well as to the compliance with the FT criteria. Solutions exist for FTSEs to control the quality of both the products and the social and environmental conditions of production. The label provides a range of guarantees on these conditions. But, although the label is less costly than, for instance, regular visits to the producer organizations, it still has a cost, both for the FTSE and for the producer organization. Another solution would be to have a network of trustworthy persons in the local countries and to ask them to negotiate with and control the producers. FTSEs such as Fierros, Silver Chilli and MMH-MFT developed such a system. But this means paying people and ensuring that they will act in the interests of the FTSE—a typical agency problem. An extreme variant of this is when the FTSE itself organizes the production process locally. Souffle de l'Inde provided a striking example in which a textile workshop in India was created and funded by the FTSE itself. Transaction costs, which are potentially very high, are lowered in this case by the fact that Souffle de l'Inde is composed of volunteers who were already in a close relationship with India (some living in India and others used to regular travels).

For most FTSEs, however, producer ownership can be seen as a more efficient cost-reducing device. Indeed, involving producers allows them to feel more responsible for the FTSE's business and to search for a stronger convergence between the interests of their organization and those of the FTSE. This is well described by Pfeffer and Salancik (1978) when they underline the advantages of cooptation for securing stakeholder support. This finds an echo in the following interviewee's statement:

*Having producers on the Board is not only symbolic. [ . . . ] They have the opportunity to better understand the constraints of our business.*

> *And they have the incentive to find solutions. [As a result], producers are definitely more committed to the partnership since they own and govern our business.*

However, having producers in the capital and on the Board does not only have advantages. First, there are the costs of inviting producers to Board meetings, to share regular information and get feedback, and so on. Second, when partnerships exist with several producer organizations, costs derive from the selection of the producer organizations and the balance of their interests in relation to those of noninvolved producers. This is one of the reasons put forward by the manager of a major pioneer FTSE to explain the inadequacy of such a system in their case, when there is a high number of producer organizations. These two costs of collective decision-making induced by producers' involvement in ownership probably explain why only few FTSEs have adopted such a system.

There are, nevertheless, solutions to decrease these costs. Again, Café-direct provides an interesting example, through the recent creation of a company specifically devoted to group the producer partners of Cafédirect. Instead of directly including producers in Cafédirect's ownership, the FTSE encourages producers to join "Cafédirect Producers Limited" (CPL), which holds shares in Cafédirect. This allows all producers to participate indirectly in Cafédirect's governance at a much lower cost. Indeed, assemblies of CPL are organized in different places in the South, so as to allow the largest number of producers possible to provide input to and receive feedback from CPL's involvement in Cafédirect. Yet, this requires a sufficient size to set up a specific structure and maintaining it over time.

Co-ownership can also be developed on the scale of smaller FTSEs. There are examples of associations between entrepreneurs in the North and South to create common ventures: in the study, Satya-Pure Elements and Karawan started in such a way. In both cases, however, producers withdrew after a short time, compromising the supply chain and pushing the entrepreneurs in the North to redevelop their business alone. The costs in this case are not so much linked to collective decision-making, but rather to a more typical "lock-in" problem in which the two participants in the transaction share assets that are crucial for each of them.

In conclusion, whatever the size of the FTSE, producer involvement offers an interesting illustration of stakeholder involvement as a solution offering many advantages but also possible costs.


## CONCLUSION

Using an economic institutional approach to understand FTSEs' organizational models appeared useful in several ways. First, legal forms adopted by FTSEs can be linked to a certain extent to the types of goods produced by these FTSEs. FTSEs involved only in private good production tend to adopt a business or individual legal form, whereas FTSEs involved also in public good production tend to favor the nonprofit form. Despite their diversity, cooperative FTSEs can be viewed somehow in the middle of this continuum. Nevertheless, many exceptions exist in which a different legal form than what would theoretically seem most appropriate given the goods produced is adopted. The costs of ownership may shed additional light on the adoption of particular organizational forms, independently from the types of goods produced. For instance, when founders are very few, the most efficient solution is likely to be the individual form, even when there is a strong focus on socio-political activities. At the other side of the spectrum, the emergence of group structures can be explained by transaction cost arguments (information, accountability, etc.) when the size and complexity of FTSEs increases.

The presence of particular stakeholders in the governance structures may also be linked to a certain extent to the types of goods produced. The focus was on the controlling functions of governance to explain this link from a contractual standpoint. Volunteer-based FTSEs seem to differ from manager or shareholder-owned FTSEs in their higher level of political involvement, their lower degree of economic activity and their lower proportion of commercial resources. On the other hand, the presence of shareholders or the managers themselves in the governance structures does not automatically result in a higher level of economic involvement. Multi-stakeholder FTSEs seem to combine high levels of economic and political involvement. Finally, customers' and producers' involvement can be analyzed as devices that both bring additional costs and allow sparing of other ones.

In brief, the economic new institutional approach helps to better understand why FTSEs adopt diverse organizational forms. However, we find several exceptions of organizational models that may seem illogical from the perspective of the types of goods produced or of other cost-reduction arguments. Moreover, this approach says little about how the adoption of particular models may vary depending on historical and geographical settings. Chapter 6 will use sociological neo-institutional arguments to help answering these pending questions.

# 6  Fair Trade Social Enterprises as Reflections of Their Environment

Sociological new institutionalism mainly focused, at least until the late 1990s, on how institutions—understood in a broad sense—constrain organizational behavior. After recalling the fundamentals of this approach and its usefulness for examining FTSEs' diverse models, the two subsequent sections take a respectively historical and geographical perspective. In the second section, the normative trends in the FT field and their consequences on FTSEs' organizational models are examined at three stages of development of the sector: foundation, mainstreaming, and entrepreneurship. Then, the third section looks at how these normative trends are translated at the local level and are intertwined with coercive and mimetic influences, revealing important differences between the four countries of the study. The chapter ends with summarizing the interplay between the different pressures at the global and local levels, and suggests possible reasons behind the persistence of organizational diversity.

## THEORETICAL BACKGROUND

Among the four already listed founding articles (Powell and DiMaggio 1991), those by Meyer and Rowan (1977) and DiMaggio and Powell (1983) are the most explicit on the institutional shaping of organizational forms. These two articles are presented here.

First, Meyer and Rowan (1991, 47) introduced the view of organizations as "dramatic enactments of the rationalized myths pervading modern societies." As organizations imitate environmental elements in their structures, they "tend to disappear as distinct and bounded units." Meyer and Rowan contest the dominant functional view of organizations by showing that "structures can become invested with socially shared meanings, and thus, in addition to their 'objective' functions, [ . . . ] serve to communicate information about the organization to both internal and external audiences" (Tolbert and Zucker 1996, 171). What they call "myths" are "rationalized and impersonal prescriptions that identify various social purposes as technical ones" (Meyer and Rowan 1991, 44). They are definitely not part of a strategic choice as they are "beyond the discretion of any individual participant or organization" (44). The existence of rationalized institutional structures as "building blocks" makes it easier and more legitimate to build formal structures. Meyer and Rowan consider that, when creating organizations, entrepreneurs do nothing more than incorporating these building blocks with "*a little entrepreneurial energy*" (52). By incorporating the blocks, organizations avoid illegitimacy.

Powell and DiMaggio (1983) deepen the notion of organizational isomorphism, distinguishing three types of institutional pressures—coercive, mimetic and normative—causing isomorphism. Coercive isomorphism "results from both formal and informal pressures exerted on organizations upon which they are dependent and by cultural expectations in the society within which organizations function" (67). The formal pressures may originate from the government, the legal environment or important stakeholders (e.g., funders), who impose particular rules and structures.

Mimetic processes refer to imitation among organizations. "When goals are ambiguous, or when the environment creates symbolic uncertainty, organizations may model themselves on other organizations" that they perceive to be more legitimate and successful (69). This converges with the notion of "path dependence": current organizational behavior will be heavily constrained by past choices made by the actors already established in the field. It is worth noting that the influent organizations may be different according to how a potential imitator perceives success and legitimacy. Powell and DiMaggio consider that new organizations in a field always model themselves upon older ones. Finally, normative pressures stem from professionalization: the importance of formal education, the hiring of people within the same industry, and the development of professional networks across which norms and models spread rapidly (promotion of "professional" practices).

The observation of organizational diversity, however, seems to contrast with early neo-institutional authors' predictions and descriptions of gradual isomorphism rather than diversity. One possible reconciliation would be the link between isomorphism and the field's maturity, suggesting that diversity in FT is a consequence of the young age of the field. This is inconsistent, however, with the observation that diversity has been increasing over time. Another characterization that may apply to FT is that is has emerged precisely to fill an "institutional void" between the market and civil society. As a consequence, it is logical that traditional institutional pressures from these fields do not directly operate, thereby avoiding isomorphism. This is consistent with Nicholls and Cho (2006) who suggest that social enterprises are inherently disruptive for existing institutional orders and are welcomed positively precisely because of their capacity to escape isomorphic pressures. Yet, this ability may be jeopardized by the powerful attraction of the market institution. Before trying to draw rapid conclusions, this chapter analyzes the early neo-institutional propositions more in detail, examining to what extent the institutional pressures they identify may be operating in the FT sector and how FTSEs may be affected by them.

## GLOBAL INSTITUTIONAL PRESSURES: A HISTORICAL PERSPECTIVE

Early neo-institutional authors suggest that institutional pressures influence the forms organizations adopt. To examine these influences, it is necessary to understand the nature, scope, and evolution of the institutional forces in an organizational field (Scott and Meyer 1991; e.g., DiMaggio 1991). Powell and DiMaggio (1983, 65) define the process of "structuration," or "institutionalization," as consisting of four parts: "an increase in the extent of interaction among organizations in the field; the emergence of sharply defined interorganizational structures of domination and patterns of coalition; an increase in the information load with which organizations in a field must contend; and the development of a mutual awareness among participants in a set of organizations that they are involved in a common enterprise." While neo-institutional authors take entire fields as the level of analysis (Kraatz and Block 2008), the focus here will lie on the *organizations* practicing FT. The perspective is thus a little different from those authors who take the FT *movement* as the level of analysis, examining it as a social movement in the process of institutionalization—i.e., of transition from a marginal position to a much broader acceptance by and influence on a variety of actors (e.g., Gendron, Bisaillon, and Rance 2009). Of course, those two levels are closely interconnected: the institutionalization of FT as a whole resulted in new ways of practicing FT at the organizational level.

The aim of this section is to expand upon the three institutionalization phases mentioned in Chapter 1 by exploring how trends, norms, and values observed during these phases have influenced FTSEs' organizational models. Several links observed in Chapter 3 (between organizational models and age, leaders' profiles, etc.) may be interpreted through the lens of these three institutionalization phases. For each of these phases, the principles as well as the dominant norms and values are described, before examining their consequences on FTSEs' organizational models.

## FOUNDATION

### Principles and Values

As mentioned in Chapter 1, the first institutionalization of a FT practice happened after the initial foundation of the movement by the FT pioneers, throughout a period that spanned across the 1970s, 1980s and early 1990s.

At that time, the participants were strongly rooted in civil society and had a central political vision (e.g., Raynolds and Long 2007; LeClair 2002; Renard 2003; Gendron 2004a). Their intent was not only to set up their own "fair" trading rules and practices, but to increase awareness in the general public, governments, and corporations, about the need to make trade fairer (e.g., Wilkinson 2007). They saw FT as an alternative to capitalism and called themselves alternative trading organizations (ATOs). Products were sold in worldshops with little emphasis on quality but much more on solidarity. Rather than only selling to consumers, it was equally important to educate them as citizens. The focus was on supporting marginalized producers and fostering their development and autonomy, not only in economic terms, but also from a social and political standpoint. This included the promotion of solidarity and economic democracy, which can be considered as the major "myths" at that time period. Partnerships with producer organizations were often "politically tinted"; for instance, certain FTSEs in the study deliberately supported producer groups in socialist countries (such as Cuba and Nicaragua). Besides solidarity, economic democracy appeared as a major criterion for choosing producers, who needed to be organized democratically and own their organization (typically through a cooperative). Solidarity and economic democracy were more important than the quality of the products, which thus tended to be low. Such lower quality, as well as the distribution strategy based on worldshops, led to a low market penetration (e.g., Low and Davenport 2005a). Important actors were the different networks created by the pioneers (IFAT, EFTA, NEWS!, etc.) as well as large NGOs involved in the foundation of FT.

## Organizational Implications

In terms of legal forms, the findings showed the prevalence of the nonprofit form in that time period. Such a model without formal owners and without any profit distribution seemed suited to values of economic democracy and solidarity. The interviews illustrated the "taken-for-granted" nature of the nonprofit form at the creation of FTSEs by groups of citizens. As reported by the manager of a French nonprofit pioneer FTSE: "at that time, all FTSEs were created with a nonprofit status. It was unimaginable to even think of adopting another legal form. Any business-form FTSE would have been forced out of the movement." Even more interesting to see the trend effect is when he added: "if our FTSE had been launched now, I'm quite certain that we would have chosen a business status [ . . . ]; the way of seeing things has much evolved since then."[1]

The democratic drive may also explain why FTSEs seeking to increase their business dimension chose the cooperative (rather than the business) form and tried to connect themselves to the broader cooperative movement. The vision of FT as a model of "cooperation among cooperatives" extended such a democratic drive to the inter-organizational level (Crowell and Reed 2009). The construction of IFAT-WFTO as a democratic forum gathering producers, importers, and worldshops—despite their very diverse forms—is an illustration of this vision.

In terms of configurations, the strength of the democratic myth may explain why pioneer FTSEs directly developed as missionaries, with a "strong system of internal beliefs, built around the organization's mission" (Mintzberg 1984b, 210). Indeed, FTSEs do not seem to have waited to reach a sufficient size and age to pursue mission goals rather than system goals—in the first place survival. This might seem in contradiction with the initial setting of most organizations (Mintzberg 1984b). But, in fact, the interviews (for instance, at Oxfam-MDM and ADM shops) suggest that system goals precisely depended on the pursuit of mission goals. Indeed, rather than constituting a preliminary condition for pursuing mission goals, survival, and growth were rather a consequence of the initial missions. It is through the development of such missions that pioneer FTSEs managed to attract resources (from volunteers, donors, public authorities, etc.), to gain legitimacy, and thus to survive and grow. This is particularly striking, for instance, for nonprofit FTSEs which developed mainly thanks to voluntary work and subsidies.

Together with mission-centered coordination, adhocratic functioning was common, typically to organize punctual education campaigns or to support producers in a well defined context and period. In several volunteer-based pioneer FTSEs, initial partnerships with producers tended to be considered "solidarity projects," similarly to the perspective of most NGOs. Groups of volunteers gathered around one specific partnership and promoted a given product during a specific period of time, typically following the political context.[2] Despite the normative environment promoting democracy and participation, however, leaders emerged from these citizen groups and brought about more centralized, entrepreneurial coordination. Moreover, organizational growth tended to temper economic democracy and hand over the strategic decision-making (typically in terms of producer support) to employees who developed more standardized and bureaucratic procedures. Yet, the key decisions in terms of producer support remained in the hands of volunteers through the "partner commissions."

In terms of governance, it was important not only to promote democratic decision-making among producers, but also to be organized democratically within the FTSE. In pioneer nonprofit FTSEs, volunteers and employees were almost automatically members of the organization and received equal voting rights at the General Assembly, in conformity with the democratic model (Cornforth 2003). Hierarchy was initially rejected, as were strong salary differences among workers. This is a clear example of a mission goal that pervaded in the organizational structure—a defining feature of a "missionary configuration" (Mintzberg 1980).

While the myths of solidarity and economic democracy were powerful in shaping FTSEs' organizational forms in the early decades of FT, they progressively declined with the subsequent institutionalizations. It is worth noting that pioneer FTSEs themselves enabled and encouraged the emergence of new ways of practicing FT that lessened the importance of economic democracy (Crowell and Reed 2009), as we will see further. While solidarity and democracy remained key values for a certain number of FTSEs, the interviews suggest that (1) these FTSEs have become a minority that is no longer representative of the FT landscape, and that (2) other myths progressively outstripped that of economic democracy, even for pioneer FTSEs.

## MAINSTREAMING

### Principles and Values

As described in Chapter 1, the second institutionalization corresponded to the development of FT labeling by national initiatives (e.g., Max Havelaar) in the late 1980s and 1990s, the subsequent distribution of FT products through mainstream channels, and the later grouping of the labeling initiatives into the FLO in 1997. Labeling opened the door to mainstreaming and offered an opportunity for the radical growth of the sales and recognition of FT. Several authors comment on the shifts in practices and values that derive from mainstreaming, typically in terms of producer support, which is described as evolving from "solidarity" to "market" (Poncelet, Defourny, and De Pelsmacker 2005), from "relationship" to "information" (Ballet and Carimentrand 2008), from "partnership" to "control" (Charlier et al. 2007), and so on. The core concept was that of "market access" for producers, which is the most straightforward avenue to improve their livelihoods and their autonomy. The relatively informal partnership rules applied by pioneer FTSEs were replaced with more formal criteria developed by Fairtrade International (e.g., González and Doppler 2006). As a result, economic democracy was much less central, as the inclusion of plantations illustrates quite strikingly (Reed and McMurtry 2009). The main concern became impact, as stated by the manager of one of the oldest FTSEs in the study: "we tended to work only with cooperative [producer] groups; now, we are relaxed about structure of producer groups, as long as benefits flow to disadvantaged producers."

Three closely related "myths" can be identified when examining this shift: market-orientation, professionalization, and accountability. Market-orientation entails a stronger reliance on market resources and mechanisms, with more attention to consumers' preferences and techniques to lure consumers and increase sales. Professionalization refers to quality improvement and efficiency, implying higher productivity, employees' specialization, cost reductions, economies of scale and scope, and so on. Although these two myths focus on different elements, they are often perceived as synonymous.

It is worth noting, nevertheless, that while professionalization is often necessary to increase the market orientation, professionalization does not necessarily require a higher market orientation (see the discussions on professionalization in the worldshops, e.g., Gateau 2008). Third, as professionalism and market-orientation were justified by the need to increase the impact on producers. There was thus a growing drive for accountability regarding impact. The constant pressure for tangible proofs of impact on producers can be considered as a "myth" on its own. The corollary was expressed by a manager as follows: "[i]f we work on how to increase value through sales and profits, we also need to work on how to make sure that producers gain the largest possible part of that value."

System goals such as economic growth, efficiency, and profit-making gained importance in comparison with traditional mission goals. Or, more precisely, the growing pursuit of system goals was increasingly justified by their contribution to the mission goals. As stated by the manager of a cooperative FTSE:

> *Making profit and increasing market shares are not our primary goal. But we have to increase sales and run the business in a professional way if we want to provide good deals for the producers [ . . . ]; and profit is necessary to make the business viable if we want to pursue our mission on the long term.*

To summarize, in the context of mainstreaming, the economic dimension was strongly reinforced as the main tool to achieve the social mission, leaving the political dimension in the periphery or, at least, not as a central and necessary element for practicing FT (Gendron, Palma Torres, and Bisaillon 2009). FTSEs thus evolved together with their broader field, increasingly occupied by mainstream businesses rarely sharing the broader political agenda of the pioneers in the FT movement.

## Organizational Implications

Certification and mainstreaming were not only characterized by the participation of "for-profit" companies in FT: they also had important consequences *for FTSEs themselves*. Some pioneer FTSEs started collaborating with mainstream retailers by importing and developing FT products for them. In the study, Oxfam Fairtrade, Fair Trade Original, Traidcraft, and CTM Altromercato provide examples of such collaborations. Other FTSEs were specifically created to develop products for mainstream channels: Cafédirect and Ethiquable are examples of this trend. These partnerships had important consequences on the organizational models of the FTSEs involved, particularly in terms of more business-oriented governance and hiring practices (Davies, Doherty, and Knox 2010). In the interviews with FTSEs involved in mainstreaming, the term "professionalization" was particularly used. This, however, translated into various organizational practices, confirming that professionalization is a vague and ambivalent myth (Lawrence and Suddaby 2006). It is worth noting that professionalization also reached pioneer FTSEs not involved in mainstreaming, as a spill-over effect which can be interpreted as mimetic isomorphism.

In terms of legal forms, cooperative and business forms were preferred to nonprofits. As the findings showed, many existing nonprofit FTSEs evolved to cooperatives and newly created FTSEs adopted cooperative or business forms. Following neo-institutional arguments, such an evolution can be considered as a symbolic reflection of the drive toward professionalism and market orientation. Yet, the case of group structures showed that such orientation could be only partial. Indeed, while part of the group still embodies economic democracy and solidarity through a nonprofit, volunteer-based, and politically active form, the other part is aligned with market-based values and language. Following Nicholls' (2010) distinction of social entrepreneurship in the FT context, this may be seen as a coexistence of "social enterprise" (type 1) and "social innovation" (type 2) logics. From a neo-institutional standpoint, group structures can thus be seen as hybrid structures that reflect the duality of the institutional trends in the field. But the interviews also suggest that the confrontation between the new norms and values coupled with mainstreaming and those promoted in the foundation period may be translated to the organizational level and result in tensions that reflect the paradoxes of the broader institutional pressures (Kraatz and Block 2008).

An interesting example is that of a pioneer group FTSE's relationships with a major coffee corporation. The FTSE's campaigning department and volunteers criticized coffee corporations for their unethical trading practices. Yet, in the meantime, the commercial department was associated to a negotiation started by the local labeling organization to have one of these corporations become a FT licensee. There was thus a fundamental disagreement within the FTSE about how to deal with that coffee corporation: through confrontation (political side) or through collaboration (economic side). The group structure did not suppress this disagreement, but rather separated and specialized the two sides. From the commercial staff, being able to take the business decisions without systematically having to consult the campaigners and the volunteers was one of the motivations for structural specialization. Some campaigners and volunteers, however, were reluctant to see the economic side acquire too much autonomy and tried to obtain control devices (typically holding a guaranteed majority of the commercial entity's shares and having a common Board for the two entities). In fact, the group structure as a whole can be seen as a compromise between the people and units embodying the different dimensions of FT, in a context of increasing specialization (Wilkinson 2007).

From a neo-institutional perspective, as put forth by Meyer and Rowan (1977), the power and autonomy gained by commercial departments thanks to the process of mainstreaming derives from the fact that they embody the most recent and powerful rationality (professionalization and market-orientation). For instance, the evolution of OFT's commercial department into the cooperative Oxfam Fairtrade was decided in the first place to professionalize the import, distribution, and marketing functions, and to appear more "credible" to commercial partners. Even if other factors explain the creation of a specific commercial entity, collaboration with supermarkets such as Delhaize and Colruyt was a major driving factor behind such an evolution.

In terms of producer support, the myth of accountability led to a formalization of structures and procedures. In several pioneer FTSEs, "partner commissions" controlled by volunteers gained increasing importance, as one manager reported:

> *The partner commission is now directly accountable to the Board of Directors. We have invited representatives of NGOs who know the field to join the commission. We have asked them [the partner commission] not only to screen and select new partners, but also to make regular assessments of the impact we have on all our partners. This is not only important for our volunteers and employees, but also towards all our stakeholders who want to know the impact we make on producers' lives.*

The increased focus on impact on the producers due to increased pressure for accountability can also be observed through the multiplication of impact assessment programs (Cafédirect, Traidcraft, OWW-OFT, ADM, etc.). Similarly, the drive for accountability may partly explain the growing trend toward producer representation in the governance structures (such as Cafédirect and Twin). In Cafédirect and Twin, producer organizations hold shares (respectively 5% and 64%) and thus participate in the GA. In each case, two representatives of the producers sit on the Board. Producer ownership may be seen as a response to a search for legitimacy, as suggested by this manager:

> *It is our deep conviction that it is necessary. We want to give the control of our organization to our partner producers so that they ensure the greatest possible impact on their communities. It is a signal both internally and towards external stakeholders to remind who is guiding our action.*

In fact, given the difficulties of systematically displaying their impact on producers, the latter's ownership allows FTSEs to gain legitimacy in a more stable and less demanding way.[3] This explanation is quite different from the one developed in Chapter 5 and illustrates the respective foci of both institutional approaches on, respectively, legitimacy versus efficiency.

ENTREPRENEURSHIP

## Principles and Values

The third notable evolution in the FT practice—still from the FTSEs' standpoint—has been the emergence and recognition of small entrepreneurial ventures, often constituted as businesses, and totally dedicated to FT.[4] The "institutionalization" of this new practice of FT is currently occurring and results of the multiplication of FT entrepreneurial ventures but also of their promotion by FT networks. Regional and national FT networks and support structures have played a major role in this regard[5], as well as promoters of (social) entrepreneurship such as chambers of commerce, business schools, foundations and so on. From a neo-institutional perspective, the emergence of this new type of FTSEs and its promotion by networks and stakeholders may be seen as reflecting a broader drive for entrepreneurial action in the social field, i.e., for social entrepreneurship. Although few FTSEs explicitly mentioned this concept, we can identify a number of values and practices that bring this "third wave" of FTSEs closer to the dynamics of social entrepreneurship than the previous two waves[6], which were closer, in terms of organizational models, to the EMES conception of social enterprise.

A first value that manifested itself in the interviews was the importance of the individual entrepreneur as the central figure, not only in the North, but also in many cases at the producers' level. The history and the "vision" of the entrepreneur thus took a much stronger place in the practice of FT- and, as we will see, in the design of the organizational model—than in the FTSEs of the previous waves, generally created by groups of citizens or coalitions of organizations. As the findings suggest, new FT entrepreneurs often had a business education and/or experience and started their project after meeting producers and developing their specific "vision" of partnership. For some of these FTSEs, smallness appeared as a choice and a value in itself. This idea seemed widespread among members of the Minga network in France, but also in the three other regions. Smallness, at least in the discourse, was presented as a way for the entrepreneurs to keep the control over their initiative and avoid the perils of formalization and bureaucracy. These perils were at the core of the criticism toward large, institutionalized FTSEs, in which producer support was seen as impersonal and growth as the only objective. Again, this was most explicit in the discourse of Minga members. But even other FTSEs showed certain defiance toward a scaling up that would compromise the social innovation and the personal relationships with the different stakeholders.

Innovation is precisely a second value shared by these "third wave" FTSEs. While FT itself can be seen as a social innovation which expressed itself to a large extent in two previous phases, newer FTSEs had to innovate even more to find their place in the sector. Such innovation has manifested itself mainly in economic terms, through "new" products compared to the traditional food and handicraft (cosmetics, garments, etc.), or new distribution channels (B2B, Internet, etc.). But we can also witness social innovation, for instance, in the emergence of "local Fair Trade"[7] or the intent to increase social impact along the supply chain.[8]

Another convergence with social entrepreneurship is the central place of risk-taking. While pioneer FTSEs grew gradually and were partly financed by noncommercial resources, and while FT companies designed for the mainstream (e.g., Cafédirect) were initially supported by well-established pioneers, the entrepreneurs of the "third wave," on the contrary, rarely enjoy such security. Relying exclusively on market resources and often engaging their personal belongings to constitute the initial capital, FT entrepreneurs are less shielded than older FTSEs, as the collapse of two FTSEs during the study showed.

Finally, the previously institutionalized values such as professionalism and market orientation also seemed central in this case. Professionalism was especially valued by new FTSEs to distinguish themselves from pioneers. The use of volunteer work, subsidies, and donations, was generally rejected and sometimes presented as disloyal competition. It was striking to note that the professionalization of most pioneer FTSEs in the context of mainstreaming was ignored, or minimized in several interviews with new business-form FTSEs. Indeed, there was a very rooted image that, until now, most FTSEs have been run by volunteers in a nonprofessional manner. Such an image was especially strong in Belgium and in France, where respectively Oxfam-MDM and ADM were seen as the typical example of volunteer, nonprofessional FT; such an image was then extrapolated to all the historical FTSEs.[9] Consequently, they saw professionalization as a goal specific to their organization that differentiated them from most other FTSEs, rather than as a value shared by the majority of FTSEs. It was as if the myth of professionalization was so deeply rooted that the managers considered it as their own finding. Such "taken-for-grantedness" typically resonates with the propositions of neo-institutional authors.

Market orientation, while shared in terms of incomes, was variable in terms of meaning. Certain FTSEs looked for growth opportunities in mainstream channels, for instance, through B2B sales (e.g., Signaléthique and Ethic Store). Other FTSEs preferred specialized shops, either to maintain personal relationships with customers, or because of their political motivation. This was especially observed among Minga members whose small-scale, alternative initiatives reflect their political opposition to the mainstream and to capitalism in general.

## Organizational Implications

The most straightforward organizational implication of the previously mentioned values is the entrepreneurial configuration. The single fact that individuals engage alone in the FT activity is symbolic and contrasts with the previous two phases. When there are a number of employees, coordination is ensured by the entrepreneur. Rather than a formal set of rules, it is the entrepreneur's vision that determines the strategy. Employees are often polyvalent and may be mobilized according to the most urgent tasks. Consequently, governance structures are manager-dominated.

In terms of legal forms, we can clearly see the impact of the professionalism and market-reliance myths. Not only is there a preference for business forms, but also explicit defiance toward nonprofit forms. The interviews with the managers of two FTSEs (a Belgian one and a British one) include direct illustrations of such defiance:

> We didn't want to create another [nonprofit] association of volunteers advocating for Fair Trade. We wanted to create a true business. We didn't want customers to buy our products only because of the social goal. We wanted to show that we could be an ethical business with social standards as high as Oxfam but with a much stronger economic dynamics and thus a much stronger impact on producers.
>
> The shop must be a viable business if it is not to be dismissed as charity.

It is interesting to note that the feeling of being "the only one to be professional" seemed to decrease with involvement in a network. Newly created FTSEs with a stronger economic focus were often more interested in joining networks where they could meet other FTSEs similar to themselves. Nevertheless, the desire for differentiation through professionalization remained strong and the business form was one way of doing so.

The Italian FTSE "Esprit Equo" is an interesting illustration of a strong differentiation process. As previously mentioned, the vast majority of FTSEs in Italy are social cooperatives. On its website[10], Esprit Equo put forth its legal form as part of its distinctive identity:

> The choice of a [business legal form] is motivated by the mainly commercial nature of the activity and by the intent of demonstrating that Fair Trade can be an economically sustainable reality, located in the market, like any other activity, if it is managed on a continued and professional basis. (author's translation)

On the same webpage, the statement that Esprit Equo is submitted to the normal tax rate of businesses and that profits are used partly to remunerate the employees can also be seen as part of the differentiation process. However, as if it were necessary to reassure the FT consumer or operator, the managers immediately linked the company to the standards and vocabulary that are commonly accepted in the FT sector. The interviews in this FTSE suggested that this proactive trust signal was motivated by the normative atmosphere in Italy, suspicious of initiatives claiming to be FT without following the FT networks' ethical standards.

> *The company aims to promote a critical and conscious consumption towards social groups and citizens, claiming to fulfill the criteria of the 'Italian Fair Trade statement' and of organic production. [ . . . ] Moreover, the statutes of the company guarantee that part of each year's profit should directly serve to support the development of projects in the context of Fair Trade.* (author's translation)

The emergence of the myth of professionalization may also explain changes in legal forms. The founder of a French FTSE having evolved from the non-profit to the business form explained:

> *The form of 'société anonyme' is more coherent to our vision of FT as a commercial, albeit ethical, initiative. It reflects our will to create a sustainable activity generating employment, instead of a volunteer-based and subsidized activity. It is a proof of seriousness, quality and professionalism towards customers and our commercial partners.*

Through the desire to rely only on market resources, the third institutionalization also brought much attention to the business model for FT. For instance, the work of BFTF on the improvement of the economic model of its members (SAW-B 2008) shows how the concern for professionalism was stimulated at the inter-organizational level.

## SYNTHESIS AND ANALYSIS

Highlighting the institutionalization of *particular practices of FT at the organizational level*, we may witness "habitualization" at each of the three phases. At the organizational level, Tolbert and Zucker characterize habitualization as "the generation of new structural arrangements in response to a specific organizational [ . . . ] set of problems, and the formalization of such arrangements in the policies and procedures of a given organization, or a set of organizations that confront the same or similar problems" (175). The "problems" or issues are, successively: the need to establish organizations able to engage in an economic activity to concretize the desire for a fairer trading system (foundation); the need to adapt to the arrival of mainstream businesses (mainstreaming); and the need for people with an entrepreneurial profile to find new, more market-oriented ways of engaging in FT (entrepreneurship).

It is interesting to note that the diffusion of new organizational practices in the mainstreaming and entrepreneurship phases required a certain "deinstitutionalization" of the previous practices (Lawrence and Suddaby 2006;

Oliver 1992). Several quotations show how managers of newer FTSEs first needed to de-legitimize the pioneers' forms and practices before presenting their own model as different and superior in meeting their perceived goals for FT. In several interviews, pioneer FTSEs that adapted their structure to deal with the mainstream clearly marked their difference either in relation to their own previous model, or regarding pioneer FTSEs that retained models characteristic of the first institutionalization—nonprofit, volunteer-based, and adhocratic. In both cases, such models were described as inappropriate to sustain the economic development of FT. FTSEs specifically

*Table 6.1* Principles and Organizational Implications of the Three Institutionalization Phases

| | Foundation | Labeling and mainstreaming | Entrepreneurship |
|---|---|---|---|
| **Period** | 1970s–1980s | 1990s | 2000s |
| **Vision** | FT as an alternative rooted in civil society | FT as an "ethical influencer" | FT as an entrepreneurial activity |
| **Producer groups** | Marginalized Focus on economic democracy Solidarity relation Control by volunteers | Large Economic democracy less central Standardized relations Control by certification | Small Economic democracy not central Personal relationship Control by managers |
| **Products** | Guided by producers' habits and identity; quality not central | Guided by consumers' preferences; focus on quality | Matching of producers and consumers' needs; focus on innovation |
| **Distribution** | Worldshops, catalogs, churches, etc. | Supermarkets | Small shops; Internet and B2B |
| **Resources** | Voluntary work Sales Subsidies Donations | Sales | Sales |
| **Networks** | WFTO, EFTA, NEWS! | FLO, national initiatives | Regional and national FT networks |
| **Org. forms** | Nonprofit Missionary-adhocratic Democratically and collectively governed | Cooperative, business or hybrid (group) Missionary with bureaucratic trends Governance including expertise (business + producer support) | Individual and business Entrepreneurial-Founder/manager-dominated (possibly with investors) |

created by pioneers to reach the mainstream had a similar discourse, as well as part of the "third wave" business-form FTSEs. Nevertheless, other FTSEs from this last category undermined the appropriateness of both the "first wave," volunteer-based, FTSEs, and the "second wave," mainstream-oriented FTSEs. Minga members in France are typically engaged in such a process of de-legitimization of the first two ways of practicing FT. These strategies will be examined in Chapter 7.

Table 6.1 briefly summarizes the principles and organizational implications of each of the three institutionalization phases.

If we observe the latest developments in terms of normative atmosphere, it seems that the values of innovation and entrepreneurship are more fertile for the emergence of business, entrepreneurial forms than for the emergence of collective, volunteer-based, and democratic organizations. Some of the interviewed managers in new FTSEs reported that the adoption of a business legal form was motivated by the fear of being misunderstood or perceived as too "alternative" by economic stakeholders (customers, retailers, suppliers, partners, etc.). A business form does not require a particular explanation, while nonprofits or even cooperatives doing business may have to justify themselves or to depict themselves as "social enterprises" (Dart 2004; Grenier 2006). As suggested by these authors, the successful adoption of the language and practices of the business world is one of the factors explaining the success of the social enterprise approaches and practices—a task in which traditional nonprofits have been less successful (see also Abzug and Webb 1999).

The resemblances among FTSEs according to the generation to which they belong could also be interpreted as being the result of imitation. Mimetic pressures are observed "when goals are ambiguous, or when the environment creates symbolic uncertainty" (DiMaggio and Powell 1983, 69). In such cases, organizations might imitate other organizations that they perceive to be more legitimate and successful. The goals of FTSEs are hybrid and thus ambiguous because there is no "one best way" to combine these hybrid goals. Moreover, the trust dimension on which the whole sector is built creates strong uncertainty; consumers might lose confidence in FT or other concepts might take its place.

Even in a given region, there was no general agreement on who should be considered as "the FT success story." Virtually each FTSE had its own model(s) according to its criteria. The main reason for such diversity probably lies in the fact that FTSEs have diverse performance criteria, as the very concept of FT allows. Moreover, it seemed difficult to be successful simultaneously in the three dimensions. Thus, there are FTSEs that are rather successful on the political side, or on the commercial side, but few are unanimously perceived as globally successful. There will often be criticism and disagreement from FTSEs and stakeholders with different views. The analysis thus contrasts with DiMaggio and Powell when they claim that "much homogeneity in organizational structures stems from the fact that despite considerable search for diversity there is relatively little variation to be selected from" (1991, 70). In the FT sector, as among social enterprises (Nicholls and Cho 2006), there is, on the contrary, a range of models that can be followed, even among the more business-oriented models.

Finally, when linking age and organizational model, several exceptions to the general trends appeared. These exceptions confirm that the distinction of these three institutionalizations is schematic: it does not correspond to three clear-cut periods that would have neatly succeeded each other. Nor does it correspond to a typology of FTSEs where all the FTSEs created in a given period would share once and for all the characteristics of the corresponding institutionalization. Most pioneer FTSEs seem to have evolved and hybridized features corresponding to the successive institutionalizations.

Such nuances highlight, in fact, the competition among several contradictory and clearly unachieved institutional orders (e.g., Friedland and Alford 1991). The nuances also echo the inability of early neo-institutional theorists to describe concretely how institutional pressures affect organizations (Scott 1991; Tolbert and Zucker 1996). Indeed, early neo-institutional work seemed to present the different types of institutional pressures as having an automatic and uniform effect on organizational structures. They thereby neglected the different degrees and ways in which organizational structures are concretely affected.

Scott (1991) distinguished seven avenues for the environment to influence organizational structures. First, the influence of institutionalization phases may be described through the process of *incorporation*. This refers to a progressive, unconscious resemblance to the environment. "Via a broad array of adaptive processes occurring over a period of time and ranging from cooptation of the representatives of relevant environmental elements to the evolution of specialized boundary roles to deal with strategic contingencies, organizations come to mirror or replicate salient aspects of environmental differentiation in their own structures" (179).

A crucial tool for incorporation is thus governance structures, especially in a stakeholder perspective. The evolution of the Board of a nonprofit FTSE offered an interesting illustration. The FTSE started with a Board composed only of volunteers. Economic democracy was clearly the main consideration, reflecting the importance of this value in the early history of FT. In the 1980s, a series of NGOs with whom it collaborated were invited to provide expertise on how to improve producer support. Some of them became official members of the GA. At that time, thanks to the contribution of these NGOs and the specialization of certain volunteers in producer support issues, the partner commission formalized its functioning and increased its importance. When a second, cooperative entity was created, people with business experience and skills were hired at all levels, including general management. This brought insights of the business world to the cooperative, including jargon, habits, and communication. The governance of the cooperative, previously exerted only by volunteers and partner NGOs, was progressively opened to people with business skills. In the first place, this happened through a business AB. But recently, a direct representation of these people on the Board was considered, although they would not be democratically elected. This has led to hostility from certain volunteers, illustrating a tension between the myth of professionalism, with Board members supposed to bring expertise and improve the organization's performance (stewardship model), and the democratic myth focusing on representation. The project of including producers' representatives on the Board, following the example of Cafédirect, and the more general drive for accountability toward producers, would bring a more stakeholder-oriented governance model, allowing the governance structures to be a vehicle for incorporation of external influences.

Another avenue that may explain the observations is *imprinting*, which can be defined as "the process by which new organizational forms acquire characteristics at the time of their founding which they tend to retain in the future" (Scott 1991, 178). Structural features were acquired not by rational choice but because they were taken for granted at the foundation. Several examples can be found in the study, among which Fair Trade Original. Since its creation in Belgium in the early 1970s, this FTSE has retained a nonprofit form, whereas its activities evolved toward a much stronger business orientation (including the payment of taxes specific to businesses). Today, the nonprofit form seems more a reminder of the pioneer's origins, as well as an additional safeguard for profit distribution, than an expression of the FTSE's current goals and activities.

A third type of avenue is *authorization* of organizational structure. The organization is not obliged to conform to the institutional pressure, but it does so in order to obtain "the attention and approval of the authorizing agent" (Scott 1991, 175). Typically, FTSEs were not forced to adopt or to evolve toward more business-oriented legal forms and manager/investor-based governance models: such a move is rather explained by the normative environment which makes that a business-oriented organizational form is much more taken for granted in the FT sector nowadays than it was a decade ago.

Finally, the role of leaders in the shaping of organizational forms may go beyond that of a passive diffusion and replication of norms and values that are supposed to be taken for granted. The link between leaders' profiles and organizational models in FT can be read through a more active avenue, namely the *acquisition* of organizational structure. Acquisition is the deliberate choice of the organizational form by managers, which contrasts with the situations described previously "in which the major impetus for the change comes from outside the organization" (178). By paying attention to the ability of managers to proactively structure their organization, Scott (1991) initiated, together with DiMaggio (1988), a new strand of institutional theory leaving much more space to agency (see Chapter 7).

## LOCAL INSTITUTIONAL PRESSURES: A GEOGRAPHICAL PERSPECTIVE

FTSEs are not only subject to the global normative pressures deriving from the successive institutionalization phases in the FT sector (and, more globally, in society). As they are located in a particular region, they are also likely to be influenced by local normative trends (which do not necessarily mirror the global ones), by imitation of local FTSEs, and by imposition or inducement of certain forms because of the legislation and the action of public authorities. This section focuses on legal forms and is structured around the four regions of the study.

### Italy

Italian FTSEs in the study—and more broadly[11]—appeared particularly uniform in terms of legal form (social cooperatives) and governance configuration (volunteer-based or multi-stakeholder with a strong representation of volunteers). What are the reasons that can explain such a situation?

#### Normative Atmosphere

A first reason behind the uniformity of Italian FTSEs seems to be the general agreement among them concerning the vision of FT as a civil society, volunteer-based, and political movement (Viganò, Glorio, and Villa 2008; Becchetti and Costantino 2010). FTSEs seemed willing to both maintain certain control over mainstream FT and differentiate themselves from the mainstream through higher ethical standards. Several managers criticized the Transfair label for not being demanding enough when dealing with corporations. Professionalism was put forth, but not as a synonym of market orientation. Several leaders insisted on the fact that they had professionalized their practice of FT without abandoning volunteer work, economic democracy, and political involvement. The common identity of Italian FTSEs seemed reinforced by their tight connections through regional and national networks. Moreover, they seemed to differentiate themselves from other countries in which FT was commonly described as much more business-oriented (Viganò, Glorio, and Villa 2008; Becchetti and Costantino 2010). Several interviewees, through their questions about the findings in the three other countries, confirmed the predominance of such an image.

#### Legislation

As the Italian legislation heavily constrains commercial activity in the nonprofit sector[12], either "volunteer organizations" (Organizazzione di Voluntariato) or NGOs, few FTSEs still have one of these forms. Indeed, for Italian FTSEs initially organized as nonprofits, law 381/1991 on "social cooperatives"[13] constituted a major opportunity. The cooperative form, in its traditional version, was mainly suited for traditional mutual interest cooperatives and was thus not associated with the pursuit of a social mission (Galera 2004). It is the combined inadequacy of the nonprofit form to run a commercial activity and of the traditional cooperative form to pursue social goals that led to the conception of this new framework (Borzaga, Galera, and Zandonai 2008, 26). Type A social cooperatives are intended to offer services to marginalized groups (elderly, homeless, etc.). Type B social cooperatives are characterized by their provision of work opportunities to disadvantaged categories of people.

The hybrid nature of social cooperatives pushed the vast majority of Italian FTSEs to choose this legal form (mainly type "A"; only one FTSE in the study chose type "B"). It should be noted that this form was also massively adopted in other sectors of social enterprise.[14] The choice of the social cooperative form was even more tempting for Italian FTSEs since they are also eligible—together with nonprofit organizations—for the fiscal category of "Onlus" ("*Organizzazione non lucrativa di utilità sociale*"). Provided that they pursue a social goal and prohibit the distribution of profits, the "Onlus" benefit from a favorable fiscal regime. Four FTSEs in the Italian study are recognized as Onlus.

The Italian legislation did not only encourage uniformity in legal forms, but also in governance practices. Indeed, the law authorizes—and encourages—various categories of stakeholders to become members of social cooperatives: employees, beneficiaries, volunteers (up to 50% of members), financial investors, and public institutions. In type B cooperatives, at least 30% of the members must be from the disadvantaged target groups. Through the legal framework for social cooperatives, Italian lawmakers seem to have encouraged uniformity.[15] Nevertheless, a more recent law (118/2005) was passed to extend the recognition of other organizational forms as social enterprises. This law "does not consider the organizational structure as a condition for eligibility as a social enterprise" (Borzaga, Galera, and Zandonai 2008, 26). While this law was precisely intended to encourage diversity, its criteria seem so restrictive that it excluded a large part of the "business-form" and other, "noncooperative" types of social enterprises. As noted by Borzaga and his colleagues, imposing a "total nondistribution constraint" is more demanding than the common characterizations of social enterprises, including the EMES approach.

In conclusion, the legislative configuration already seems to explain much of the homogeneity in Italian FTSEs. The choice of social cooperative form seemed moreover reinforced by the particular normative setting in the context of networks.

### Networks

FT networks seem to have played an important role in promoting nonbusiness forms, and social cooperatives in particular. From its creation in 2003, Agices—the main FT network—reserved its membership to nonprofit and cooperative FTSEs only. This requirement reflects the fact that all the initial members of Agices were social cooperatives or, to a lesser extent, nonprofits. As stated by the founder of a pioneer FTSE: "any other legal form, particularly from the business world, would have been considered as inappropriate." Besides discouraging changes of legal form among the current members, this requirement also encouraged new FTSEs to adopt a similar form if willing to join Agices.

At this stage, the role of both legislation and networks in favoring organizational uniformity among FTSEs is not explicitly coercive but rather normative, which means that there is strong pressure, although no explicit obligation, to conform to institutional expectations (DiMaggio and Powell 1983). This is described by Scott (1991) as an *inducement* of the organizational structure. In other words, there is no sufficient authority to impose a particular organizational form, but certain agents provide strong incentives for organizations to conform to their expectations. Favorable legislation, funding opportunities, and fiscal preferences are typical such incentives.

If, however, Agices succeeded in influencing the Italian law project in a way in which the nonprofit or cooperative form would be required to be recognized as a "Fair Trade organization," this would move from inducement to *imposition* of organizational forms (Scott 1991). The outcome would be the strengthening of organizational uniformity. The lobbying role of Agices also consisted of putting pressure on lawmakers to include FT in the recognized sectors of activities for social cooperatives and by organizing seminars for FTSEs about how to fill the requirements of the social cooperative form. Finally, it lobbied to open the "Onlus" status to FTSEs.

### Mimetism

Besides coercion, organizational uniformity in Italy may also be explained through mimetism. As there is no guide of "best practices" about how to create an FTSE, it is likely that imitation based on personal relationships will play a major role. Indeed, several volunteers were involved in other FTSEs before creating their own organization. The most striking example is that of Niente-Troppo, which designed its structure on the model of Pangea, with several volunteers and employees having followed specific training at Pangea. Such imitation, as well as the regular contacts between the two FTSEs, facilitated the later absorption of Niente Troppo by Pangea. Unlike on other countries, most pioneers still seemed nearly unanimously considered as successful from an economic, social and political standpoint, even by the recently created FTSEs.

## Belgium

In Belgium, as the findings show, there is a large diversity of operators: "first wave," volunteer-based nonprofit FTSEs (Oxfam-MDM, Sjamma, etc.), pioneers having reinforced their economic profile in the context of the mainstreaming their products (OWW-OFT, MMH-MFT, Fair Trade Original, etc.) and new FT businesses (Ethic Store, Fierros, Citizen Dream, etc.). Within these three broad categories, especially the last one, there is a great diversity of legal forms, architectures, and governance structures.

### Normative Atmosphere

There are clear differences among the three previously mentioned categories regarding their vision of FT. The contrast is particularly strong between the first- and the third-wave FTSEs. Nevertheless, the general trend is clearly toward the strengthening and the legitimization of a more business-oriented practice of FT, including a high emphasis on professionalization and on mainstreaming strategies. Moreover, the differences of vision are no longer obstacles to the dialogue among and networking of all types of FTSEs. Organizational diversity, moreover, is recognized and encouraged by support structures (TDC), networks (BFTF) and public authorities (Huybrechts 2010b).

### Legislation

Pioneers such as Oxfam, MMH, and Fair Trade Original were able to import products and open shops while adopting a nonprofit form. This can be explained by the fact that the legal requirements concerning nonprofit organizations ("associations sans but lucratif") are quite flexible in terms of commercial activity (Dubois 2003; Nyssens 2008). Nonprofit organizations are allowed to engage, to a certain extent, in trading activities, provided that they remain accessory to the main social goal—defined in terms of priorities rather than volume (Dubois 2003, 56). There is no restriction on profit-making either, but only on its explicit distribution. This explains why major FTSEs such as Oxfam-MDM and Fair Trade Original still have a nonprofit form, although their turnover is high and their commercial activity well developed (especially in the second case).

As explained in Chapter 3, however, three pioneer nonprofit FTSEs (Oxfam-WW, Max Havelaar, and MMH) had to split their organization into two entities, isolating the commercial activity from the nonprofit entity. This was due to the decision of the subsidising authority (the DGD) to fund only the activities of producer support, education, and regulation, organized through a nonprofit form. There was no requirement concerning the legal form of the commercial activity, but only on the fact that it should be clearly and legally isolated from the funded activities.

For their commercial activity, the three FTSEs forced to split up their structure chose the cooperative form. Two other FTSEs in the study chose the same form. Besides economic assets (see Chapter 5), other reasons for choosing this form may be found in the Belgian legislation on cooperatives. Such legislation only requires cooperatives to have a variable capital (Dubois 2003).

Thus, in Belgium, the cooperative form does not necessarily imply the respect of the cooperative values and principles[16]. Only the cooperatives recognized by the CNC ("Conseil National de la Coopération") are expected to limit the distribution of their profits and to make their decisions democratically–if not "one member, one vote," at least a voting right that is not linked to the number of shares (Defourny, Simon, and Adam 2002). Yet, in the study, only one FTSE asked for such recognition. In fact, the loose legal framework for cooperatives had paradoxical consequences: on the hand, with no requirements to prove democratic decision-making or the pursuit of a social mission, it made the adoption of this form relatively easy; on the other hand, adopting this form did not signal any specific "social" commitment.

This may partly explain why an additional social-oriented framework was developed in 1995. With the development of social enterprises running a commercial activity but pursuing a primarily social mission, Belgian lawmakers introduced a variant to be added to a cooperative or a business form: the "société à finalité sociale" (SFS).[17] It was recognized that a business company could formally pursue a social goal, which constituted a revolution in Belgian commercial law (Dubois 2003).

Such a framework could have been an opportunity for FTSEs to see their specific nature legally recognized, which could have led to more organizational isomorphism if many FTSEs had adopted this framework. In the study, however, only two FTSEs adopted the SFS framework. Such minimal success among FTSEs can be explained by the fact that the organizational requirements of this framework were not offset against advantages such as fiscal preferences (Cannella 2003; Nyssens 2008).

In fact, SFS companies are widespread in given sectors in which this form is required by public authorities, for instance, work integration companies in the Walloon Region (Nyssens 2008). In FT, on the other hand, public authorities have not promoted one particular model. Moreover, they seem to acknowledge and foster the diversity of FTSEs.[18]

## France

As we have seen, French FTSEs in the study are mainly nonprofits and businesses, which correspond relatively well to, respectively, the first and third waves. While French legislation may explain the poor success of cooperatives, other reasons are required to explain why most other FTSEs are structured either as nonprofits or as businesses.

### Why so few cooperative FTSEs?

In the French part of the study, Ethiquable and Soli'gren were the only cooperatives—the first one as a "SCOP"[19] (workers' cooperative) and the second as a "SCIC"[20] (general interest cooperative). The interviews suggest that French legislation made the adoption of the cooperative form difficult.

Indeed, the administrative requirements on French cooperatives include limited profit distribution and various rules in terms of governance.[21] In all French cooperatives, members must have equal voting rights (one member, one vote). In a SCOP, workers must have at least 65% of the voting rights at the GA and form the majority of the Board (Hiez 2006). In a SCIC, members must be at least of three types (Margado 2002): workers, beneficiaries, and supporters (individuals or institutions who bring funding or other types of support to the cooperative). In Soli'gren, the SCIC form was motivated by the city of Grenoble and local NGOs willing to be associated in the governance structure in exchange for their support to the FTSE.

Many leaders of French FTSEs not organized as cooperatives declared that they were interested in the cooperative idea *a priori*, but that they had rejected the cooperative legal form because of its heavy administrative requirements. Such complexity may explain why the SCIC form, although inspired by the Italian experience of social cooperatives, has known limited success in France (Fraisse 2008). As a consequence, it seems reasonable to suggest that the legal framework on cooperatives, more than, for instance, an unfavorable normative context, explains the fact that most French FTSEs have adopted either nonprofit or business legal forms.

### Nonprofits

The law on nonprofits (1901) allows for commercial activity only to a certain extent. It was quite striking that French nonprofit FTSEs in the study were relatively small. This could be explained by the legislative constraints, but also by a lesser focus on the economic activity and much more on solidarity projects (e.g., Ayllu, Aux 4 coins du Monde, Souffle de l'Inde, etc.). When ADM formalized its importing activity under the central "Solidar'Monde" (in 1984), it replaced the nonprofit form by a conventional business legal form, anticipating the future trend of group structures. Nevertheless, the ADM Federation remained as a nonprofit structure. Similarly, the local shops of ADM were obliged to be organized as nonprofits. This explains why several newly created worldshops were nonprofits and why their proportion in the study was high. Nevertheless, when excluding ADM worldshops, there were few nonprofit FTSEs, and their proportion was decreasing as new FTSEs massively adopted business forms. The interviews with FT support structures suggested that this reflected a shift in the normative atmosphere, with criticism toward the volunteer-based nonprofit form coming simultaneously from the new mainstream-oriented FTSEs (such as Ethiquable or Signaléthique) and from Minga members (such as Saldac and Karawan).

### Business Forms

Most recent FTSEs in the study chose a business form. Since the creation of Alter Eco as the first privately held FTSE in the late 1990s, many FTSEs were created following their model.[22] More generally, the success of business forms can be explained by reluctance toward the nonprofit form and attraction of a market-based avenue to FT, stimulated by Max Havelaar France and its regional platforms.

A different drive for business forms comes from the Minga network. The promotion of the combination of business forms and political involvement by Minga entails mimetic but also normative isomorphism: FTSEs adhering to Minga show a striking uniformity in their discourses but also, progressively, in their organizational models (Diaz Pedregal 2007). Minga offers an example of normative isomorphism through a professional network, as described by DiMaggio and Powell (1983). Indeed, the professional training organized for current and potential FT entrepreneurs, although not directly addressing organizational forms, promotes a particular model of practicing FT that is likely to strengthen the uniformity among Minga members.[23] Three interviewees in Rhône-Alpes reported this training as a crucial step in the creation of their FTSE. In conclusion, in Rhône-Alpes and more generally in France, the context seems favorable to business-form FTSEs, whose proportion should be increasing in the coming years.

## United Kingdom

In the UK, similarly to Belgium, there is a wide variety of organizational models. It is quite striking to observe that, contrarily to the three other countries, the landscape seems particularly open, which may partly be explained by the absence of monopolistic behavior of pioneer FTSEs or networks. Another factor that may play a role is the very flexible legal context. The analysis is structured around the main types of forms.

### Charities

Nonprofit FTSEs, although not very numerous, were present either as such (Gateway) or in the context of group structures (Traidcraft and Twin). But, contrarily to the situation in the three other countries, pioneer FTSEs did not necessarily adopt a nonprofit form: Traidcraft began as a public limited company, One Village and Siesta developed as family businesses, and so on. The legal form closest to nonprofit organizations is the "volunteer organization." Many volunteer organizations are additionally "charitable organizations" or "charities." To deserve this name, they must serve a public purpose and be active in one of the fields listed by the "Charities Act" (poverty alleviation, human rights, etc.). Among the available legal structures for charities, most British nonprofit FTSEs chose the the Company limited by guarantee, because of the broader possibilities for engaging in diverse economic activities (hiring people, selling products, etc.) while protecting members from personal liability.[24] Companies limited by a guarantee are allowed to run commercial activities, provided that they serve the charitable purpose. Contrarily to what was observed in France and in Belgium, the interviews and observations did not reveal particular criticism from other FTSEs or networks toward the nonprofit form and the use of volunteer work. Nevertheless, it is worth noting that few British FTSEs in the study remained as charities.

### Cooperatives and CICs

The adoption of the cooperative form is particularly easy because there is no specific form for cooperatives. Indeed, in the UK, cooperatives must register as corporations and may then freely choose to apply the cooperative principles (Galera 2004). This is the scenario followed by a cooperative FTSE, which was launched by several people wishing to be involved in the FTSE not as volunteers but as workers. This led to the creation of a workers' cooperative, considered by the manager as "one of the forms that is most coherent with the philosophy of Fair Trade." Although the "Community Interest Company" (CIC), created in 2005 specifically for businesses with social purposes, has known a certain degree of success in the UK (Spear 2008), only one British FTSE in the study (Zaytoun) had this form. The CIC enjoys the flexibility of a conventional business company, while having to fulfill a number of compliances to ensure the pursuit of the social goal (Low 2006). The CIC legal form includes a community interest test and an asset lock to ensure that the new entity is dedicated to its expressed community purposes (Low 2006; Spear 2008). However, the CIC does not benefit from the same tax advantages as charities. It is especially suited for social entrepreneurs who want to pursue a social goal in a more flexible and business-oriented way than through a charity. As in Belgium with the SFS, and unlike the Italian social cooperative form, the CIC form was not particularly advocated by FT networks or large FTSEs. This, together with the administrative requirements of the CIC form, might explain its weak success among British FTSEs. But more globally, the fact that British FTSEs have not been searching for and promoting specific forms to run the FT activity, thereby fostering organizational diversity, can be explained by the very relaxed view on legal forms. These forms did not seem to be perceived by the interviewed leaders as important "signals"—at least, much less than in the three other countries.

### Business Forms

The apparent absence of normative resistances from pioneers, volunteers, and campaigners toward business models is another factor that contrasts with the situation in the three other countries. This explains why many British FTSEs, including the pioneers, were free to adopt a business form (private or public company limited by shares). The trend of professionalization and accountability, as well as the opening up to mainstream distribution, also developed much earlier than in the other countries, as described in Chapter 3. The creation of Cafédirect and other FT businesses was another signal that professionalism and market orientation were encouraged to meet the social ends of FT. The "Cafédirect model," with producers' involvement and high FT standards, served as an example of a social enterprise combining market penetration and social mission. This example was mimicked in the UK and in other countries. It is thus a mix of normative and mimetic factors, rather than coercive pressures, which may explain the success of business forms. Yet, contrarily to the situation in the other countries, the emergence of business forms among FTSEs did not imply the undermining of other—typically nonprofit—forms. Rather, the different forms seemed to coexist, in a context emphasizing values of professionalism and accountability but without suggesting particular models to implement these values.

## SYNTHESIS AND CONCLUSION

In the following table, the nature and salience of the diverse types of institutional pressures are summarized in the four regions/countries of the study.

From this table and from the whole chapter's analysis, several conclusions can be drawn. At the global level, normative pressures and myths derive from the successive institutionalization phases. Throughout the interviews, these myths were regularly used to justify, explicitly or not, the adoption of particular models. The links between age and leaders' profiles on the one hand, and the organizational models on the other, were neither automatic, nor uniform. FTSEs indeed differed in the way in which they have adapted their structure to the successive institutionalization phases. This confirms that the practice of FT has not emerged on the basis of one universally shared myth or vision. It has rather emerged in a sort of "institutional void" or at least in an "interstice" between different institutional orders (Renard 2003). As a consequence, FTSEs have not been passively led into one common mould. They have rather been influenced by norms originating from, successively, the activist side of civil society, the mainstream market, and the promoters of (social) entrepreneurship. These norms, however, have not imposed themselves exogenously, making the FTSEs of each generation dependent on a specific path. It is FTSEs themselves that have adapted the organizational path to FT using "bricolage," combining elements from these different worlds (Di Domenico, Haugh, and Tracey 2010). In the future, the further penetration and concretization of the trends toward professionalization and accountability could lead to more uniformity through business-like forms. This is consistent with several authors who analyze the growing success of business-oriented approaches to social enterprise (e.g., Dart 2004).

*Table 6.2*   Synthesis of the Institutional Pressures in the Four Countries

| | Belgium | France | Italy | United Kingdom |
|---|---|---|---|---|
| **General normative pressures** | Foundation: economic democracy and solidarity = generally weakening, although still shared by some pioneersMainstreaming: professionalization, market orientation and accountability = established trends shared by largest FTSEs, supported by networksEntrepreneurship: individual, risk-taking, innovation, professionalism and market orientation = emerging trends | | | |
| **Local normative pressures** | Dominance of values linked to mainstreaming - entrepreneurship Economic democracy and solidarity pursued by few pioneers | Democracy and solidarity applied differently in ADM & Minga Entrepreneurial values strong; politically tinted by Minga | Economic democracy and solidarity much stronger than elsewhere Professionalism but limited market orientation | Dominance of values linked to mainstreaming; accountability stronger than elsewhere; small FT entrepreneurial ventures less developed |
| **Local coercive pressures** | Generally weak Pressure toward specialization in the case of public funding | Generally weak Nonprofit form imposed in the ADM network | Strong; social cooperative or nonprofit form required for Agices members | Very weak |
| **Local mimetic pressures** | Nonprofit form in earlier decades; now rather business forms as a differentiation mechanism | Idem: from nonprofit to business forms Mimetism within networks (ADM, Minga, etc.) | Social cooperative model, with inclusion of volunteers and employees, imitated by newer FTSEs | Some imitation in business forms and participatory governance (producers' ownership) |

Normative pressures also exist at the local level and are especially important since the global trends seem multiple and vague. First, regional differences appeared at the normative level, with, for instance, Italy and the UK differing much in the salience of economic democracy and solidarity in relation to market orientation. The interviews with the Roman FTSEs confirmed Becchetti and Costantino' (2010) observation that Italian FTSEs constitute a relatively homogeneous political movement, which expresses itself through a common organizational model. But local differences could also be explained by diverging coercive and mimetic pressures. Indeed, through legislation and funding, public authorities may induce the adoption of particular organizational forms. The emergence of group structures in Belgium illustrated such an influence. Moreover, networks may play a role in rendering certain forms more easily available for FTSEs, and even in requiring these particular forms, as the Italian case has shown.

Another factor explaining diversity is the absence of a general imitation process, typical in a field in which different institutional logics coexist (Kraatz and Block 2008). While uniformity existed because of imitation in specific networks (for instance, Minga in France), there did not seem to be commonly recognized success stories that could be imitated by all FTSEs. Imitation seemed to occur mainly within similar regions and generations. Nevertheless, generally speaking, new FTSEs seemed more likely to imitate successful business-oriented FTSEs than volunteer-based nonprofit FTSEs. The pioneering examples of business-oriented FTSEs such as Ethiquable in France, Cafédirect in the UK, and Citizen Dream in Belgium, despite their different sizes and economic performances, all demonstrated, to various extents, that market orientation and social mission could be combined, thereby inspiring new generations of FTSEs.

In most cases, global and local pressures acted in the same direction, i.e., toward more business-oriented forms relying increasingly on market resources. For instance, in Belgium, the public requirement of organizational splitting for large nonprofit FTSEs converged with the normative trend toward professionalism: both pressures favored the emergence of cooperatives focused on the economic activity (in the context of group structures). In France, Minga's criticism of voluntary work and nonprofit forms reinforced the global normative trend. Nevertheless, in other cases such as Italy's, the local coercive and mimetic pressures seemed to contradict the global trend. This may obviously lead to tensions. The case of Esprit Equo illustrates how FTSEs may be caught between global trends (in this case, the imitation of business-form FTSEs in other countries) and local trends (making it difficult to implement such a contrasting model).

In brief, the diversity of organizational forms in FT challenges the isomorphic predictions of early sociological neo-institutional theory. Isomorphism is observed only in specific segments of FTSEs, i.e., in a particular region or within a particular generation. Other theoretical approaches are thus needed, particularly to examine the strategic ability of FTSEs to react differently to and influence institutional settings. These approaches draw on the intuitions of DiMaggio (1988) and Scott (1992), examining the two-sided interactions between organizations and their environment. As will be discussed in Chapter 7, the institutional work approach shows that diversity is not only the result of weak and contradictory institutional demands, but also of the ability of the field actors to manage and alter them through different strategies. This is in the line of DiMaggio when he suggests that "multiple, conflicting constraints provide opportunities for various kinds of organizational forms to be established. These cross-cutting institutional pressures provide a space for entrepreneurs to construct an organization out of a diverse set of legitimated practices" (1988, 197). Such view is also embraced by Nicholls and Cho (2006) when they emphasize the disruptive and innovative capacity of social entrepreneurs, enabling them to escape isomorphic pressures.

# 7 Fair Trade Social Enterprises as Institutional Bricolage

This chapter aims to introduce a more strategic component in the institutional analysis. Case studies representing the different organizational models show how these models have been used as strategic tools to influence and shape the FTSEs' institutional environment. They display the role of FTSEs as "institutional entrepreneurs" promoting their own model as a superior avenue for the pursuit of FT. Organizational models are seen as "institutional bricolage" meant to garner legitimacy, and thus resources, from different stakeholders. Access to networks is central in this regard. Diversity is interpreted here as the result of these different strategies adapted to each FTSE's specific environment.

First, the theoretical propositions relating to institutional work and (hybrid) institutional logics are recalled and deepened. Then, the management and diffusion of hybrid models are extensively described in the context of six case studies (one for each model, plus an additional one for the second, entrepreneurial business model). The final section discusses the case study findings and links them to the strategic institutional literature.

## THEORETICAL BACKGROUND

Up to this point, the focus has been laid on the forces that drive FTSEs to adopt diverse organizational models. Yet, both economic and sociological neo-institutional perspectives ignore much of the actors' abilities to shape and give meaning to their organizational model. This chapter aims to address the *strategic role* and the diffusion of organizational models by FTSEs themselves. To this end, the focus is laid on a few case studies that show how FTSEs have been shaped and managed from the perspective of various organizational actors and stakeholders. Using "institutional bricolage," FTSEs are not only able to choose among a range of options, but they can also create or alter these options through influencing their environment in a more favorable way. Such dynamics constitute the focus of the emerging literature on "institutional entrepreneurship" or, more largely, "institutional work," defined as "the purposive action of individuals and organizations aimed at creating, maintaining, and disrupting institutions" (Lawrence and Suddaby 2006, 224). Such work implies "the generation of new organizational models and policies that change the direction and flow of organizational activity" (Hwang and Powell 2005, 180).

In institutional terms, FTSEs are typical examples of hybrid organizations. What we labeled earlier as a "combination of dimensions" can be interpreted, from an agency-based institutional perspective, as a hybridization of institutional logics. Hybridity of logics has been described and explained mostly at the field level, either as a temporary situation ultimately leading to the emergence of one of the logics (Lounsbury, Ventresca, and Hirsch 2003; Lounsbury 2007; den Hond and de Bakker 2007), or as the result of distinct sub-groups each bearing its own logic within a field (Townley 2002; Marquis and Lounsbury 2007; Purdy and Gray 2009). Little research, however, has examined the contribution of hybrid organizations themselves to creating and fostering hybridity of logics at the field level.

The notion of hybrid organization has received a growing attention in the literature, particularly in fields relating to social entrepreneurship dynamics (Billis 2010) such as microfinance (Battilana and Dorado 2010) and integration of low-skilled workers (Pache and Santos 2010). Yet, most of the current work focuses on organizational hybridity only as a consequence of field-level hybridity, in the line of what was examined in Chapter 6. This section aims to reverse the relationship and examine how FTSEs, either individually or in coalition, act as hybrid organizations fostering and maintaining institutional pluralism.

Using cases representing the different organizational models, the remainder of this section examines how the FTSEs have (1) integrated conflicting logics within their organizational model; (2) legitimated their model and sought access to resources; and (3) diffused their hybridized models through individual and collective institutional work. For each FTSE, the construction of the organizational model is analyzed, highlighting the role of "institutional entrepreneur" played by one or several people in the organization and the links to various stakeholders and other social actors. Then, the findings of these case studies are discussed in relation with the theoretical framework.

## CASE STUDIES

### Esprit Equo (Type 1)

#### *Organizational Model and Institutional Setting*

As already explained, the founders of Esprit Equo explicitly chose to focus on the economic and social dimensions, leaving the political activity aside. In their view, their business should be professional and profitable so as to allow them to live from it while having a maximal impact on producers. Esprit Equo's entrepreneurs were not critical about the model of other FTSEs, recognizing that education, regulation and advocacy may be important in the FT movement and require "nonbusiness" forms. What they regretted, however, is the monopolistic vision of the established FTSEs and networks, who consider that FT must necessarily be undertaken through a not-for-profit—nonprofit or cooperative—form.

Esprit Equo's turnover was exclusively composed of sales. The governance and architecture were quite simple, with only the couple of founders/ entrepreneurs. Most of the activities were of a commercial nature: product development together with Comercio Alternativo, building of the supply chain and sales of the products (through wholesale and, to a lesser extent, in their own shop). Producer support was a central dimension, but it was carried out in a quite informal way by the founding couple through regular travels to Morocco.

Within the study, Esprit Equo is probably the most striking example of a "black swan," i.e., an organization that seems unaligned with the general trend. Indeed, in a legal and socio-economic environment that associates FT to social cooperatives, and with a network of FTSEs that restricts its membership to not-for-profit forms, Esprit Equo appears to be an exception. In terms of networking and legitimacy, the business form of Esprit Equo seemed to constitute a handicap in many aspects. First, it was isolated and could not engage in partnerships with most other Italian FTSEs. Since Esprit Equo is absent from the local (RES) and national (Agices) networks, it had no access to common facilities (presence on fairs, advertising, shared logistics, etc.). Second, the entrepreneurial approach to FT has not been well represented in the negotiations for an Italian law on FT. If such a law happened to consider only social cooperatives as FTSEs, this would obviously constitute an obstacle for Esprit Equo. Third, there is the threat of customers used to the worldshop model being suspicious about the ethical nature of Esprit Equo's products. Fourthly, resources such as subsidies and donations were out of reach because of the business form.

Given these obstacles, one may wonder why Esprit Equo did not choose a more legitimate model. From the interviews, it appeared that the unaligned model was also the symbol and the result of a differentiation process through which the founders wished to signal that their way of practicing FT was different than the one shared by most other FTSEs. Moreover, in order to counter or at least alleviate the obstacles inherent in their "nonalignment," the entrepreneurs deployed—consciously or not—a number of legitimating and resource-raising strategies.

First, in terms of collaborations in the Italian FT sector, Esprit Equo established contacts with Transfair Italy, participating in some of their training sessions and national events on FT. Moreover, Esprit Equo engaged in a fruitful partnership with Commercio Alternativo[1]. This importing FTSE from Northern Italy, number two in terms of sales, is characterized by a stronger commercial orientation than the number one, CTM. This translated into tight partnerships with supermarket chains and the acceptance of labeling for all its food products (contrarily to most Italian FTSEs[2]). Commercio Alternativo initially distributed the products of Esprit Equo in its own retail network. This allowed Esprit Equo to increase its turnover, but also to gain legitimacy in the eyes of other FTSEs. Indeed, despite a more commercial orientation, Commercio Alternativo is recognized as a pioneer FTSE in Italy and its products are distributed in most worldshops. Commercio Alternativo is a member of WFTO—which probably offers the strongest possible legitimacy in the eyes of the pioneer FTSEs. In a second step, Esprit Equo and Commercio Alternativo developed a whole range of cosmetics together. This allowed Commercio Alternativo to develop an offer of cosmetics competing to that of CTM, which launched "Natyr" in the early 2000s. For Esprit Equo, being "endorsed" by a WFTO member such as Commercio Alternativo allowed it to be better accepted in the Italian FT sector. The alliance between these two FTSEs is an interesting example of "alternative" to the established Italian FT actors.

In this quest for legitimacy, much relied on the relationship with producers and on the way of communicating about it. Regular contacts and visits were eased as one of the two entrepreneurs has Moroccan origins. Even more, he became a Board member of the Moroccan FT platform[3] and helped Moroccan producers establish contacts with other European FTSEs. In the communication about their cosmetics line, Esprit Equo and Commercio Alternativo particularly insisted on the high ethical standards of the partnerships with the producers' organizations.

Moreover, Esprit Equo compensated for the small number of potential partners in Italy by developing partnerships with FTSEs in France, Belgium and the UK. The international profile of the founders facilitated these partnerships—which contrasted with the more local anchorage of most other Roman FTSEs. The presence of business-form FTSEs in other countries was an opportunity not only to find commercial partners but also to find inspiration about how to run FT under an entrepreneurial model. It is interesting to note that Esprit Equo also developed a fruitful relationship with a very politically involved FTSE, at the opposite extreme of the organizational continuum: Il Fiore. This is an interesting example of collaboration between FTSEs with a totally different profile.

Finally, like many other business-form FTSEs, Esprit Equo compensated for the lack of noncommercial resources (subsidies, donations, volunteer work, etc.) by focusing on sales. The diversification of selling channels—another advantage of the collaboration with Commercio Alternativo—and the ability to receive bank loans thanks to a coherent business plan were part of the solutions implemented by Esprit Equo to secure resources despite their exclusively commercial origin.

## Toward an Institution?

Esprit Equo can be seen as one of the path-breaking business-form FTSEs in Rome and more generally in Italy. Although other FTSEs structured as businesses were rare in Italy, the innovative experience of Esprit Equo could pave the way for similar initiatives by demonstrating how social mission and profitability may be combined efficiently. Despite the adverse environment and suspicion on the part of not-for-profit FTSEs, Esprit Equo managed to grow, thanks to the partnerships it succeeded in establishing, both in Italy and abroad. Thanks to these assets, Esprit Equo was not only able to survive and develop as an FTSE, but also to start influencing the normative environment in a way that would be more favorable to the development of other business-oriented FTSEs.

## Citizen Dream (Type 2)

### Toward a New Organizational Model

At the time of its creation, in 1998, Citizen Dream also clearly looked like a "black swan." Its business legal form, 100% market resources, and its "soft" communication toward customers[4] contrasted sharply with the existing models of FTSEs. Although the business focus was increasing for most Belgian pioneer FTSEs, Citizen Dream was among the first entrepreneurial business-form FTSEs in Belgium.

Similarly to Esprit Equo, the explicit focus of the entrepreneurs on "private good" production and the desire to differentiate their way of viewing and implementing FT from the pioneer, nonprofit FTSEs led to the choice of the business form. The business form also corresponded to the preferences of the entrepreneurs, reluctant toward the volunteer-based nonprofit form. The adoption of a business form was thus a clear strategic choice of the entrepreneurs, with the support of the founding shareholders. Much like Esprit Equo in Italy, Citizen Dream operated strategically to be accepted in the FT sector despite its unusual form. First and most strikingly, it asked and obtained WFTO membership, which appeared as a powerful signal of trustworthiness and legitimacy concerning its FT activity. Such a signal was useful in the organization's relations with the established pioneer FTSEs, especially Oxfam-MDM, who was initially suspicious.[5] Not only were the producer partners of Citizen Dream—themselves WFTO members—recognized, but the structure of Citizen Dream itself was considered to be compatible with FT standards. This required, nevertheless, a commitment of Citizen Dream to FT as its central activity[6] and to employees' participation in governance.

Second, as the interviews with each of the two entrepreneurs revealed, Citizen Dream consciously shaped its shareholders' structure and thus its governance so as to include stakeholders that were perceived as legitimate in the FT movement. The involvement of development NGOs, recognized individuals[7] and other FTSEs[8] in the GA and on the Board probably facilitated the legitimization of Citizen Dream's organizational model. These stakeholders embodied the combination of an ambitious economic project with a strong social mission. There was, however, no claimed political message. Franchisee shops also had a clear interest in the economic health of the FTSE. Concerning producer support, besides the presence of development NGOs in the governance structures and the legitimating role of WFTO, another asset was the entrepreneurs' personal contacts with the producers in India. In conclusion, Citizen Dream was an example of a business-oriented, sales-financed FTSE, with very little political involvement, and with a social mission endorsed by an international FT network and secured by an advanced multi-stakeholder governance structure.

### Toward an Institution?

Despite its collapse in 2008, Citizen Dream had an influence on the Belgian FT landscape. Unlike Esprit Equo, Citizen Dream did not remain an exception for long, as several other business-form FTSEs emerged after 2000.[9] As previously mentioned, other factors explained this emergence, such as the proactive role of support structures and networks (mainly the TDC and the BFTF) in promoting new entrepreneurial FTSEs. But the example of Citizen Dream showed potential entrepreneurs that the road was open for entrepreneurial models—albeit paved with obstacles, as its own collapse showed. Several entrepreneurs engaged in FT took this experience both as a warning about the importance of avoiding a certain number of mistakes[10] and as a challenge to succeed where Citizen Dream had failed.[11]

The development of the "Belgian Fair Trade Federation" and its crucial role in recognizing and federating small FTSEs—beside the pioneers— further contributed to promote other models for practicing FT, thereby fostering organizational diversity in the sector. It is no coincidence that the report on FT handicraft, which recommended the creation of a FT federation and asked public support for the FT economic model, was written by Citizen Dream's founder. The federation was thus created with the goal of supporting FTSEs in their economic development[12] and the people in charge of it have been enthusiastic regarding the emergence of business-oriented organizational models.[13] In conclusion, in a few years, the institutional context of FT in Belgium has evolved very much toward a legitimization of business forms.

The following figure illustrates the extension, or rather the transformation, of Citizen Dream's organizational model into an institution in itself (Kraatz and Block 2008). Although other "institutional entrepreneurs" intervene (particularly the TDC and SAW-B), it appears that Citizen Dream's founders, through their innovative organizational model, their involvement in the study on FT handicraft, and their relationships with

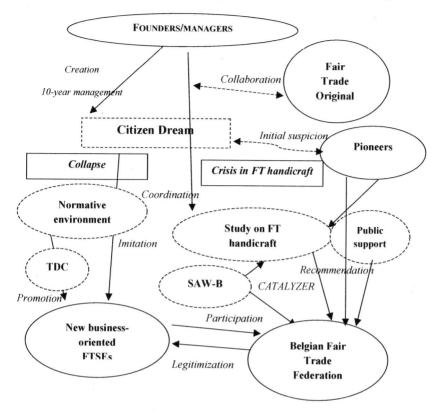

*Figure 7.1*   Institutional legitimization of business-form FTSEs in Belgium.

other FTSEs and networks (e.g., SAW-B), have played an important role in the evolution of the FT institutional environment in Belgium, with a recognition of newcomer business-form FTSEs and an increasing networking of the diverse types of FTSEs.

## Saldac (Type 2)

### *Origins of the Organizational Model*

As already mentioned, the FT cooperative "Andines," in the Ile-de-France region, developed a model that fitted neither the ADM model of nonprofit, volunteer-based FTSEs, nor the "Alter Eco" model of business-form FTSEs addressing the mainstream. The criticism of Andines toward these two models led to serious disputes. Andines participated in the PFCE platform but remained critical toward both collaboration with supermarket chains and the use of voluntary work and subsidies. As previously mentioned, in

2002, during the discussions that subsequently led to a French law on FT, the tensions were too high and Andines exited the PFCE, creating its own network, called Minga.

Through Minga, Andines institutionalized its model for practicing FT and promoted its replication by other FTSEs. The main idea of this model is that of combining a central economic activity with a radical political message, through the development of an alternative to the capitalist, market-oriented system that both FTSEs collaborating with supermarkets and volunteer-based FTSEs are accused of favoring and strengthening. The Minga model rapidly developed and influenced the whole French FT sector. Existing FTSEs joined the network and new FTSEs were conceived on the same model. In this respect, the development of a professional training scheme was a crucial step. In Chapter 6, Minga was presented as a strong source of normative isomorphism that pushed FTSEs to adopt similar organizational models. But we should not forget that Minga is a network created and managed by FTSEs themselves, many of which are not just passively influenced but also act as influencers.

Saldac was gradually influenced by the Minga model. Initially, Saldac was created as a nonprofit FTSE but refused to follow the path of ADM. Besides the entrepreneur, who had personal contacts with several producer groups in Latin America, two persons, who were previously active in ADM, joined the project with the willingness to create an alternative to ADM. The FTSE remained, however, small and confidential until the early 2000s. The creation of Minga was taken as an opportunity by Saldac to legitimize its model and find commercial and political partners. Saldac evolved into a business legal form for reasons that were not just symbolic. Indeed, the intent was to send a signal to the different stakeholders that the FTSE was not a charitable project but rather a trustworthy commercial partner, albeit with an alternative vision of business. Becoming one of the standard-bearers of Minga in its region, Saldac developed partnerships with other FTSEs at the local level. This confirms that relationships between the different strands are easier at the local than at the national level. Several—not all—ADM shops in the region offered Saldac products. Other local FTSEs willing to combine a business orientation and a desire for political involvement were influenced by Saldac.

The organizational model of Saldac differs from that of most business-form FTSEs (such as Citizen Dream) in that the political project is much more central and "radical." Such a project is explicitly "anti-mainstream" and sees the economic activity as a political symbol in itself rather than only as a mean to support a social mission. At the organizational level, this translated into the stronger polyvalence of the staff compared with other business-form FTSEs. In Saldac, as in other "political businesses" (e.g., One Village in the UK), all the employees were encouraged to participate in the broader political movement. "Coherence" was a guiding principle, with more attention, at all the levels of the supply chain, to economic democracy, to small-scale work, and to a "fair price" for all the suppliers and the employees. This led to rejecting voluntary work, following the argument that any work deserves a fair wage. The expertise of small-scale producers and intermediaries was favored both in the South and in the North (transport, transformation, etc.), and all the employees were invited to participate in the exchanges. Selling channels were local and personalized, aiming to build a dialogue with customers as active citizens. Fostering integration led the functions to be less specialized than in the previous model of business-form FTSEs: there is no clear-cut division between, for instance, advocacy and sales.

## Oxfam- Magasins du Monde (Type 3)

The threefold structure of Oxfam-MDM echoes its three missions— namely being a citizen movement; advocating for FT; and commercializing FT products based on solid partnerships with producer groups. It is striking that neither the structure nor the legal form or the governance model have changed over the last decades. This could convey an image of a passive organization, with limited influence on its environment. The reality is, instead, that of a permanent struggle aiming to protect the specific features of the organization from the shifts in the environment.

Until the late 1990s, Oxfam-MDM shared the FT sector with its sister organization Oxfam-WW and a number of other pioneer FTSEs (such as MMH, Weltladen and Fair Trade Original). These FTSEs had a nonprofit, volunteer-based form and shared the same vision of FT as an alternative to the capitalist model. However, while other FTSEs dealt mainly with food products and had to adapt their structure to both compete and collaborate with mainstream businesses, Oxfam-MDM's focus on handicraft shielded it from such a structural adaptation. Unlike other pioneers that became more market-oriented and often evolved into group structures, Oxfam-MDM, with its volunteer-based and "integrated" structure, remained in a position where it could embed its trading activity in its socio-political project and remain critical toward supermarkets and corporations in general. Moreover, through a certain lobbying, Oxfam resisted the pressure from the DGD to isolate the education and producer support activities in a separate, noncommercial organization. A splitting project was nevertheless conceived, but never implemented.[14] The only concrete impact was that Oxfam's accounting was split into two distinct parts.

The reluctance of Oxfam-MDM to formally separate the economic and socio-political activities is more emblematic than it may seem. As in the previous model of political businesses, it reveals their conception of FT as an integrated activity, where worldshops are both sales outlets and vectors of political activity, and where relationships with producers entail both a socio-economic and a political dimension[15]. But, unlike these businesses, Oxfam uses subsidies and voluntary work to achieve its goal. Moreover, because of its larger size and recognition, it is also more exposed to institutional pressures. This probably makes the tensions more explicit than in smaller structures. These tensions may be dealt with in the day-to-day practice through dialogue between the employees of the different units, who work in the same building and know each other well. The tensions and the need for a permanent equilibrium between the different dimensions of FT, between the business and the movement, explain the challenge of finding a leader capable of simultaneously running the ambitious political project and supporting the economic development, feeling at ease with both campaigners and salespeople.

As an institution in itself, Oxfam-MDM initially tried to slow down the emergence and the development of business-form FTSEs in Belgium. Many leaders of newcomer FTSEs reported that, when making contact with Oxfam-MDM to ask for advice before launching their project, they were discouraged to do so. The staff changes and the participation in networking, however, brought an important change in this perception.

The history of Oxfam-MDM shows how this organization has tried not only to resist external pressures considered as hostile, but also to influence the environment and to reduce the threats and competition from other FTSEs. The organizational model of Oxfam-MDM can in fact be seen as an inheritance of the early period of FT. The results of Oxfam-MDM's strategy are mixed. One one hand, it remains a tone-setting FTSE with much expertise in producer support and education, regulation, and advocacy. The involvement of thousands of volunteers, the high recognition in the public opinion, the many linkages within civil society and the international connections within the FT movement (mainly through WFTO and EFTA) have certainly helped it to maintain its institutional power. On the other hand, the FTSE's ambition to reinforce its economic dimension is difficult to implement and is slowed down by certain resistances from volunteers. While the past records of Oxfam-MDM are impressive, the ambiguity of its strategy and the risks related to its future directions lead to certain preference for the *status quo*.

## Pangea-Niente Troppo (Type 4)

### *Toward an Organizational Model*

As previously mentioned, Pangea started its activity in 1991, only three years after the emergence of CTM. Created as a nonprofit ("associazione"), it evolved to the social cooperative form in 1993, soon after the latter was instituted and implemented in Italy. Pangea quickly became the main Roman worldshop in the CTM network, at the expense of ComES, the other Roman pioneer CTM worldshop.[16]

Pangea's organizational model is characterized, first, by the social cooperative form. As previously mentioned, much work had to be done by

Agices—including Pangea's staff—to convince public authorities that FT constituted a coherent field of activity for social cooperatives, on the one hand, and to help FTSEs fill their annual social report so as to fit the legal requirements, on the other hand. The successful adoption of a legal form that was initially not intended for FTSEs was the result of intense lobbying, which constitutes a striking example of how leading FTSEs can influence the legislative context in their favor.

A second characteristic of Pangea's model is linked to its high level of political involvement. This translates, in Pangea but also in other multi-stakeholder cooperatives, into units specifically devoted to education, regulation and advocacy. In Pangea, the "Info-Cultura" unit is composed of three full-time equivalents (out of a total of nine). Even in the "commercial" unit, people—for instance, those working in the worldshops—are involved to a certain extent in education campaigns. Pangea's managers insisted on the need to professionalize not only the commercial activity but also the political involvement of employees and volunteers. The strong focus on economic democracy and participation in decision-making is a third feature of this type of organizational model. Governance structures, including employees, volunteers, customers, and other supporters, are shaped in a sense that encourages democracy and participation.

### Toward an Institution?

As one of the pioneer Roman worldshops and a central CTM member, Pangea's role and influence in the Roman region have been strong. The founding role of Pangea in the Agices network, concretized by one of Pangea's managers occupying the presidency of the network, reinforced its tone-setting role. Of course, it would be exaggerated to suggest that all Roman worldshops were inspired by Pangea's organizational model. But Pangea was one of the actors that helped to create the institutional environment legitimizing the social cooperative, volunteer-based, and politically oriented way of practicing FT.

Pangea's organizational model spread to other Roman worldshops, partly through the legitimization of this model in Italian FT networks (including the RES network), but also partly through direct imitation. Such imitation occurred, for instance, in the case of two FTSEs that were founded by former Pangea employees (Equociquà and Niente-Troppo). In conclusion, we may say that Pangea played a crucial role in the Roman area. Through its own experience and through its active contribution to networking, Pangea fostered and translated at the local level the socio-political avenue to FT as promoted at the national level.

In the case of Pangea, as with many other cooperative and nonprofit FTSEs, the "institutional work" was rather collective—despite the role of individuals in leading these organizations. Such work was mostly undertaken by a generation of employees different from the founders, who previously worked as volunteers. These "managing employees" seemed to combine a high level of political involvement with a certain pragmatism, which appeared useful to deal with the Roman supermarkets selling CTM products.

## MMH-MFT (Type 5)

### From Institutional Pressure to Organizational Model

FTSEs impacted by their environment are not necessarily passively influenced by it. Indeed, organizations adapting their structure to institutional pressures may use that change as an opportunity to re-think their activity and find a new balance between structure, strategy, and environment. The case of MMH-MFT is a nice example of such an appropriation of an exogenous pressure for change. In the late 1990s, before it evolved into a group structure, MMH was doing well: both the sales of honey and related products and the development and education projects were successful. When the FTSE split into two legally distinct entities[17], it was rather by obligation than by choice. Nevertheless, MMH decided to split its activities not only on paper but also in practice. This did not mean that the two structures would go their separate ways. But, rather, it was decided to take this organizational evolution as an opportunity for each structure to specialize and develop its own strategy.

MFT, the cooperative entity, was given complete operational autonomy, with a specific manager and a small staff with business skills and experience. The warehouse and the offices were moved to another location. While governance was exerted by volunteers in the early years of the splitting, people with business expertise progressively joined the Board to make it more efficient in business-related decision-making—an evolution toward the stewardship model, as described in Chapter 3.

As for the nonprofit part, it specialized in extra-economic producer support and education. Regarding the first point, it is interesting to observe that, from 2003, MMH developed producer support projects with groups that are not necessarily furnishing honey to MFT. MMH rather aims those organizations that are the most in need of support—some of which are partners of MFT, but others not. This is quite exceptional in the FT sector: generally, only partner producer organizations receive social support and training, beside the commercial partnership. The rationale here is that the training and support capacities of FTSEs are best used for small producer groups in a fragile situation than for more developed groups that have already received such support and do not "need" it anymore.

Regarding the other points—education and regulation—MMH acquired much expertise in presentations for schools, with three specific employees. One of the education programs, called "Fair Kids," was developed with the DGD—precisely the funding agency that pushed for a splitting of the activities. Consisting of small movies made by children all over the world and aiming to increase awareness among children living in the North about the economic and social gaps between North and South, "Fair Kids" received the "Innovation Trophy" at the first European FT Fair in Lyon (2008). The development of an advanced and independent program of producer support, as well as the recognized expertise in education, can be seen as two signs of professionalization of the social and political dimensions.

Of course, one could argue that professionalization in the different dimensions of FT could have occurred even without an organizational splitting. The interviews, however, suggested that the organizational splitting brought a strategic rethinking of each activity, to devote the most suited financial and social resources to each of them, and to associate the most adequate people in the governance structures. Parallel to the specialization through organizational splitting, specific coordination mechanisms were established. Although the respective managers and staff of the two entities are organizationally and geographically separate, there was coordination at both the governance and the operational level. In the governance structures, although the cooperative's capital was opened to diverse stakeholders (partners, supporters, customers, etc.) a core group of volunteers still contributed to decision-making in both entities. Moreover, at the operational level, clear formal rules of collaboration were established. For instance, part of MFT's profits was transferred to MMH. Conversely, MFT committed itself to promoting FT in the context of its commercial activities. Finally, the two directors had regular exchanges and contribute to insufflating a common vision to this dual organizational structure in which an NGO and a business collaborate to better achieve the hybrid goals of FT.

## DISCUSSION

All these cases show, in one or another way, that organizational actors within FTSEs were not only able to choose among a range of options. Indeed, they could also influence their environment and other FTSEs in order to shape these options in a way that suits them. The discussion is structured in three interrelated sections: (1) the introduction and management of hybridity; (2) the legitimization of hybrid models and the access to resources; and (3) the diffusion of hybrid models.

### Introducing and Managing Hybridity

Of course, the experimentation and management of hybrid logics differed substantially with the organizational model. In the individual and manager-owned models, hybridity was introduced by the entrepreneurs themselves. Their commitment to the social mission combined with their pursuit of economic efficiency naturally favored hybridity. This is the most flexible but also the most fragile avenue to hybridity. Indeed, very little safeguard exists against a reorientation toward a purely profit-making logic: without any compulsory legal or organizational safeguard, hybridity depended very much on the entrepreneurs' willingness. It is worth noting that several entrepreneurs secured their commitment to the social mission. For instance, Citizen Dream integrated people with a more specific attention to the mission on their board. Other FTSEs (e.g., Saldac) asked for peer control within a network. Networks were also a way for isolated entrepreneurs to participate, even modestly, in the political project of the movement.

Volunteer-based FTSEs could be characterized in the opposite way, with socio-political logics taking the precedence over the market logic, even if the latter took an increasing importance. Oxfam-MDM offered an interesting example of an attempt to shift the balance toward a stronger business orientation. This was not easy in an organizational model conceived to devote a large place to the social and political missions: "pure" nonprofit form, board composed almost exclusively of worldshop volunteers, accountability to civil society through the diverse networks in which it is involved, etc. Reluctant to formalize a stronger business orientation, Oxfam-MDM seemed to use more informal mechanisms to introduce a minimum dosis of market logic, including advisory business experts, slight changes in hiring practices, introduction of performance assessment for worldshops, etc. Discursive action was key in the sense that board members and managers in search of a reinforcement of the business logic constantly needed to show how the changes they introduced contributed to the socio-political project and give guarantees about the limited scope of these changes. This case showed hybridity as sustained through the permanent search of compromises between organizational members each carrying different logics, especially at the board level and among employees from different units.

The emergence of group structures consisting of both a nonprofit and a business entity and involving multiple stakeholders in their governance corresponded to the most formal avenue to hybridity. In Chapter 6, the influence of external factors was highlighted to explain this evolution, particularly the role of the Belgian subsidizing authority. The case of Miel Maya, however, showed how internal factors also played a major role. The external demand for a dualization of the organizational structure was seized by the FTSE as an opportunity to formalize its hybrid nature. This evolution meant to enable integration in mainstream markets and partnerships with corporations while conserving a formal link with civil society stakeholders can be seen as an advanced example of what Kraatz and Block (2008) call a "compartmentalization" strategy. According to the interviews in Miel Maya, this was not a strategy of "decoupling" aiming to respectively satisfy social/civic and market-oriented institutional demands without actually changing the practices. It rather led to a model in which hybridity was clarified and signaled in the context of a group composed of distinct yet interrelated entities.

## Legitimating Hybrid Models and Accessing Resources

The different cases showed how legitimacy is crucial in accessing resources. As noted by Lawrence and Suddaby (2006, 292), "all of the practices [of] institutional work require resources, which are available to some actors and not others. A critical view of institutional work could begin to examine how those resources are distributed and controlled, and by whom." This seems in line with many arguments of "resource dependence theory" (Pfeffer and Salancik 1978), with which institutional theory has been hybridized (Tolbert and Zucker 1996). Legitimacy contributes to survival "because audiences are most likely to supply resources to organizations that appear desirable, proper, or appropriate" (Suchman 1995, 574). The focus on the organizational model also leads to considering primarily *structural* legitimacy: "audiences see the organization as valuable and worthy of support because its structural characteristics locate it within a morally favored taxonomic category" (Suchman 1995, 581). In other words, "[t]he structurally legitimate organization becomes a repository of public confidence because it is 'the right organization for the job'" (581).

The role of networks in securing structural legitimacy was key for the legitimization of new models. Saldac and Pangea took an active participation respectively in Minga and in Agices to legitimate their own organizational model. Such a participation in the decision-making at the network level allowed these FTSEs to reduce their dependence on the environment by precisely trying to control part of this environment (what Pfeffer and Salancik describe as "enacting" the environment). Indeed, these FTSEs are in a good position to ensure that the network remains aligned on their interests. In other words, Saldac and Pangea are able to shape—at least partly—the network in a way that secures their organizational model, thereby reducing uncertainty.

Moreover, the relative control of the network also allows the FTSEs to better control their interaction with the stakeholders from the broader environment. For instance, it is through its role in the Agices network that Pangea was involved in discussing with public authorities about the adequacy of FT as specific field for social cooperatives and the promotion of FTSEs under a not-for-profit form. In the same sense, Citizen Dream, through piloting the study on FT handicraft, promoted the support from public authorities that would not take the form of subsidies but rather of entrepreneurial stimulation. Even if Citizen Dream eventually collapsed, its involvement in the research of a viable economic model for business-form FTSEs aimed to protect and improve its own way of practicing FT.

The case of Oxfam-MDM also illustrated the strategic reaction of an FTSE to a shift in the environment. Oxfam-MDM traditionally enjoyed a very good reputation and certain legitimacy as "the" reference FTSE (at least in French-speaking Belgium). The relationships within civil society and the political world allowed Oxfam-MDM to escape the coercive pressure toward organizational splitting from the DGD. This alone illustrates the relative independence of Oxfam-MDM regarding the regulatory environment. Moreover, the structural legitimacy of Oxfam-MDM guaranteed a continuous resource flow consisting of subsidies, regular buying by sympathetic customers, and large provision of voluntary work. The latter was particularly secured through the systematic representation of volunteers from different regions in the governance structures. However, the normative shift toward market orientation and entrepreneurial approaches to FT, translated into changes in other FTSEs' organizational models, endangered Oxfam's legitimacy and brought uncertainty concerning a number of resources (through criticism about voluntary work, subsidies, political action, etc.). The gradual awareness about this shifting environment partly pushed Oxfam-MDM to adapt its management and to participate to the creation of the BFTF. Indeed, through resuming collaboration with other FTSEs and hiring a manager with a stronger business profile—enjoying a higher legitimacy in the eyes of business-form FTSEs—Oxfam-MDM tried to regain partial control over its environment. This echoes Pfeffer and Salancik's observation (1978, 2):

> *Problems arise not merely because organizations are dependent on their environment, but because this environment is not dependable. Environments can change, new organizations enter and exit, and the supply of resources becomes more or less scarce. When environments change, organizations face the prospect either of not surviving or of changing their activities in response to these environmental factors.*

Cooptation of stakeholders is a second tool for legitimating specific models by gaining support from various "institutional demanders." In the study, this was the strategy developed, for instance, by Citizen Dream or Max Havelaar Belgium. The advantages are clear: "when an organization appoints an individual to a board, it expects the individual will come to support the organization, will concern himself with its problems, will favorably present it to others, and will try to aid it" (Pfeffer and Salancik 1978, 163). Throughout the case studies, we saw how cooptation allowed FTSEs to gain expertise and resources in a much more regular and secured way than if the stakeholders were not involved.

The securement of resources via the governance structures seemed to vary with the types of organizational models. In individual and business-form FTSEs, as well as in the business parts of group structures, the high need for financial resources led to a much stronger presence of individual and institutional investors. In group structures such as Miel Maya or OWW-OFT, it is interesting to note that such need for financial resources, before leading to involve new stakeholders, led to reconsidering the relationship with existing ones. Volunteers, customers, supporters and employees were invited to evolve from being "members" to being "shareholders," implying at least a small financial investment in the FTSE. Other stakeholders were involved specifically to gain access to financial resources. This was particularly striking in Cafédirect, which issued for £5 million new shares in 2004, thereby improving its financial breathing space and involving a broader range of individuals and institutions in its governance.

At a smaller scale, Citizen Dream obtained access to long-term credit at a regional public investment agency in exchange for a representation of the latter on its Board. Another member of Citizen Dream's Board was Fair Trade Original, which had a commercial relationship with the former. The mutual participation in governance allowed more systematic exchange of knowledge and skills, thereby leading to a stronger "mutual dependence" (Pfeffer and Salancik 1978). More particularly, Citizen Dream secured its access to certain categories of handicraft products and Fair Trade Original secured their retailing in a dozen of shops.

The interviews in volunteer-based FTSEs and the nonprofit parts of group structures indicated that the involvement of volunteers in governance was crucial to stimulate their participation and their loyalty. Indeed, for these FTSEs, volunteer's loyalty was one the most crucial resources. For large FTSEs such as Oxfam-MDM and OWW-OFT, participation of local volunteers to the Board was also a manner to communicate concerns of local worldshops to the central organization. One leader suggested that, without a representation in the governance bodies, volunteers would probably feel less concerned by the evolution of the organization and thus be less motivated in their work. Through a presence on the Board, volunteers' representatives can ensure that the organization's projects and functioning are worth the time they give (typically in the worldshops). They are thus able to confirm the trustworthiness of the organization toward the broader community of volunteers (Harrow and Palmer 2003).

The cooptation of NGOs, for instance in Citizen Dream, Oxfam, Max Havelaar, or Traidcraft, entailed various advantages in terms of resource dependences. In both OWW-OFT and Oxfam-MDM, the role of NGOs in the identification, the selection and the evaluation of the producer groups, not only formally through the "partner committee" but also informally, appeared clearly. Since the access to information in the South is particularly difficult, the help of these NGOs through their cooptation on the Board allowed the FTSEs to reduce the uncertainty and thus improve their support to the producers. Finally, it is worth noting that the cooptation of certain stakeholder groups such as NGOs and volunteers facilitated (or even conditioned) the provision of these resources by increasing the legitimacy of the FTSEs. The presence of these "trustworthy" stakeholders visibly functioned as a positive signal toward stakeholders willing to provide financial resources, primarily donors and public institutions.

## Diffusing Hybrid Models

Most of the FTSEs described earlier were involved in institutionalizing their practice of hybridity partly through the promotion of their own organizational model. This appeared particularly strikingly when these FTSEs contributed to networks in which their form and practice is somehow "celebrated" (Meyer and Rowan 1991), as is the case of Pangea-NT with Agices and of Saldac with Minga. These cases illustrate the different steps toward institutional creation such as advocacy, normative networking, and theorizing of the new model (Maguire, Hardy, and Lawrence 2004; Lawrence and Suddaby 2006). It is worth noting that the actors creating institutions do not necessarily need to be in a powerful position to do so. The case of the members of Minga provides a good illustration of the "potential for institutional entrepreneurship on the part of relatively small, peripheral or isolated actors" (Lawrence and Suddaby 2006, 249). The promotion of what is increasingly referred to as the "Minga model," together with the regular publication of reports, books, and press releases, is an example of theorizing, defined as the "naming of new concepts and practices so that they might become a part of the cognitive map of the field" (Lawrence and Suddaby 2006, 249).

Certain actors attempt to create institutions parallel to previous arrangements, suggesting new avenues without undermining those followed by extant actors. The action of Citizen Dream and Esprit Equo did not intend to undermine the forms and practices of pioneer FTSEs. Rather, particularly with Esprit Equo, the pioneers' role in developing and advocating for FT was acknowledged. Moreover, in both cases, there was an expressed concern for highlighting the conformity of their model with the missions of FT (through WFTO membership in the case of Citizen Dream and through a partnership with a recognized FTSE in the case of Esprit Equo). This can be related to the "juxtaposition of old and new templates" in order to "simultaneously make the new structure understandable and accessible, while pointing to potential problems or shortcomings of past practices" (Lawrence and Suddaby 2006, 242).

In other cases, however, institutional entrepreneurship includes disrupting pre-existing arrangements, i.e., "attacking or undermining the mechanisms that lead members to comply with institutions" (Lawrence and Suddaby 2006, 262). This is particularly strong in the case of Minga members, who seek to undermine not only the already less legitimated practices of the "first wave" of FT (embodied by ADM), but also the much more institutionalized ones from the "second wave." Most striking in this respect is Minga's criticism of the use of the term "label" by Max Havelaar France and, more broadly, by FLO. Depicting Max Havelaar as a private brand that monopolizes the FT field and integrates it into the capitalist model (Minga 2005) is an example of definitional work, i.e., "defining and redefining sets of concepts in ways that reconstitute actors and reconfigure relationships between actors" (Lawrence and Suddaby 2006, 264).

Facing real or perceived threats of disruption, older FTSEs such as Oxfam-MDM, MMH-MFT or Pangea-NT seemed rather active in *maintaining* the institutions linked to their respective forms and practices. The active role of

Oxfam-MDM in protecting itself from the shifts in its normative environment confirms Lawrence and Suddaby's (2006) suggestion that "the maintaining of institutions must be distinguished from simple stability or the absence of change: rather, institutional work that maintains institutions involves considerable effort" (261). The action of Pangea-NT and other FTSEs in Agices to reserve membership—and thus legitimacy—to the sole nonprofit and social cooperative FTSEs is also illustrative of a defensive strategy.

The high degree of institutional work in an emerging field such as FT confirms that institutional entrepreneurship is favored by "the presence of multiple institutional orders or alternatives" (Leca, Battilana, and Boxenbaum 2008, 7), as underlined in Chapter 6. The importance of discourse and normative competition in FT gives actors with few resources the opportunity to engage in institutional work. Disruption, particularly, does not require "a powerful or culturally sophisticated actor, but one capable of working in highly original and potentially counter-cultural ways" (Lawrence and Suddaby 2006, 270). The action of Minga members, located at the periphery of the dominant FT structures and networks, is an example of a "counter-cultural" actor that is little influenced by the dominant institutional discourses—typically those linked to mainstreaming. As a consequence, its attempts of disrupting these dominant institutions are more powerful because they are less subject to the paradox of embedded agency (e.g., Leca, Battilana, and Boxenbaum 2008; Battilana and D'Aunno 2009).

Finally, it is worth noting that the cases featured different types of institutional entrepreneurs, which can be linked to those highlighted by Dorado (1999). Newcomer FTSEs often played the role of "institutional innovators," as illustrated with Esprit Equo, Citizen Dream and Saldac. These FTSEs introduced and started to institutionalize new approaches to FT. Although pioneers also played such an innovating role, for instance when creating new arrangements such as group structures, they rather intervened as "institutional engineers," i.e., "powerful gatekeepers who affect the flow of resources in a field" (Hinings et al. 2004, 309). Third, "institutional catalysts" are often external actors who intervene to concretize the institutional evolution (Hinings et al. 2004; Dorado 1999). Several illustrations were given through support structures and networks.

## CONCLUSION

In the emergent literature on FT, other authors already examined the institutionalization of the FT movement by major networks (Diaz Pedregal 2007; Raynolds and Long 2007), or the role of FT as a whole as an "institutional entrepreneur" toward the global market (Nicholls 2010). The contribution here has been to highlight the role of FTSEs themselves as entrepreneurs using their organizational model—and thereby their way of practicing FT—as a driver of institutional change.

This chapter aimed to use the framework of institutional work to analyze FTSE's organizational models not just as reflections of their environment, but as genuine strategic tools able to influence their environment. The case studies featured different strategies through which FTSEs both experienced and diffused their organizational models as superior avenues to managing the hybrid goals of FT. First, the structuration of organizational models appeared as "institutional bricolage" through displaying combinations of different legitimating and resource-raising mechanisms (particular legal forms, governance models such as the multi-stakeholder configuration, etc.). Second, the promotion and the diffusion of the hybrid models, particularly through networks, seemed to explain much of the configuration of the organizational landscape in the four countries. Different types of institutional entrepreneurs were highlighted to help understanding how FTSEs are both influenced by their environment (typically by the choices made by pioneers or other stakeholders) and capable of creating or altering the path for newcomer FTSEs.

# Part III
# Managing Hybridity in Fair Trade

# 8   Managing Hybrid Organizational Models

Based on the different theoretical interpretations, we now better understand the roles and dynamics of the different types of social enterprises in the FT field. This last chapter aims to deepen the strategic perspective of Chapter 7, through examining how each organizational model offers particular opportunities and threats (in the form of tensions) for FT entrepreneurs. The contribution of each model to the practice of FT in its different dimensions is reviewed based on both the sample and case study findings. Recommendations are made to the (current or potential) FT entrepreneurs regarding how to seize the opportunities, overcome the dilemmas and manage their relationships with the other FTSEs and stakeholders. The chapter ends by revisiting the organizational trajectories (evolution from one model to another) from a strategic standpoint.

## OPPORTUNITIES AND TENSIONS IN EACH MODEL

### Individual Ventures (Type 1)

As, in this case, the governance structure and the architecture are reduced to one or two individuals, the main difficulty is that all the expertise must come from the entrepreneurs themselves. Such an expertise may be limited to the development and the commercialization of high-quality products, i.e., on the economic dimension of FT. Indeed, seizing a valuable market opportunity (new product, new distribution channel, etc.) is even more crucial than in other types of FTSEs, simply because entrepreneurs are totally dependent on the venture in terms of revenues: most of them have invested their own money in it. This is why certain entrepreneurs seek additional expertise in economic matters, for instance, through an advisory board. Several tools have also been developed by FT networks (e.g., in France and in Belgium) to advice the entrepreneurs at the different steps of the entrepreneurial process. But even with much advice, the risks remain entirely beared by the entrepreneur.

The social dimension may be handled either directly, through the personal involvement of the entrepreneur, or through partners (NGOs, other

FTSEs, etc.). In the retail FTSEs, producer support is dependent on the importing FTSEs. In both cases, the entrepreneurs should give the priority to small producer groups with whom they can establish personal contacts (even for entrepreneurs active only at the retail level). While practices were diverse, the entrepreneurs had in common the absence of organizational governance, leading to a very low control of producer support. This is why several of the entrepreneurs put a high value in participating in a network, thereby benefitting to a certain extent of an extra-organizational governance mechanism able to monitor the pursuit of their social mission. Regarding the political involvement, this depended much on the entrepreneur's profile. But, generally speaking, it is the dimension that was least present in the day-to-day activities. Even the individual entrepreneurs members of Minga, for instance, considered that it was their way of practicing FT in an alternative way that constituted a political symbol, as they did not have the time for concrete activities relating to education and advocacy. FT entrepreneurs should thus not be too ambitious regarding their own political involvement; they may participate in the FT project merely through bringing their own example; they may also build partnerships with other actors. To summarize, the individual FTSE is a vector that may be used very differently according to the entrepreneur's visions (Spence and Rutherfoord 2001).

The tensions between the different dimensions are obviously less visible because they are embodied by the entrepreneurs themselves. But this does not mean that the tensions are absent. The dependence of the entrepreneurs on the economic performance of their venture might suggest that this dimension will necessarily have the primacy over the others in the case of a conflict. But this did not seem confirmed in the study. Indeed, the focus on producer support seemed central, and certain entrepreneurs were particularly involved in education and advocacy activities which had little link with their economic project. In certain cases, confirmed not only through the interviews but also by other stakeholders, it appeared that entrepreneurs sacrificed a significant part of their potential revenue to maintain high prices for the producers.

The study showed that certain entrepreneurs fought to maintain the 100% FT origin of their products, which probably did not constitute the choice maximizing the economic performance. In this case, the tensions between the economic and the social goals were handled in the benefit of the latter. At the opposite, other entrepreneurs decreased the proportion of FT products for economic reasons. This evacuated part of the tensions and boosted the economic performance, but it also faded the FT characteristic of their ventures. Finally, tensions were also observed between the economic and the political dimensions. For reasons linked to his political vision of FT, certain entrepreneurs decided to suppress FT labeled products from their shops and to favor products responding to perceived higher ethical standards offered by smaller and more alternative FTSEs such as members of Minga. This was clearly inefficient in economic terms: the quality of the products was generally lower, their price equal or higher, and they required much more efforts in terms of supply management and communication about their FT nature.

The main challenge of individual FTSEs is the lack of expertise and governance mechanisms that make the simultaneous management of hybrid dimensions difficult. While certain individual entrepreneurs explicitly favored their economic development, others were more focused on personalized producer support or participation in a political project. Therefore, individual entrepreneurs should exploit the opportunities of broadening the scope of their ventures, particularly through linkages with other FTSEs (bilateral contacts or networks) and FT supporters. While this may appear as a recommendation for all FTSEs, it is particularly the case for individual FTSEs that would otherwise remain both isolated and confined to their particular conception of FT. As they cannot create complex governance structures, individual entrepreneurs should explore other ways of broadening their governance, through a network as "guardian" of their social mission, and/or through advisory groups aiming to capture lacking expertise. Finally, although the fear of several entrepreneurs to lose the control of their venture may be understood, organizational growth should lead them to consider evolving to the next category after some time.

## Entrepreneurial Businesses (Type 2)

Common with the previous category is the high importance of the economic dimension. But, again, there may be much diversity on the other features. As already commented, there is a strong difference between, on the one hand, businesses for whom the political dimension is not part of their goals and that leave it to the pioneers, and, on the other hand, a minority of highly politicised businesses. The cases of Citizen Dream and Saldac showed that, while their organizational model was common, the meaning given to it fundamentally diverged.

The tensions are quite different depending upon the level of political involvement. When the latter is low, the main balance that has to be sought is between the economic and the social dimensions. Sometimes, the social mission is seen only as an automatic consequence of the economic activity, provided that the FT criteria are complied with—a rationale similar to that of labeling. This was observed in FT shops in which there is no direct import. In such cases, the shop can focus on selling, delegating the responsibility of producer support—and thus the tensions linked to it—to the importer. If doubts arise regarding the ethical nature of the importer, the shop is able to switch quite easily.

In the case of direct import, the social mission is more likely to translate into organizational arrangements with people or units responsible for producer support. This may lead to a stronger specialization of tasks, but also to higher internal tensions. For instance, in one FTSE, the initial intent was to buy 100% of the products from WFTO producer groups. Nevertheless, fearing quality problems and low margins, and wishing to extend the scope of products for customers, the managers decided to include products from non-FT producer groups (through partnerships that were qualified by the FTSE as "ethical trade"). This decision brought criticism from certain FT pioneers. This example illustrates a typical tension between quality and financial margins, on the one hand, and support to small-scale, marginalized producers, on the other hand. Given the entrepreneurial nature of these businesses, it is the founder/manager—rather than, for instance, the shareholders—who has to deal with these tensions.

When the political involvement is high, as is the case for Minga members, the ambition is to integrate the three dimensions of FT not only within the organization but also in the activities of each employee. As we have seen with Saldac, polyvalence—rather than specialization—is encouraged. But the ambition of integration, without a structure that formally "settles" the tensions, is difficult to achieve. One central tension to which these particular FTSEs are confronted is the tension between the social mission, i.e., the desire to support small-scale producers in the South, and the political promotion of a local approach to FT. In Saldac, the local approach dominated, for instance, when the staff preferred honey and wine from the Rhône-Alpes region than from Latin America. Another tension may arise for instance, between the political opposition to mainstream channels and the socio-economic advantages for producers resulting from the use of these channels. One Minga member in the study faced such a dilemma and decided to reject an opportunity of large-scale distribution of its products and to favor local small-scale shops.

While the business *expertise* available to the entrepreneurs is generally significant, through their education and experience but also through the possible advice of the shareholders associated in the venture, this does not necessarily lead, as already mentioned, to effective *monitoring*. This is even more striking concerning the social mission, the adequacy and coherence of which reside in the hands of the entrepreneur alone. Similarly to the previous category, the entrepreneurs of business-form FTSEs should consider joining networks that might "endorse" their trustworthiness. This could also increase their legitimacy and their link with the broader FT movement, as observed for instance in the case of Signaléthique (working with the PFCE and WFTO). Peer-to-peer monitoring in the context of a network may, however, be insufficient. And, contrarily to individual ventures, business-form FTSEs have the possibility to set up self-governance structures that bring monitoring, expertise, resources, and linkages with the diverse stakeholders. The combination of intra- and inter-organizational governance may particularly stimulate the legitimacy and the efficiency of business-form FTSEs.

## Volunteer-based Nonprofits and Cooperatives (Type 3)

Despite nuances in practices, the study has shown that volunteer-based FTSEs have a clearly higher political involvement and a lower economic focus than the other types of FTSEs. These features were accounted for, in the economic neo-institutional approach, by the existence, in these FTSEs, of a number of organizational assets that allow them to overcome the failures of other institutional arrangements (typically the market and the state): limited profit distribution, explicit social mission, trust-instigating role of volunteers, access to noncommercial resources, etc. From a sociological neo-institutional perspective, volunteer-based forms appeared as "logical" reflections of the drives for economic democracy and solidarity that were powerful ideals in the early decades of FT. However, these ideals were progressively marginalized with the emergence of values promoting professionalism and market orientation. In Belgium, and even more so in France, this model and the FTSEs representing it—respectively Oxfam-MDM and ADM—were explicitly criticized. Consequently, volunteer-based FTSEs in these two countries had to resist and justify the adequacy of their model, as the case of Oxfam-MDM has shown. In Italy, the volunteer-based model remained dominant. In the UK, volunteers gradually moved from the FTSEs to the broader movement of FT supporters (typically in the context of FT towns, universities, Churches, etc.).

Yet, this organizational model is still currently adopted when a group of people with limited financial resources and economic skills but with high idealism wish to launch a FT project. These new volunteer-based FTSEs are widespread in Italy, where they are still institutionally favored, but they are much less common in other countries (examples in the study include D'ici, d'ailleurs and new ADM shops in France). Since the institutional context is much less favorable, creating—and maintaining—a volunteer-based FTSE involves a more conscious and explicit choice than it was in the early decades of the movement. Volunteer-based FTSEs could also specialize only on education and advocacy and leave the economic activity to others, as the case of Oxfam UK has shown. But the interviews suggested that most volunteers and stakeholders were hostile to this strategy. Indeed, the economic activity is necessary both to support the social mission and to concretize the political project (for instance through the worldshops). The economic activity is thus considered as important albeit subordinated to the socio-political goals that constitute the priority for most volunteers and stakeholders. As the Oxfam-MDM case has shown, this may lead to tensions when certain actors wish to develop the commercial activity in a more autonomous way.

Indeed, when analyzing the case of Oxfam-MDM, especially during its most threatening economic situation, it appeared that the FTSE was somehow "caught" between the need to reinforce its economic strategy and profile, and the desire to leave the primacy to the socio-political project in the context of a democratic governance and functioning. This fundamental tension may partly explain the difficulty of finding managers able to overcome this paradox without losing the volunteers' support.

Globally speaking, we may distinguish the tensions according to whether they arise within the operational context (i.e., mainly among employees), within the governance structures (i.e., with the participation of the volunteers) or between the staff and the Board members. At the first, operational level, the interviews with employees from the different departments of Oxfam-MDM showed that the cultures and perceptions of FT were different, especially between the political and the commercial departments. In the meantime, however, the interviewed employees saw the work of the other departments as necessary and complementary to theirs. Several employees suggested that the integrated structure and the common location of all the units provided many possibilities for conversing and dealing with the tensions at the interpersonal level. The tensions at the operational level were more explicit, for instance, when resources had to be allocated to events that were not clearly linked to one or another department. Contacts with the producers were established both by people in charge of purchasing and by people from the political unit. These "grey zones" seem much more numerous in integrated FTSEs such as Oxfam-MDM than in group structures, thus requiring a more systematic bargaining in the former than in the latter, in which more explicit rules of repartition exist. Such a permanent bargaining locates these FTSEs close to Mintzberg's description (1986) of a "political" organization (in the broad sense of the term). In an integrated structure, the general director's role is crucial in dealing with the tensions and maintaining the equilibrium between the different sensitivities.

The second type of circumstances causing explicit tensions is when fundamental strategic decisions have to be taken in the General Assembly. When debates arose in volunteer-based FTSEs such as Oxfam-MDM and, previously, OWW-OFT and Miel Maya, to decide whether products should be made available in the mainstream, tensions were particularly strong. As observed by Davies and Crane (2003), the economic dimension was justified by its contribution to the social mission. In other debates, however, the volunteers favored socio-political considerations.

Finally, examples of tensions stemming from the operational activities but used by the volunteers at the governance's level were also numerous. They appeared to be quite strong, for instance, when it came to external communication. Several advertising and/or education campaigns—the precise nature of which as "advertising" or "education" is not always clear—were criticized afterwards by part of the volunteers, both for the content and for the fact that the volunteers had not been consulted. Volunteers claimed the right to give their opinion before the launch of such campaigns. This and other examples show that when volunteers have strong, democratic-based representation in the governance structures (as is the case in Oxfam-MDM), the socio-political dimensions are likely to remain strong, thereby countering the institutional pressures for "commercialization" and reinforcing the alternative character of this type of FTSE.

To avoid ambiguity, often a synonym for a certain organizational paralysis, volunteer-based FTSEs should deal with the following dilemma. One possibility is to see themselves as a socio-political movement and to articulate their activities (including the economic ones but also the support to producers) around this project. The sales of FT products may find their place in this context, with worldshops appearing as places of education and campaigning more than as channels to increase the turnover. This involves accepting: a limited economic scope compared to other FTSEs; a social mission that does not rely so much on increasing volumes for producers but rather on qualitative and political aspects of partnerships; an understanding of professionalism that is not mixed up with market orientation; and a secondary place for profitability (for instance as a criterion for evaluating the worldshops). This option seems often favored by volunteer-based FTSEs; an extreme example is Oxfam UK that stopped importing FT goods. But another possibility for volunteer-FTSEs is to boost the economic activity besides the socio-political project. This requires, however, giving a significant autonomy to the economic activity. Several architectures can be built for this purpose, with different types of control by volunteers and stakeholders regarding the economic activity. The group structure is the most common one and should be considered when a large size is reached, in order to exploit the possibilities of the combination of legal forms and the specialization of governance structures and managerial posts. But it is also possible to imagine other architectures in the context of a single legal structure, in which it may be easier for employees and managers to converse and deal with the tensions at an interpersonal level in the day-to-day operational context.

## Multi-Stakeholder Cooperatives (Type 4)

The economic neo-institutional approach describes cooperatives as intermediates between nonprofits and businesses, potentially combining assets in both economic and socio-political domains. Moreover, the multi-stakeholder model enables to span expertise over the three dimensions. But this does not mean that this possibility is always concretized. Furthermore, the concrete implementation of such a combination may vary quite a lot according to the profiles of the managers and the expectations of the stakeholders. For instance, Soli'gren, owned by the city of Grenoble, local NGOs, volunteers, local producers, and customers, seemed more focused on the socio-political dimensions than other, more business-oriented multi-stakeholder cooperatives such as Ethiquable. Much depends on which types of stakeholder coalitions are dominant. There is thus much latitude regarding the meaning given to the vehicle that the multi-stakeholder cooperative constitutes.

While the presence of diverse stakeholders in the decision-making structures may provide expertise and resources, the likelihood of divergent views among them—leading to high "costs of ownership"—is an evident source of tensions. Part of the literature on cooperatives addresses the tensions between economic and social goals in these organizations; it suggests that there may be a tendency to give priority to economic development over the social mission (Levi 1998). The tensions are even stronger since the social (and political) dimensions are intended to be translated at the internal level (democracy and participation). In the FTSEs of this category, the staff seemed to play a crucial role. For instance, in Pangea-NT, a new generation of highly motivated leaders took the succession of the founders. Most of these younger leaders were themselves previously volunteers and were thus particularly legitimate in the eyes of the broader community of volunteers and supporters. In the meantime, they seemed able to cope with commercial issues, such as dealing with supermarkets for the distribution of CTM products. The leading role of these employees was reinforced by their involvement in the Agices and RES networks.

While multi-stakeholdership has a number of assets, it is also a huge challenge. The first challenge comes from the evolution from a single-stakeholder model (generally volunteers and/or employees) to a multi-stakeholder one: in order for the latter to exist not only on the paper, as something that is nice to communicate, stakeholders must receive significant voting rights. Second, FTSEs must accept that involving multiple stakeholders inevitably leads to tensions, which may not be handled *a priori*. This is a condition for the governance structures to be a place of constructive debate about the articulation of the hybrid dimensions in the organizational missions and activities. Participants in multi-stakeholder governance are thus not only responsible for the good functioning of the organization, but also for the strategic management of hybridity.

## Group Structures (Type 5)

The case of group structures appeared most interesting in both the economic and the sociological neo-institutional approaches. The first approach stressed the opportunity to combine the organizational assets of both forms, as well as the advantages in terms of incentives and access to information. The second approach viewed this form as a reflection of the values of professionalism and market orientation linked to the phase of mainstreaming, coexisting with the previous myths of solidarity and economic democracy. The institutional acceptance of groups may also be seen as the result of their intermediate position and their multi-stakeholder configuration, in the sense that several stakeholders are likely to recognize themselves in at least one of the group's components.

The case of MMH-MFT showed how the institutional pressures pushing FTSEs to render their economic activity autonomous were taken as an opportunity to develop the specialization of different entities while ensuring their coordination. In other words, thanks to its large size and to the creation of various autonomous units and departments, the group structure may be purposively designed to deal with the hybrid nature of FT. The variety of group systems and of coordination mechanisms shows that there is much room for strategic design. Moreover, the age and size of groups make them powerful institutional tone-givers: they influence the FT sector at least as much as they are influenced by it.

It is not because the different entities and departments that compose group structures have their specific tasks and do not necessarily interact with each other in their day-to-day activities that tensions are absent. Several examples showed the contradictions that may emerge between the different entities. The question is thus not so much whether there are tensions in such FTSEs, but rather how and by whom these tensions will be handled. It seems that the structural separation and the large size of groups may decrease the day-to-day tensions but also the opportunities for interpersonal dialogue. In this context, the ultimate decision-making in the case of conflicts may be done either by mutual adjustment of the entities or by an "umbrella" person or structure.

For instance, OWW-OFT and Traidcraft evolved from a situation with two directors to the appointment of one common director for the two entities. In Traidcraft, instead of having one of the two directors taking control over the whole group, which might have given the impression that one part was taken over by the other, the appointment of a new external director meant to symbolize a "fresh start." At OWW-OFT, the director of the nonprofit part was appointed to manage the whole group, which symbolized the fact that the nonprofit controlled the cooperative, and not the opposite. Another solution may lie in regular interactions between the two directors, as in the case of MMH-MFT. The governance structures are also a crucial place for dealing with the tensions. OWW-OFT and Traidcraft chose for a common Board (with an additional overall "guardian" structure in the second FTSE). MMH-MFT evolved to separate Boards but with part of the members belonging to the two Boards. These FTSEs should not lose sight, on the long term, of the importance of maintaining strong coordination mechanisms to balance specialization and avoid seeing the two entities go their separate way, evolving isomorphically toward, respectively, a pure business and a pure NGO.

## Managing Tensions: A Synthesis

The following figure synthesizes the way in which the different organizational models manage the tensions that may occur in their practice of FT as a hybrid construct. It gives a number of examples of such tensions and indicates at which level they are managed in each organizational category. The figure indicates how, the more we move to the right (older and larger

|  | Type 1 | Type 2 | Type 3 | Type 4 | Type 5 |
|---|---|---|---|---|---|
| **Case** | Esprit Equo | Saldac | MDM-Oxfam | Pangea-NT | Oxfam-WW |
| **Examples of tensions** | 100% FT origin vs profitability Political vision vs socio-economic performance | | Producer support Volunteers and shops Allocation of resources Communication | Campaigning against vs. collaborating with supermarkets Producer support | |
| **Governance** | Entrepreneur | Entrepreneur vs shareholders | Among volunteers Between volunteers and managers | Stakeholders | NGO-side (+ volunteers) vs business-side (+ shareholders) |
| **Management operations** | Entrepreneur vs employees | | Political vs "commercial" employees Director(s) | | Director(s) |

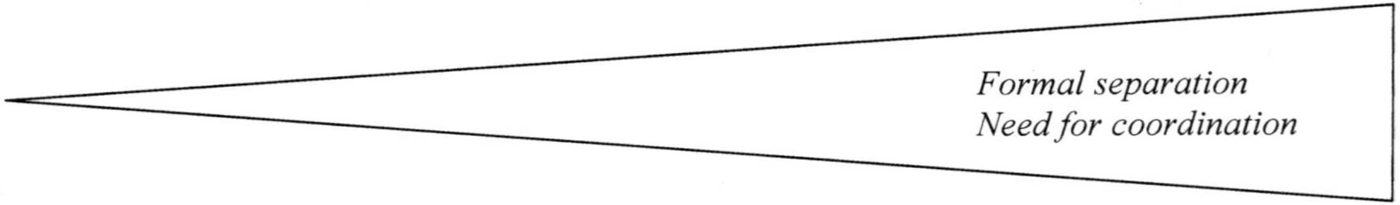

*Formal separation
Need for coordination*

*Figure 8.1*  Managing tensions in FTSEs.

FTSEs), the more organizational entities are specialized in the management of each dimension, and the more formal coordination mechanisms must be established to ensure a coherent strategy.

## ORGANIZATIONAL CHANGE

FTSEs should be aware of the different organizational possibilities and considering evolving when it is appropriate. Different common changes were already highlighted, such as from individual ventures (type 1) to entrepreneurial businesses (type 2), or from nonprofits (type 3) to group structures (type 5). These evolutions can now be understood not only as reflections of broader institutional changes in the FT sector, but also as strategic moves through which FTSEs adapt their way of managing the hybrid dimensions of FT. For instance, the emergence of group structures has been explained by coercive and normative pressures as well as by contractual arguments. But the case of MMH-MFT showed that the evolution towards a group structure also corresponded to a strategy with multiple goals: aligning the organizational form on the specific pursuit of each of the three dimensions of FT; clarifying the goals of each entity; obtaining specific resources for the pursuit of each dimension (sales on the one hand, and subsidies, donations, and voluntary work on the other); seeking expertise, both at the operational level (managers and employees) and at the governance level; increasing the linkages with both the business world and with civil society etc.

The shift in missions rather than in organizational models is also worth discussing. Indeed, individual or business-form FTSEs may evolve from a predominantly business focus to a more hybrid mission, including stronger attention to socio-political issues, without changing their organizational model. We find interesting examples of such dynamics in France, with business-form FTSEs (e.g., Karawan) being "converted" to the political vision of Minga. This vision may be integrated into the existing organizational model without changing the latter, precisely because the members of Minga wish to affirm their political vision *through*—and not *despite*—the economic activity. The impact of this evolution towards a stronger political profile will rather be observed, for instance, in the distribution strategy (with a reluctance to deal with mainstream businesses), in the selection of products to be sold in the shop (with a reluctance to sell labeled products) and, more generally, in the philosophy (with a preference for small-scale and local approaches).

## CONCLUSION

This chapter examined the opportunities and tensions related to the different organizational models. Each model enables to combine the hybrid dimensions of FT to various extents, even when the predominance is given to one of these dimensions (typically, economic or political in respectively type-1 and 2 and type-3 FTSEs). At the same time, none of the models escaped tensions between these hybrid dimensions. What differentiates the models is not so much the presence of tensions, but rather the way through which they are handled: by the entrepreneur alone, by the staff, at the governance level or through the network. The evolution of FTSEs from one model to another was also better understood as a strategic step enabling to better adapt the model to the evolution of the FTSE's practice.

# Conclusion

Several conclusions can be drawn at the end of this work. First, the main findings of the study are reviewed, including further recommendations for the FTSEs. Second, contributions are underlined based on the findings and the design of this work. Trails for future research are proposed in the third section. A final section is devoted to the future of organizational diversity in FT and beyond.

## FINDINGS AND RECOMMENDATIONS

### Taxonomy

To explore the way in which organizational diversity may be structured, a taxonomy was developed including five categories: individual ventures (type 1); entrepreneurial, business-form FTSEs (type 2); volunteer-based FTSEs (type 3); multi-stakeholder cooperatives (type 4); and group structures (type 5). These categories seemed relatively homogeneous, with, however, a few exceptions that could not be definitively placed in one of the categories. The different categories seemed to correspond to different stages of the organizational trajectories. While most FTSEs started either as volunteer-based FTSEs (type 3), or as entrepreneurial businesses (types 1 and 2), the two other categories (types 4 and 5) seemed to be adopted only beyond a certain age and size. FTSEs could use this taxonomy to situate themselves in the broader landscape and analyze other FTSEs in their field, and to examine their possible evolution along the organizational trajectories drawn. It could be an even more useful tool for networks, public and private support structures, and researchers, who could have a more realistic picture of the organizational landscape when examining the FT movement. Training, public support or consultancy could be focused on certain categories of FTSEs. Based on the common organizational trajectories, FTSEs in crisis could be specifically supported and advised regarding the evolution of their organizational model and the management of similar challenges by other FTSEs.

## Deterministic Approaches to Organizational Diversity

We saw how, over time, the organizational landscape evolved from mainly volunteer-based nonprofit or cooperative FTSEs, towards other forms such as businesses, individual ventures and group structures. Age and size brought more complexity as well as a stronger specialization of the organizational units on one particular dimension of FT. This appeared particularly clearly for group structures composed of a business (economic activity) and an NGO (socio-political activities). Regional differences were strong, with a relative uniformity in Italy (social cooperatives), a divide between volunteer-based nonprofits and businesses in France, and a larger diversity in Belgium and the UK. Organizational models differed much on the basis of the profiles of their leaders, with, logically, more "activist" profiles in volunteer-based FTSEs and more "business" profiles in manager-owned and cooperative FTSEs. Beyond this logical link, however, it was interesting to observe how, despite the growing importance of business profiles in all FTSEs, certain leaders of individual and business-form FTSEs developed a more activist vision. In terms of resources, only the volunteer-based nonprofits and cooperatives (either as a whole or as part of a group structure, i.e., types 3 and 5) raised nonmarket resources such as subsidies, gifts, and voluntary work. Even then, however, more than two thirds of their resources originated from sales. This proportion was close to 100% for the other FTSEs (individuals, businesses, and multi-stakeholder cooperatives). Finally, concerning the FTSEs' goals and activities, putting their social mission aside, three main patterns were observed. A dominance of economic goals and activities was observed in the individual and part of the business-form FTSEs (types 1 and 2); socio-political goals were particularly central in volunteer-based FTSEs (type 3), with the economic activity rather considered as tool to serve these goals; and the different types of goals were combined more explicitly in multi-stakeholder cooperatives and groups (types 4 and 5), as well as, more surprisingly, in a minority of "politicized" businesses.

From an economic institutional standpoint, organizational diversity was explained by the fact that FTSEs do not all produce the same mix of dimensions or "goods." The emergence of FT pioneers as volunteer-based, nonprofit FTSEs was analyzed because of the trustworthiness of such a form, especially in the absence of labeling, as well as because of its assets in the political, "public good" dimension of FT (regulation, education, and advocacy). The cooperative form was then examined as a device that offers similar assets in terms of trustworthiness and production of public goods, while better enabling the development of the economic activity through the mobilization of capital and higher economic incentives. This explains why several nonprofit pioneers wishing to expand their economic activity evolved into cooperatives, and why new FTSEs emerged with such a form. The growth of the FT market and the development of certification were suggested as major arguments explaining the arrival of business-form or "investor-owned" FTSEs. Yet, the analysis showed that these FTSEs were not necessarily focused only on the economic activity, and that they were able to engage in the production of trust and public goods as well. These forms were also explained by their low costs of ownership, especially in individual FTSEs. Finally, group structures were presented as organizational models allowing for the combination of a large number of assets and cost reductions in terms of information and incentives.

From this perspective, the recommendations for FTSEs are simple. They should ensure that their organizational model is effectively aligned with their product mix in a way that minimizes their transaction costs. FTSEs should avoid inefficiencies (weak alignment) so as to ensure their long-term survival. While useful in many aspects, this theoretical framework does not account for the whole extent and complexity of organizational diversity in FT.

Using the sociological neo-institutional analysis, organizational diversity was further explained by the nonexistent, weak and/or conflicting isomorphic pressures affecting FTSEs. From a normative stand, three phases of institutionalization of the FT practice were distinguished: foundation, mainstreaming, and entrepreneurship. Each of these phases seemed to constrain the organizational models of FTSEs of the corresponding generation. Pioneer FTSEs modelled their form on the values of economic democracy and solidarity, which were predominant in the early decades of FT. Then, the mainstreaming phase brought values of professionalism and market orientation to the forefront, leading new FTSEs to adopt more business-oriented forms, and pushing a large proportion of pioneers to adapt their structures (typically towards a stronger specialization, which culminated in the evolution towards multi-stakeholder cooperatives and group structures). Group structures were interpreted as reflections of these first two institutionalization phases; accordingly, the tensions between the business and the nonprofit part could be seen as mirroring the broader tensions between these two institutional orders. Finally, a third institutional phase consisted of the emergence of entrepreneurial ventures, in the context of the promotion of (social) entrepreneurship. This included a focus on individual action, risk-taking, and innovation).

Nevertheless, despite such trends, even within the same generations of FTSEs, uniformity seemed limited. One reason for the differences among FTSEs was that the organizational implications of the normative settings of the different phases were rather vague. Indeed, while certain implications could be drawn in terms of legal forms, architecture, and governance models, there was still much latitude for diverging interpretations of and reactions to the normative pressures. Another reason for the global diversity was geographical. Indeed, the normative, coercive, and mimetic trends seemed different from one region to another. For instance, while in Italy, the social cooperative form and the use of voluntary work seemed encouraged by the networks and the legislation, there was no such drive in Belgium and the UK. In France, the diversity seemed to result from the coexistence of different networks with very different visions of FT. Nevertheless, a dominant trend towards a stronger business orientation was observed, suggesting that the uniformity within FT is likely to increase in the future (see the end of this conclusion).

The sociological neo-institutional approach brings useful insights for organizations to situate themselves in their institutional context. Not only is efficiency important for their survival, but also legitimacy in the eyes of other FTSEs, FT supporters, public authorities, the general public, etc. When adopting their initial organizational model, or when changing it, FTSEs should take into account the perception of these stakeholders and the broader normative atmosphere. This does not mean that FTSEs should strictly conform to their institutional environment: as we have seen, they have the ability to alter this environment in a way that is more favorable to their organizational model. But such institutional work requires efforts (see the case of Esprit Equo), which should be submitted to a strategic decision and undertaken with other partners.

## Agency-based Approach to Organizational Diversity

Through the analysis of the concrete shaping of the organizational model in six different cases, FTSEs appeared able to act as "institutional entrepreneurs" capable of influencing the environment in a way that recognized and promoted their own organizational model and secured their access to crucial resources. FTSEs combined the different logics associated with the hybrid dimensions of FT through a process of "bricolage." Indeed, the construction of the organizational model as embodying hybrid logics appeared as particularly crucial to legitimize certain visions of FT, i.e., certain ways of combining these logics. In contexts in which pioneer FTSEs were dominant and seemed suspicious towards newer, more business-oriented forms, certain FTSEs had to struggle to have such a type of form accepted and diffused. While this process happened successfully in Belgium (with the experience of Citizen Dream and the creation of the BFTF), the situation seemed more locked for FTSEs such as Esprit Equo in Italy.

In Belgium and in the UK, most pioneers anticipated mainstreaming, or at least adapted to its requirements, thereby becoming able to compete with mainstream players. In Belgium, such an adaptation was partly stimulated by the public administration, which pushed FTSEs to isolate the socio-political activities in a separate, nonprofit entity. The study showed how MMH-MFT re-appropriated this forced evolution into a group structure through a gradual specialization at the operational level, and later at the governance level. Such evolution was not really observed in the craft sector, where Oxfam-MDM tried to maintain its model and was initially suspicious to the emergence of business-form FTSEs. Eventually, in the context of a difficult economic situation, and after changes in its leadership (both the person and the profile requirement), it preferred openness over isolation, as its involvement in the BFTF shows. ADM's position appeared even more difficult as it was caught between mainstream-oriented business FTSEs that were much more successful economically, and a growing stream of political businesses that criticized the use of subsidies and voluntary work. The latter's political vision, entailing a strong hostility towards mainstreaming, and capitalism in general, was embodied by the Minga network. Saldac relayed such a vision locally in Rhône-Alpes, influencing other FTSEs and offering an alternative to employees and supporters who were unsatisfied by the ADM model.

The strategic contribution of governance structures to institutional bricolage seems particularly worth examining. As hybrid organizations, FTSEs should determine *ex ante* the types of resources they aim and identify the stakeholders who could facilitate the access to these resources. The involvement of particular stakeholders would thus not only be the result of historical or interpersonal proximities with particular groups, but it would also be guided by the FTSE's strategic control over key constituents in its environment. Following Pfeffer and Salancik (1978), FTSEs should thus consider the cooptation of diverse resource-rich stakeholders in order to also gain expertise and loyalty from these stakeholders, even though this may bring about challenges in terms of decision-making and lead the existing "governants" to give away part of their control of the organization. It is worth noting that the inclusion of stakeholders can also be achieved in other ways than through formal involvement in governance. In the study, the most advanced example of stakeholder dialogue was provided by Traidcraft. Although such a large-scale dialogue is more difficult for smaller FTSEs, it allows FTSEs to gain "a clear and detailed picture of each stakeholder's expectations, and to engage into concrete actions to meet these expectations" (Traidcraft's Chief executive).

The legal form is also a matter of strategic choice. This is particularly highlighted in the literature on social entrepreneurship, as suggested by Battle Anderson and Dees (2006), "[w]hile many social entrepreneurs do adopt a not-for-profit form of organization, they, and those researching them, should view the choice of the legal form as a strategic decision, not a state of being. Legal forms of organization are artefacts; tools people have designed to serve various purposes" (156). FTSEs can exert a strategic management of their legal form when they do not consider it as a static, given element imposed by the environment but rather as a tool that may evolve with the organization and be a part of the innovative institutional bricolage process. Indeed, both through the initial conception of the legal form and through its subsequent change, certain FTSEs showed to be very innovative. In several cases, the managers had to spend much time in collecting information about the legal form, explaining it to employees and other stakeholders, and meeting its requirements. Another possible innovation is the combination of several legal forms each corresponding to a particular logic. The FT activity seems to require organizational innovation as part of the broader social innovation. In such a sense, the experimentation made by FTSEs with new forms and combinations may open new organizational paths suited for other FTSEs, social enterprises, and hybrid organizations in general.

## Tensions

On the basis of the lessons learned from the case studies, this work examined the nature and the level of the tensions facing each type of FTSE regarding the hybrid nature of the FT practice. For each organizational category, the specific situation is summarized here and recommendations are formulated.

Individual FTSEs (type 1) appeared as very specific cases in which it is the entrepreneur who embodies a particular mix of dimensions. But given the limited expertise and resources of the entrepreneur, the "mix" was often reduced to one dominant dimension. This reduced the emergence of tensions. These tensions were not absent (for instance the typical tension between profitability and proportion of FT products) but they were often implicit and situated at the entrepreneur's level.

Entrepreneurial business-form FTSEs (type 2) were homogeneous in their focus on their economic activity, on which the entrepreneurs were dependent for their survival. Only a minority, however, particularly within the Minga network in France, had a very strong political message that they wished to express through a deliberately local, small-scale and anti-mainstream economic project. This led to tensions, for instance, between the reluctance to deal with large volumes, and the willingness to bring significant support to producers in the South. Again, these tensions were often managed by the entrepreneurs alone, leaving much room for their particular vision of FT.

In individual and business-form FTSEs, a broader combination of the different dimensions of FT may be achieved through a greater polyvalence of the staff. Polyvalence may also be a value in itself, particularly when FTSEs do not see business, producer support and political activity as three separate domains. This is the case when the alternative way of doing business entails a political dimension. This may then translate into rather polyvalent structures, with a manager or a small team performing various tasks and aiming to be similarly at ease in a shop, in a negotiation with producers or in a political debate. In medium-sized FTSEs, volunteers or employees may be specialized in one domain but simultaneously master basic knowledge on the other dimensions. For example, it may be useful for salespeople to know from which producer groups each product originates; and people in charge of relationships with the producers may find an interest in knowing the market configuration and consumers' preferences for each type of product.

The third, volunteer-based category was generally characterized by a high level of political involvement and relatively low economic development (compared to other FTSEs). The trading activity was often considered mainly as a tool subordinated to the broader socio-political project. This led to debates concerning the degree to which, and the cost at which, the economic development was allowed. In Oxfam-MDM, but also in other volunteer-based FTSEs, this led to tensions both at the operational level (between the employees working in different units), which were handled by the general director, and at the governance level, where the volunteers generally seemed to give primacy to the socio-political missions over the economic performance.

Multi-stakeholder cooperatives were characterized by stronger specialization in each domain. The case of Pangea-NT showed the opportunities of such a specialization, through the ability of both leading campaigns against multinationals and negotiating with supermarkets. These opportunities also brought tensions, which were mainly dealt with through the governance structures.

Finally, group structures went relatively far in the specialization of each of their entities: resources, managers and employees, governance models, etc. The tensions tended to be reduced at the operational level by the fact that the goals and tasks were attributed to each entity through explicit rules. Yet, tensions could arise from the lack of information exchange between the two entities, for instance concerning campaigns against the unethical practices of multinational companies.

## CONTRIBUTIONS

### Combination of Theoretical Frameworks and Methodologies

A first key contribution of this work has been to bridge different theoretical frameworks. While such a combination has not been straightforward, it has provided interesting insights concerning the contributions of each perspective and on their possible dialogue in understanding the reasons and the meaning of organizational diversity in FT.

Using economic new institutionalism, FTSEs can be seen as diverse because they perform different roles. Organizational models are reflections of the actors' ability to minimize transaction costs for the production of particular goods. Such a functional view is one way of seeing things and has shown useful to interpret the study findings; however, several weaknesses and inconsistencies have highlighted the need for other approaches. Sociological new institutionalism has brought the emphasis on the symbolic role of organizational models, as reflections of norms, values and other pressures originating from the environment. In such sense, organizations adopt certain forms not because they are the most efficient but because they are the most appropriated and legitimate. Institutional work also draws on the legitimacy of the organizational model, but sees it as a strategic construction aiming to contribute to the creation or the modification of institutional orders rather than as a mere process of conformance to given institutional pressures.

Neither of the approaches has offered a global and undisputable understanding of organizational diversity in FT. It seems clear that organizational models have both a functional *and* a symbolic role; they are both constrained by their environment, and able to influence such environment through individual and collective institutional work. These types of roles may be more or less important according to the situation and the time period. Indeed, legitimacy issues are probably more important at the founding of the organization, when the dependence on external appraisal is highest, and when newcomers are facing uniform and thus strong normative pressures from other actors. The latter situation can be defined through the notion of "path dependence." When previous FTSEs have followed a rather uniform path in terms of form and way of practicing FT, then it is much easier for newcomer FTSEs to simply follow the path than to explore alternative models. On the other hand, when normative pressures are diverse and/or weak (a situation faced, for instance, by pioneer FTSEs in Belgium and in the UK), several paths can be followed or created, leaving more room for creativity. Large and established organizations may more easily create new avenues, as the cases of Cafédirect and OWW-OFT have shown.

As the most recent approach, institutional work is also probably the most complete and the most realistic approach. Through the notion of institutional logics, it has enabled to link structural and agency-based arguments. Combining sample findings and case studies is another advantage of using different theoretical perspectives entailing different methodologies. It has enabled to gain both a general picture of the rationale of organizational diversity in FT, and an in-depth understanding of the meaning and the implications of such diversity at the organizational level.

## Bringing Organization Theory into Fair Trade and Social Enterprise

As mentioned in the introduction, there has been little work using organization theory in the context of social enterprises, and Fair Trade in particular. Yet, the insights of organization theory are crucial to open the "black boxes" of FTSEs, which, as stated in the introduction, are much more than simple and homogeneous units linking ethical consumers in the North with small-scale producers in the South. Using the metaphor suggested by neo-institutional economists, a major contribution of this work has thus been to "open the black box" of FTSEs. This work should help researchers and practitioners to situate particular FTSEs in their broader organizational landscape, and to understand the role and the implications of diverse organizational models. The strategic perspectives analyzed in Chapter 7 should be particularly useful to understand hybrid organizational models as institutional bricolage tools for garnering legitimacy and capturing crucial resources.

## Bringing Fair Trade and Social Enterprise into Organization Theory

Conversely, the study of FT and, more generally, social enterprise, brings specific challenges to organization theory, part of which have been dealt with in this study. First, it appears that the notion of organizational model has often been reduced to the sole architecture or design. Yet, since, in FT and among social enterprises in general, several legal forms may be adopted and seem to be linked to different foci, the choice of the legal form becomes much more strategic than in other fields. Moreover, with the presence of several social groups holding a stake in the FT project, the governance model may also be shaped in a way that enables a certain balance between the different organizational goals. The decision-making power thereby does not depend on one's financial contribution as a shareholder and becomes shared between groups that are involved in a common project. Hence, the legal form and the governance model should be taken into account in the study of organizational models, especially in hybrid organizations such as social enterprises. As this study has shown, the possible congruence between legal form, architecture and governance model may give more consistence to the study of organizational models.

In this context, a major contribution of studying FTSEs and social enterprises is, as this work has suggested, to examine the link between the hybrid nature of a given field and the diverse organizational models of its participants. Such a hybrid nature gives a particular flavour and interest to organizational variables such as goals and resources. Indeed, the origin of the resources or the nature of the goals and activities appear particularly crucial in the sectors in which social enterprises operate. Each of the theoretical approaches may be enriched by the observation and the explanation of organizational diversity in a given field. For neo-institutional economists, the existence of complex, hybrid "goods" such as those inherent in FT brings nuances to the classification of organizational models in terms of assets, as analyzed in Chapter 5. For neo-institutional sociologists and organization theorists, the apparent persistence of organizational diversity over time seems to challenge the isomorphic predictions and to reflect situations of "institutional void" and/or "institutional plurality" (Kraatz & Block 2008). Neo-institutional theory should thus not only take into account the strategic abilities of organizations in the context of institutional work, but also examine the influence of ideological factors in the shaping of organizational models and the persistence of their diversity. The disruptive power of social enterprises as emblematic hybrid organizations and their ability to recompose extant institutional orders (Mair and Marti 2006; Nicholls 2010) may enrich the theoretical perspectives and offer exciting fields of investigation.

## FUTURE DIRECTIONS

Since this study is among the first to use organization theory to examine FTSEs, there is clearly much room left for research in this area. Here is a nonexhaustive list of organizational issues that seem worth exploring.

Taking the taxonomy developed in this work as a background, each organizational category could be examined on its own, with case studies that would highlight the features and challenges of each model regarding the practice of FT. The study of individual FTSEs could for instance, be linked with the broader literature on (social) entrepreneurs. Another interesting case could be that of "political businesses" and their institutionalization through networks (such as Minga). Concerning more mainstream-oriented businesses, a key question would be how far they may follow the logic of turnover and profit maximization, feeding the debate about the boundaries of FTSEs and, more broadly, social enterprise. The challenges of maintaining volunteer-based FTSEs in an increasingly market-oriented and competitive field would also be worth examining, including the degree to which the economic activity can be developed and given autonomy. The case of group structures as explicit hybrid organizations is particularly challenging and should be explored further, drawing on the rich and complementary interpretations offered by the diverse theoretical approaches used in this work. Studies could be devoted to examining different tools for balancing the specialization in each dimension and the coordination of the specialized entities. The study of some of the most innovative coordination schemes such as multi-stakeholdership seems particularly promising. Finally, the taxonomy could be refined, completed and "tested" in other contexts, including more in-depth international comparisons of how and why the organizational landscape of FT differs across the countries (following, among others, Huybrechts and Reed 2010).

Researchers could also focus specifically on organizational change in FT, trying to explain how and why it occurs and whether this is different from what is described in other sectors. A closer look at how changes in organizational models may reflect or cause shifts in the missions would be insightful. Also worth examining is the relation between the different categories of FTSEs, drawing on the different types of relations highlighted in previous work on FTSEs (Becchetti and Huybrechts 2008) and in the broader social enterprise literature (e.g., Austin 2000). Special attention could be paid to the way in which the organizational model impacts the relationships of FTSEs with mainstream corporations. The complementarities between the two major components of FT, highlighted by several authors at the movement's level (e.g., Gendron, Bisaillon, and Rance 2009; Wilkinson 2007; Nicholls 2010), could be explored further at the inter-organizational level. The different categories could also be compared on a range of precise issues. A major but tricky issue would be to compare the impact on the producers according to the type of FTSE involved. Finally, further empirical material about how the tensions inherent to the FT activity manifest themselves in the different types of FTSEs would be welcome.

## THE FUTURE OF ORGANIZATIONAL DIVERSITY

A key question at the end of this work is that of the future prospects of FTSEs and hybrid organizations in general. The mainstreaming of FT brought a new generation of FTSEs and pushed a large part of the pioneers to evolve towards a more market-oriented profile. The recent emergence of entrepreneurial forms has further increased the predominance of business-like FTSEs. This might announce an increasing isomorphic trend towards the for-profit business form as the main organizational model for practicing FT.

Several factors may point in this direction. First, as the business forms have gradually been accepted by pioneers, and as the business path to FT has become institutionalized, the obstacles to the multiplication of business forms have disappeared. While in France and in Belgium business-form FTSEs already constitute the majority in terms of the number of organizations, it is likely that these organizations will gain increasing power in the future. Moreover, the tendency in pioneer FTSEs, especially in cooperatives and group structures, suggests that "professionalism" and market orientation are increasingly powerful guidelines. From a functionalist perspective, these orientations are often justified as being required for the very survival of the FTSEs. But, as highlighted by the early sociological new institutionalists, normative trends such as professionalism and market orientation are precisely presented as technical requirements by influential stakeholders (business experts and consultants, public authorities, commercial partners, etc.). Finally, the development of certification schemes, both in the context of Fairtrade International (broadening of the range of labeled products) and outside of it (labels such as Ecocert) is likely to attract a growing number of for-profit companies, which may push FTSEs into a more business-oriented path.

Despite all these factors, it has been suggested throughout this book that there still is a place for diversity and hybridity in FTSEs. This may enable certain "resistance" to the uniformization of the market logics. It seems clear that the pioneers' approach to FT, with volunteer-based, non-profit models, will become a minority in most countries (with maybe a few exceptions for instance in Italy). But other, more innovative models to maintain socio-political logics and linkages with civil society exist. The examples of OWW-OFT and Cafédirect show how NGOs and volunteer groups may remain involved in market-oriented FTSEs by becoming influential shareholders that act as watchdogs of the social mission. Moreover, the marginalization of volunteer-based FTSEs in terms of economic weight and number of organizations does not mean that these FTSEs will lose their influence. By situating themselves more at the periphery of the FT sector, they may continue to monitor its evolution, and formulate new avenues for high(er) FT standards. As stated by an interviewee in a pioneer volunteer-based FTSE: "probably in twenty years time we won't be in the FT market any more: our role will rather be to come up with the next 'big idea' that will bring more fairness into the globalized economy."

Moreover, the dominance of market resources, business legal forms, and entrepreneurial dynamics in the other FTSEs does not prevent them from pursuing nonmarket logics. The case of Minga has shown that a business-like form may precisely be used to legitimate very alternative and anti-mainstream logics. In such a sense, the FT sector may remain a laboratory in which innovative hybrid models are conceived. This will only be possible if FT and social enterprise networks act as global governance structures advising the entrepreneurs on all the dimensions of FT and prevent that the businesses lose sight of the social mission and the broader political message of the movement.

Despite the broader institutional forces, particularly pressure from the conventional business world, FTSEs have managed to practice FT under a wide array of models, integrating hybrid logics. In this sense, the different models, including corporate actors not focusing on FT, may be complementary to each other. To a certain extent, FT needs both its more business-oriented FTSEs and corporations to explore new economic opportunities, and its ideological "guardians" (Wilkinson 2007). The FTSEs that combine these two aspects should particularly serve as examples of these complementarities. This does not mean that the differences among FTSEs should be minimized and their internal and external tensions ignored. But, if the FTSEs manage to conserve the control over the FT standards and maintain their ethical quality, then their role will remain crucial as "mediators" between civil society and the market (Nicholls 2010). The demanding ethical standards of FT may frighten some corporations and accelerate the development of alternative certification schemes. But as this process is already happening, FTSEs should focus on maintaining the movement's credibility and legitimacy, at the risk of losing part of the corporate participation. Through pursuing "unity in diversity" thanks to the networking processes (Huybrechts 2010b), and developing collaborations in spite of the diverging "affiliations," FTSEs may be able to resist isomorphic pressures and dilution in the process of mainstreaming (Jaffee 2010). In this respect, their innovative organizational models can be sources of inspiration for other social enterprises seeking to pursue hybrid goals.

# Notes

## NOTES TO THE INTRODUCTION

1. If we compare FT sales in 2009 with world trade figures as provided by the World Trade Organization, the proportion varies between 0.03% (labeled sales) and 0.035% (estimate of total FT sales).
2. In 2009, FT (labeled) sales reached €3.4 billion worldwide and €2.5 billion in Europe (FLO-I 2010); market shares ranged from 1 or 2% for several products up to 20% for coffee in the UK and even 50% for bananas in Switzerland (Krier 2005, 2008; FLO-I 2010).
3. Annual growth for products labeled by Fairtrade International (previously Fairtrade Labeling Organizations International, FLO-I) was 30 to 40% (figures based on the annual reports from 2001 to 2009).
4. Note that "Fairtrade" (one word) is used to refer to the products certified by Fairtrade International. "Fair Trade" (two words) remains the correct expression for designing the whole sector or movement, whatever the products and affiliations.
5. Retail, transformation, import, and also, as will be described in Chapter 1, production.
6. For instance, the British FT companies Cafédirect (coffee) and Divine (chocolate).
7. Initially International Federation for Alternative Trade, now World Fair Trade Organization.
8. The website www.fairtrade-institute.org references more than 300 journal articles related to FT (accessed on June 22, 2011).
9. Here is a nonexhaustive list of French- and English-language journals that have published one or more special issue(s) on Fair Trade: *Agriculture and Human Values, Canadian Journal of Development Studies, Cahiers Agricultures, Critical Perspectives on International Business, Development in Practice, Economie et Solidarités, International Journal of Tourism, Journal of Business Ethics, Journal of International Development, Journal of Strategic Marketing, Revue Internationale de Gestion, Sustainable Development.*
10. See www.fairtradeinternationalsymposium.org
11. For a more complete review of the FT literature, see for instance, Lemay (2007).
12. In part of the literature on FT, and more broadly on development, the terms "North" and "South" refer to the geopolitical division of the world between, respectively and broadly speaking, "developed" and "developing" countries.
13. It is worth noting here that the perspective of organization theory is missing.

## NOTES TO CHAPTER 1

1. In the growing literature on FT, much attention has been devoted to the origins and evolution of FT. The aim here is to provide a brief summary of the story, the full account of which can be found, for instance, in Raynolds et al. (2007), Diaz-Pedregal (2007), or Gendron et al. (2009). For a more critical review of the "usual story," see Anderson (2009a; 2009b).
2. Several authors (e.g., Nicholls and Opal 2005) consider the initiatives previously referred to as "charity trade" as constituting the "first wave" of FT. Without neglecting the contribution of these previous initiatives to FT, the rise of ATOs in the 1970s can be considered here as the first concretization of FT as we know it nowadays (Anderson, 2009b; Gendron et al., 2009a).
3. Later changed into International Fair Trade Association, and finally World Fair Trade Organization in 2009.
4. In Edouard Douwes Dekker's ("Multatuli") books, "Max Havelaar" is the name of a fictive hero who takes the defense of small-scale tea producers in Dutch colonies.
5. Certification will be used here as the term encompassing different types of labeling practices.
6. One example, among others, can be found at http://www.WFTO.com/index.php?option=com_docman&task=doc_download&gid=612 (accessed May 1, 2009).
7. IFAT (now WFTO) website (www.ifat.org; accessed April 21, 2007); emphasis added.
8. Nonfood products certified by FLO are few at this date (e.g., cotton or roses) but are likely to expand in the future.
9. FINE is an informal network set up in 1998 and gathering the four main Fair Trade umbrella organizations of the time: FLO, IFAT, NEWS!, and EFTA.
10. www.fairtrade-advocacy.org
11. One hundred percent is generally understood in a flexible sense, considering that many FT retailers also include part of products that are not strictly speaking FT but follow the same principles (local FT, products from social economy networks, etc.).
12. http://www.fairtrade-advocacy.org/images/charterfairtradeprinciples.pdf (accessed April 20, 2009).
13. International Labour Office. FT standards aim to complete ILO standards, which are considered as the minimum basis for any trading relationship.
14. Different expressions in the FINE definition reflect this hybrid character: "market access," "sustainable and equitable trading partnership," "equity in international trade," "sustainable development," "better trading conditions," "securing rights," "raising awareness and campaigning," etc.
15. It is worth noting that other authors identify three similar dimensions, albeit with other names (Diaz Pedregal 2007).
16. The main Fair Trade label is managed by Fairtrade International and applies to most food products (coffee, bananas, etc.). Such a label guarantees the respect of a range of social and environmental standards, beyond which FTSEs are free to bring additional producer-oriented benefits. The Gold Standards developed by Cafédirect, a British FT coffee company, are an example of such benefits. In the craft sector, where no product-related label exists but where WFTO proposes a certification system for FTSEs, producer support practices are also heterogeneous among FTSEs.
17. The FT practice and literature also use the notions of "marginalized" or "small" (see Lemay 2007 for a discussion of these notions).

18. To differentiate FT from ethical labels in which part of the sales are donated to social projects involving producer organizations, FT operators and networks often underline the fact that in FT, the social mission is rooted in the economic partnership itself, through the payment of a fair price and a long-term relationship.

19. FT is seen as located, for instance, between "market" and "solidarity" (Poncelet, Defourny, and De Pelsmacker 2005), or between "social movement" and "business" (Raynolds and Long 2007).

20. http://www.WFTO.com/index.php?option=com_content&task=view&id=1 53&Itemid=186&lang=en (accessed September 13, 2009). This excludes the organizations and networks that are only engaged in promoting and advocating for FT from the scope of this study. These structures are viewed here as major stakeholders of FTSEs, but not as FTSEs themselves.

21. http://www.ica.coop/coop/principles.html (accessed April 18, 2008).

22. A fourth legal form, gaining increasing importance, is that of foundations.

23. "Economie sociale marchande."

24. For instance, the "Chantier de l'économie sociale" in Québec (from the nineties up to now), the resolution of the European Parliament (1997), the recent Walloon legislation (2008), etc.

25. Listings including FT are often observed in books and reports mapping the social economy (e.g., Defourny *et al.* 1999; Chavez and Monzón, 2007) or in public recognition schemes.

26. After having coordinated a report on FT handicraft (2008), SAW-B initiated and hosted the Belgian Fair Trade Federation (BFTF) during the process of its creation.

27. The "Chantier" organizes an annual "Fair of social economy and fair trade" (Gendron et al., 2009b).

28. For analyses of FT producer groups as social economy organizations, see Poncelet et al. (2005).

29. Legislation on FT has been developed in France and is in preparation in Belgium and Italy. The European Commission officially recognized FT, first in a 1999 statement, and recently through a more complete statement, issued on May 5, 2009 (http://trade.ec.europa.eu/doclib/docs/2009/may/tradoc_143089.pdf). The European parliament adopted a resolution in favor of FT in 2006. A key element in the public support to FT is the setting up of public procurement policies favoring FT. Besides the different national initiatives, EFTA initiated the Fair Procura project (now Buy Fair [www.buyfair. org]) to share practices and develop legal justifications for preferences to FT in the context of public tenders. Finally, the development of FT towns and countries, initiated in the UK and later replicated in Europe through the "Fairtrade Towns in Europe" EU-funded program, is a concrete example of public involvement in FT.

30. For example, Twin and Soli'gren, patronized by, respectively, the Greater London Council (1985) and the city of Grenoble (2005).

31. The link between democracy and voluntary work will be explored further.

32. In which all members, from the North and the South, have equal voting rights, leading to much control by producer groups, who represent the majority of the members.

33. Initially, only national labeling initiatives participated in FLO (now Fairtrade International). Producer groups were later associated with the definition of the labeling criteria. In December 2008, after a two-year reformation process, FLO formulated a new strategy, including a governance model that gives greater representation to producer groups, organized in three continental networks. Producers now represent one third of FLO's Board

members. (http://www.fairtrade.net/how_we_are_run.html, accessed May 27, 2009).

34. The concept of "public space" was inspired by Habermas (1974; 1992) and Giddens (1994), cited in Laville and Nyssens (2001).

35. For about a decade in WFTO, and much more recently in the case of FLO.

36. It has to be noted, though, that while UK scholars seem to have been historically more connected with American authors and approaches, Peattie and Morley (2008) suggest that, in terms of content, they are closer to continental European approaches.

37. The term social enterprise seems to be used more frequently in the UK than elsewhere, both by practitioners (e.g., Social Enterprise Coalition, Social Enterprise London, etc.), by academics and by the state (Social Enterprise Unit).

38. In a footnote (41), Dees and Battle Anderson explain that the term "Social Enterprise" has been chosen for this school of thought on the basis of a "convention," probably rooted in the American practice. They admit that such a term should ideally not be linked to one particular school of thought but that it should be left as a generic name. This work follows Defourny and Nyssens (2008a) who propose to call this school of thought the "Enterprising Nonprofit" school.

39. Examples include numerous collaborations between FTSEs and social enterprise networks (e.g., Social Enterprise London) or the examplification of FTSEs' leaders as social entrepreneurs (e.g., Penny Newman, former CEO of British FTSE Cafédirect, designated as "Social Enterprise Ambassador" in 2007).

40. "Social enterprises are part of the growing 'social economy'. The social economy is a thriving and growing collection of organizations that exist between the traditional private sector on the one hand, and the public sector on the other. Sometimes referred to as the "'third sector," it includes voluntary and community organizations, foundations and associations of many types. A social enterprise is a business with primarily social objectives whose surpluses are principally reinvested for that purpose in the business or the community, rather than being driven by the need to maximise profit for shareholders and owners." (Social Enterprise: A Strategy for Success, http://www.cabinetoffice.gov.uk/upload/assets/third_sector/se_strategy_2002.pdf (accessed June 16, 2009).

41. Notable exceptions include the work of several authors of the EMES network that link social enterprise with the intuitions of the solidarity economy (e.g., Laville and Nyssens, 2001).

## NOTES TO CHAPTER 2

1. This section is based on the author's general knowledge of the Belgian FT sector, interviews, several websites, reports written by the former Fair Trade Centre, Krier's reports (2005 and 2008), and Biélande, 2007. This text was reviewed and corrected by several people at the Trade for Development Centre and the Belgian Fair Trade Federation. The author acknowledges their useful help and comments.

2. Concerning the other pioneer nonprofit FTSEs, Fair Trade Original and Sjamma were not subsidized, whereas Weltladen was, but mainly at the local level.

3. www.befair.be

4. Fédération des entreprises de Belgique.

5. See the 2008 report "Les entreprises font la différence avec le commerce durable" (Vancronenburg 2008)
6. See www.befair.be, and particularly the 2008 report written by Samuel Poos and available at http://www.befair.be/site/download.cfm?SAVE=17774&LG=2.
7. This section is based on the interviews, several websites, reports (Krier, 2005; 2008; Sarrazin-Biteye, 2009) and a book on FT in France (Diaz-Pedregal, 2007). The PFCE as well as several French academics (Carimentrand, Diaz-Pedregal, Gateau, and Ozcaglar-Toulouse) kindly helped improving this text.
8. A good example is that of Christian Jacquiau's book "Les coulisses du commerce equitable." While criticizing part of the FT system—the labeling function of Max Havelaar—his book had an impact on the whole French FT sector, leading to serious debates and to reinforced divisions among FTSEs.
9. This section is based on the interviews, several websites (BAFTS, Fairtrade Foundation, etc.), Anderson (2009a, 2009b), Moore (2004; 2006; 2009), Nicholls (2010), Krier's reports (2005 and 2008) and the Fair Trade Knowledge Transfer Workshop in Cardiff.
10. Traidcraft was created by people from Tearcraft, an older FTSEs with an even clearer and exclusive Christian identity (Anderson, 2009a).
11. http://www.fairtrade.org.uk/what_is_fairtrade/history.aspx
12. Cooperative supermarket chains have been pionners in retailing FT products in countries such as the UK, Italy, and Switzerland. This is why certain authors from these countries suggest that the involvement of these supermarkets in FT should be distinguished from that of conventional supermarkets (e.g., Nicholls and Opal, 2005).
13. This section is based on the interviews, several websites, Krier's reports (2005 and 2008), and the articles by Viganò et al. (2008) and Becchetti and Costantino (2010).
14. Translated and adapted from http://www.altromercato.it/it/info/chi_siamo/storia.
15. Associazione Italiana dei Parlementari per il Commercio Equo.
16. Indeed, the observation of any set of organizations could lead to the conclusion of organizational diversity. The goal here is to show that the diversity of forms is fundamental and reflects different visions of FT, as explained in the Chapter 1.
17. More details about the way in which the information was compiled and processed may be found in the PhD thesis on which this book is based (Huybrechts 2010a).
18. The PFCE suggested avoiding the central region of Ile-de-France, in which FTSEs were regularly solicited for various studies. The PFCE was, moreover, also interested in having more information about FTSEs from other regions.
19. www.equisol.org
20. Coordination lyonnaise des acteurs du commerce équitable.
21. www.bafts.org.uk

## NOTES TO CHAPTER 3

1. Mintzberg's 1980 article only mentions the first five mechanisms.
2. FTSEs in which other stakcholders besides volunteers are involved to a significant extent, with real influence on decision-making—at least from the standpoint of the manager—are included in the multi-stakeholder category.
3. Readers interested in the statistical construction of this cluster analysis may find more details in the PhD thesis on which this book is based (Huybrechts 2010).

4. These associates may have invested in the venture only to support the entrepreneur, or they may participate more actively in the decision-making.
5. At Oxfam-MDM, for instance, such equality has declined with the growth of the organization, and even more so since people with business experience were hired at the management level. Such a differentiation has been even stronger in group structures such as Oxfam-WW and Max Havelaar.
6. Traidcraft website (accessed January 30, 2008).
7. These exceptions partly correspond to the FTSEs that were difficult to categorize completely in type 2, for instance, Fair Trade Original (which is manager-owned but nonprofit) and Cafédirect (which has a business form but which is not manager-owned).
8. Internal documents elaborated in 2007 and 2008.

## NOTES TO CHAPTER 4

1. Also in political science, feeding approaches such as resource dependence theory, which will be mentioned further. The focus for this work, however, is laid on sociology and economics.
2. Certain authors, however, question Williamson's and other contractual authors' use of rationality, which appears boundless in several aspects (Slitter and Spencer 2000, 71): "It makes little sense to speak of people suffering from bounded rationality when they simultaneously retain the capacity for farsightedness, allowing them to foresee a way round the problems of complexity and uncertainty at the outset of contracting."
3. Including its two schools of thought, although it is the second, transaction cost approach which will primarily be used here.
4. For an analysis of the opposition between the deterministic, system-based view, and the actor-based view, a classical reference is Crozier and Friedberg (1977).

## NOTES TO CHAPTER 5

1. "Ownership arrangement," "institutional arrangement," "contractual configuration," and "governance structure" are terms that are used more or less as synonyms in the contractual literature. The terms "organizational form" or "organizational model" will be used uniformly throughout the theoretical approaches.
2. For instance, Milgrom and Roberts, in their handbook on organizational economics, state as given that the structure and design of organizations is determined by the desire of economic agents to minimize their transaction costs (40).
3. It is worth noting that consumers (and not just producers) are also indirect beneficiaries of producer support (Becchetti and Huybrechts 2008). Recent theoretical advances in experimental economics have documented that fairness and inequity aversion play an important role in consumer preferences. Consumers with such preferences buy FT products not for pure altruism but also to satisfy their specific preferences (Fehr and Schmidt 1999, 2002; Sobel 2005).
4. The complexity of the information asymmetry in FT products is that the social dimension of producer support does not correspond to an "experience good." In other words, while many dimensions of information asymmetries about product quality may be overcome by purchase and taste, repeated

purchase of FT products cannot help consumers to verify the truthfulness of the FTSE regarding the ethical dimension of the products.

5. As we have seen in the theoretical chapter, the second contractual school of thought, largely centered around transaction cost theory, has a more complex and "extra-contractual" view on organizations that takes into account bounded rationality and the incompleteness of contracts.

6. A category of stakeholders who have the right to claim the profits of the organization (Milgrom and Roberts 1992).

7. Obviously, there is always some interest, at least symbolic, in the participation of any stakeholder. In this context, "selfless" means that these stakeholders have no explicitly recognized material interest in the success of the organization in which they are involved.

8. Although authors like Davies and Crane (2003) describe FTSEs such as Divine Chocolate as "for-profit."

9. Other terms such as "mainstream" (as opposed to "alternative") or "capitalist" are even more ambiguous because they refer to the philosophy rather than the form. Indeed, a cooperative or even a nonprofit can appear to display very mainstream, capitalist behavior.

10. Because most of the shares are invested on the long term and because the remuneration depends on the firm's results.

11. With already a few exceptions of pioneer FTSEs such as Solidar'monde or Siesta, although the "investor-owned" nature of these FTSEs may be discussed.

12. Large at least on the scale of FT.

13. It should be noted that economists such as Hansmann totally disagree with this, considering cooperatives closer to mainstream corporations than to nonprofits.

14I. ndeed, each FTSE is governed by people who are very likely to be customers of the FTSE. But it is not their principal relationship with the FTSE: they are primarily volunteers, employees, etc.

15. Advantages include special offers, free "goodies" and regular news about the FTSE.

## NOTES TO CHAPTER 6

1. Author's translation; nonprofit is originally "association."

2. For instance, Nicaraguan coffee imported during the 1980 revolution.

3. If we translate this into Suchman's (1995) distinctions of legitimacies, it would correspond to "structural legitimacy"—the fact that producers own the FTSE make it legitimate—rather than "consequential legitimacy"—the FTSE is legitimate because it proves to have a real impact on producers.

4. As already mentioned, this does not necessarily mean that 100% of the products are strictly speaking FT, but that the majority of them are, with the remainder being coherent with the FT principles (local FT, social economy, organic, etc.).

5. Examples include Equisol and the PFCE in France, and the Trade for Development Centre in Belgium.

6. This is not to say that social entrepreneurial dynamics cannot be found in the two previous waves, especially in the context of mainstreaming). But the individual-centered, innovative, and risk-taking description of social entrepreneurial dynamics has been much more explicitly observed in FTSEs of the "third wave."

7. In France, Italy, and Belgium, it is new FT shops that first proposed local products (for instance, organic wine from Rhône-Alpes winegrowers, food

produced on Sicilian fields taken back from the Mafia, etc.). These products have been considered coherent with the "traditional" Southern FT products and have generally been successful among FT consumers.

8. For instance, having the products transformed or packaged by work integration enterprises or small artisans, or looking for more ethical transportation and storing companies.

9. Most of these new entrepreneurs have thus limited knowledge of the changes that certain pioneer FTSEs have undertaken, as described in the previous section (for instance, at Oxfam-WW).

10. www.espritequo.com (accessed April 18, 2008).

11. The observations in the Roman area seem convergent with the analyses of Viganò *et al.* (2005), and Becchetti and Costantino (2010) at the country's level.

12. In Italy, the term "nonprofit" is used by many field actors and academics to designate both nonprofit and cooperative organizations. Here, "nonprofit" is used the narrow sense as defined in the economic literature.

13. Initially "social solidarity cooperatives"

14. In 2005, there where 7,300 social cooperatives, employing nearly 250,000 people. The number of social cooperatives has been increasing by 10 to 20% each year (Borzaga, Galera, and Zandonai 2008, 26).

15. This does not mean that this was a purposive action, especially since FT was only timidly emerging at the time of the formulation of the law. But the fact is that there was a massive adoption of that form by Italian FTSEs. Funding opportunities did not play an important role, since the Italian FTSEs mostly chose the "type A" model, which is not accompanied by particular funding opportunities or fiscal preferences (contrarily to the "type B" model).

16. See Chapter 1 for a brief description of these principles.

17. These are the main principles to which the SFS have to subscribe: limitation of profit distribution to a maximum rate (currently 6%); pursuit of a social mission; prohibition to appropriate the assets of the organization in case of liquidation; limitation of the maximal voting power in the GA (5%).

18. As shown through the support of the Walloon Minister of Economy for the strengthening of the BFTF.

19. "Société coopérative de production" as defined by the law of July 19, 1978.

20. "Société coopérative d'intérêt collectif," as defined by the law of July 17, 2001, and completed by the law of February 21, 2002.

21. The French law on cooperatives dates back to September 10, 1947, and recognizes the specific identity of cooperatives (Conseil Supérieur de la Coopération, *Le mouvement coopératif en France*, Rapport 2007).

22. Two business-form FTSEs in the French study explicitly mentioned Alter Eco as their "model."

23. The focus is on the entrepreneur as the central figure (www.quatre-mats.org).

24. Contrary to the unincorporated association, where members are personally liable for the association's actions.

## NOTES TO CHAPTER 7

1. www.commercioalternativo.it (accessed June 15, 2008).

2. Although CTM, whose products were available in supermarkets but without a label, resumed its collaboration with Transfair Italy in 2008.

3. Plate-forme marocaine pour le commerce équitable—www.pmce-info.org (accessed June 15, 2008).

4. In the sense that references to FT in communication and marketing were only implicit.
5. Oxfam-MDM depicted Citizen Dream as an example of a "FT light" initiative.
6. Part of the products, however, were not explicitly FT and were referred to as "ethical trade."
7. For instance, a WFTO consultant.
8. Such as Fair Trade Original.
9. Another business-form FTSE, Fierros, was even active in FT before this date, but it had much less recognition.
10. Particularly the rapid growth and the lack of awareness about the fixed costs inherent in retailing.
11. The task, however, is even more difficult because the failure of Citizen Dream made certain banks particularly reluctant to give loans to FT businesses.
12. This is a strong difference, for instance, with the Agices network.
13. This does not mean that they have been less favorable to the pioneers' participation, which has been crucial for the success and the legitimacy of this federation. But there has been a real intent to network beyond the pioneer FTSEs, by including the growing category of small business-form FTSEs, seen as a promising path to the further extension of FT.
14. The project is described in an internal, confidential document.
15. Recently, the political unit precisely explored and promoted the political dimension of partnerships with producers.
16. According to one of its managers, ComES stopped its collaboration with CTM in 1998 because it no longer wanted to be limited to and thus constrained by one importer only. ComES rather preferred to open its shops to the diverse importers that emerged during the 1990s.
17. Officially, there are in fact three entities: two nonprofit associations and one cooperative. One of the nonprofits, however, is mainly a formal structure that has currently no operational activity.

# Bibliography

Abzug, Rikki, and Natalie J. Webb. 1999. "Relationships Between Nonprofit and For-Profit Organizations: A Stakeholder Perspective." *Nonprofit and Voluntary Sector Quarterly* no. 28 (4):416–431.

Akerlof, George. 1970. "The Market for 'Lemons': Quality Uncertainty and the Market Mechanism." *Quarterly Journal of Economics* no. 84:487–500.

Alchian, Armen, and Harold Demsetz. 1972. "Production, Information Costs and Economic Organization." *American Economic Review* no. 62:77–95.

Anderson, Matthew. 2009a. "'Cost of Cup of Tea': Fair Trade and the British Co-operative Movement, c. 1960–2000." In *Consumerism and the Co-operative movement in modern British history*, edited by L. Black and N. Robertson. Manchester: Manchester University Press.

———. 2009b. "NGOs and Fair Trade: The Social Movement Behind the Label." In *NGOs in Contemporary Britain: Non-state Actors in Society and Politics since 1945*, edited by N. Crowson, M. Hilton and J. McKay. Houndmills: Palgrave Macmillan.

Andreoni, James. 1990. "Impure Altruism and Donations to Public Goods: A Theory of Warm-Glow." *Economic Journal* no. 100 (464–477).

Anheier, Helmut K. 2005. *Nonprofit Organizations: Theory, Management, Policy*. London: Routledge.

Anheier, Helmut K., and Walter Seibel. 1990. *The third sector: comparative studies of non-profit organizations*. New York: De Gruyter.

Arrow, Kenneth. 1987. "Reflections on the Essays." In *Arrow and the Foundations of the Theory of Economic Policy*, edited by George Feiwel, 727–734. New York: New York University Press.

Auroi, Claude, and Isabel Yepez del Castillo. 2006. *Economie solidaire et commerce équitable : acteurs et actrices d'Europe et d'Amérique Latine*. Louvain-la-Neuve: Presses Universitaires de Louvain.

Austin, James B. 1998. "Business Leaders and Nonprofits." *Nonprofit Management & Leadership* no. 9:39.

Austin, James E. 2000. "Strategic Collaboration Between Nonprofits and Businesses." *Nonprofit and Voluntary Sector Quarterly* no. 29 (1):69–97.

Austin, James, and Ezequiel Reficco. 2005. "Corporate Social Entrepreneurship." *Harvard Business School Working Paper* no. 09–101.

Austin, James, Howard Stevenson, and Jane Wei-Skillern. 2006. "Social and Commercial Entrepreneurship: Same, Different, or Both?" *Entrepreneurship: Theory & Practice* no. 30 (1):1–22.

Bacchiega, Alberto, and Carlo Borzaga. 2001. "Social Enterprises as Incentive Structures." In *The Emergence of Social Enterprise*, edited by Carlo Borzaga and Jacques Defourny, 273–295. London and New York: Routledge.

BAFTS. 2003. The story so far. London: British Association for Fair Trade Shops.

Balineau, Gaëlle, and Ivan Dufeu. 2010. "Are Fair Trade Goods Credence Goods? A New Proposal, with French Illustrations." *Journal of Business Ethics* no. 92 (0):331–345.

Ballet, Jérôme, and Aurélie Carimentrand. 2008. La transformation du commerce équitable : de l'éthique relationnelle à l'éthique informationnelle. Paper read at 3ième colloque RIODD : Responsabilité sociale et environnementale, nouvelles formes organisationnelles, 6–8 Juin 2008, at Lyon.

———. 2010. "Fair Trade and the Depersonalization of Ethics." *Journal of Business Ethics* no. 92 (0):317–330.

Barney, Jay B., and William Hesterly. 1996. "Organizational Economics: Understanding the Relationship between Organizations and Economic Analysis." In *Studying Organization. Theory & Method*, edited by Stewart R. Clegg and Cynthia Hardy. London: Sage Publications.

Battilana, Julie, and Thomas D'Aunno. 2009. "Institutional work and the paradox of embedded agency." In *Institutional Work*, edited by Thomas B. Lawrence, Roy Suddaby and Bernard Leca. Cambridge: Cambridge University Press.

Battilana, Julie, and Silvia Dorado. 2010. "Building sustainable hybrid organizations: the case of commercial microfinance organizations." *Academy of Management Journal* no. 53 (6):1419–1440.

Battle Anderson, Beth , and J. Gregory Dees. 2006. "Rhetoric, Reality, and Research: Building a Solid Foundation for the Practice of Social Entrepreneurship." In *Social Entrepreneurship. New Models of Sustainable Social Change*, edited by Alex Nicholls, 144–168. Oxford: Oxford University Press.

Becchetti, Leonardo, and Fabrizio Adriani. 2002. Fair Trade: A 'Third Generation Welfare' Mechanism to make Globalisation Sustainable. In *CEIS Working Paper*. Rome: Centre of International Studies on Economic Growth.

Becchetti, Leonardo, and Marco Costantino. 2010. "Fair Trade in Italy: Too Much 'Movement' in the Shop?" *Journal of Business Ethics* no. 92 (0):181–203.

Becchetti, Leonardo, and Benjamin Huybrechts. 2008. "The Dynamics of Fair Trade as a Mixed-form Market." *Journal of Business Ethics* no. 81 (4):733–750.

Becchetti, Leonardo, and Furio Rosati. 2005. The demand for socially responsible products: empirical evidence from a pilot study on fair trade consumers. Palma de Mallorca: Society for the Study of Economic Inequality.

Ben-Ner, Avner. 2002. "The shifting boundaries of the mixed economy and the future of the nonprofit sector." *Annals of Public and Cooperative Economics* no. 73 (1):5–40.

Ben-Ner, Avner, and Benedetto Gui. 2000. "The Theory of Nonprofit Organizations Revisited " In *The Study of the Nonprofit Enterprise: Theories and Approaches*, edited by Helmut K. Anheier and Avner Ben-Ner, 3–26. New York: Kluwer Academic/Plenum Publishers.

Ben-Ner, Avner, and Teresa Van Hoomissen. 1991. "Nonprofit Organizations in the Mixed Economy: A Demand and Supply Analysis." *Annals of Public and Cooperative Economics* no. 62 (4):519–550.

Bezençon, Valéry, and Sam Blili. 2009. "Fair Trade Managerial Practices: Strategy, Organisation and Engagement." *Journal of Business Ethics* no. 90 (1):95–113.

Billis, David. 2010. *Hybrid Organizations and the Third Sector. Challenges for Practice, Theory and Policy*. New York: Palgrave-MacMillan.

Birchall, J. 1997. *The International Cooperative Movement*. Manchester: Manchester University Press.

Bisaillon, Véronique, Corinne Gendron, and Marie-France Turcotte. 2005a. "Commerce équitable comme vecteur de développement durable." *Nouvelles pratiques sociales* no. 18 (1):73–90.

———. 2005b. Commerce équitable et économie solidaire : les défis pour l'avenir. In *Synthèse des activités du Chantier Commerce Equitable*. Montréal: Chaire de responsabilité sociale et de développement durable—UQAM.

Black, Duncan. 1948. "On the Rationale of Group Decision-making." *Journal of Political Economy* no. 56:23–34.

Blumberg, Boris, Donald R. Cooper, and Pamela S. Schindler. 2005. *Business Research Methods*. Maidenhead: McGraw-Hill.

Borzaga, Carlo, Giulia Galera, and Flaviano Zandonai. 2008. "Italy." In *Social Enterprise in Europe: Recent Trends and Developments*, edited by Jacques Defourny and Marthe Nyssens. Liège: EMES European Research Network.

Borzaga, Carlo, and Roger Spear. 2004. *Trends and challenges for Co-operatives and Social Enterprises in developed and transition countries*. Trento: Edizione 31.

Boyne, George A. 1998. "Bureaucratic Theory Meets Reality: Public Choice and Service Contracting in U.S. Local Government." *Public Administration Review* no. 58 (6):474–484.

Campi, Sarah, Jacques Defourny, and Olivier Grégoire. 2006. "Work integration social enterprises: are they multiple-goal and multi-stakeholder organizations?" In *Social Enterprise. At the crossroads of market, public policies and civil society.*, edited by Marthe Nyssens. London: Routledge.

Cannella, Marilèna. 2003. *La société à finalité sociale. Un succès ou un coup dans l'eau?, Prix Roger Vanthournout*. Bruxelles: Luc Pire.

Charlier, Sophie, Isabelle Haynes, Amandine Bach, Alexis Mayet, Isabel Yepez del Castillo, and Marc Mormont. 2007. Fair trade facing new commercial challenges: evolution of the actors' dynamics. Brussels: Belgian Science Policy.

Charreaux, Gérard. 1997. *Le gouvernement des entreprises—Corporate Governance, Théorie et Faits*. Paris: Economica.

Chavez, Rafael, and José Luis Monzón Campos. 2007. The Social Economy in the European Union. Brussels: CIRIEC International & The European Economic and Social Committee (EESC).

Clegg, Stewart R., and Cynthia Hardy. 1999. "Introduction." In *Studying Organization. Theory & Method*, edited by Stewart R. Clegg and Cynthia Hardy. London: Sage Publications.

Coase, Ronald. 1937. "The Nature of the Firm." *Economica* no. 4:386–405.

———. 1998. "The New Institutional Economics." *American Economic Review* no. 88:72–74.

Cornforth, Chris. 2003. "Introduction: the changing context of governance—emerging issues and paradoxes." In *The Governance of Public and Non-Profit Organisations. What do boards do?*, edited by Chris Cornforth. New York: Routledge.

———. 2004. "The Governance of Cooperatives and Mutual Associations: a Paradox Perspective." *Annals of Public and Cooperative Economics* no. 75 (1):11–32.

Cornforth, Chris, and Charles Edwards. 1999. "Board Roles in the Strategic Management of Non-profit Organisations: theory and practice." *Corporate Governance: An International Review* no. 7 (4):346–362.

Cornforth, Chris, and Claire Simpson. 2002. "Change and Continuity in the Governance of Nonprofit Organizations in the United Kingdom." *Nonprofit Management & Leadership* no. 12 (4):451–468.

Crowell, Erbin, and Darryl Reed. 2009. "Fair Trade: A Model for International Co-operation Among Co-operatives?" In *Co-operatives in a Global Economy: The Challenges of Co-operation Across Borders*, edited by Darryl Reed and J.J. McMurtry, 141–177. Newcastle upon Tyne: Cambridge Scholars Publishing.

Crozier, Michel, and Erhard Friedberg. 1977. *L'acteur et le système*. Paris: Editions du Seuil.

Dart, Raymond. 2004. "The legitimacy of social enterprise." *Nonprofit Management & Leadership* no. 14 (4):411–424.

Davies, Iain. 2009. "Alliances and Networks: Creating Success in the UK Fair Trade Market." *Journal of Business Ethics* no. 86 (0):109–126.

Davies, Iain A., and Andrew Crane. 2003. "Ethical Decision Making in Fair Trade Companies." *Journal of Business Ethics* no. 45:79–92.

Davies, Iain, Bob Doherty, and Simon Knox. 2010. "The Rise and Stall of a Fair Trade Pioneer: The Cafédirect Story." *Journal of Business Ethics* no. 92 (1):127–147.

Davis, Lance E., and Douglass C. North. 1971. *Institutional Change and American Economic Growth*. Cambridge: Cambridge University Press.

De Pelsmacker, P. , L. Driesen, and G. Rayp. 2005. "Do Consumers Care about Ethics? Willingness-to-pay for Fair Trade Coffee." *Journal of Consumer Affairs* no. 39 (2):363–385.

Dees, J. Gregory. 2001. The Meaning of "Social Entrepreneurship". The Fuqua School of Business, Duke University.

Dees, J. Gregory, and B. Beth Anderson. 2006. Framing a Theory of Social Entrepreneurship: Building on Two Schools of Practice and Thought. In *Research on Social Entrepreneurship: Understanding and Contributing to an Emerging Field*: Association for Research on Nonprofit Organizations and Voluntary Action (ARNOVA).

Defourny, Jacques. 2001. "From Third Sector to Social Enterprise." In *The Emergence of Social Enterprise*, edited by Carlo Borzaga and Jacques Defourny, 1–28. London: Routledge.

Defourny, Jacques, and Patrick Develtere. 1999. "Origines et contours de l'économie sociale au Nord et au Sud." In *L'économie sociale au Nord et au Sud*, edited by Jacques Defourny, Patrick Develtere and Bénédicte Fonteneau, 25–56. Bruxelles: De Boeck.

Defourny, Jacques, Patrick Develtere, and Bénédicte Fonteneau. 2000. *Social Economy North and South*. Leuven: Katholieke Universiteit Leuven.

Defourny, Jacques, and José Luis Monzón Campos. 1992. *The Third Sector. Cooperative, Mutual and Non-profit Organizations*. Brussels: De Boeck.

Defourny, Jacques, and Marthe Nyssens. 2006. "Defining social enterprise." In *Social Enterprise. At the crossroads of market, public policies and civil society*, edited by Marthe Nyssens, 3–26. London: Routledge.

———. 2008a. Conceptions of Social Enterprise in Europe and in the United States. A Comparative Analysis. Paper read at 8th ISTR International Conference and 2nd EMES-ISTR European Conference: "The Third Sector and Sustainable Social Change: New Frontiers for Research", at Barcelona.

———. 2008b. "Social Enterprise in Europe: Recent Trends and Developments." *EMES Working Paper* no. 08 (01).

Defourny, Jacques, Michel Simon, and Sophie Adam. 2002. *Les coopératives en Belgique, un mouvement d'avenir ?* Bruxelles: Luc Pire.

Delaval, Jean-Michel. 2003. Le commerce équitable : un défi lancé à la théorie économique. In *Working Paper*. Liège: Université de Liège.

den Hond, Frank, and Frank de Bakker. 2007. "Ideologically Motivated Activism: How Activist Groups Influence Corporate Social Change Activities." *Academy of Management Review* no. 32 (3):901–924.

Develtere, Patrick, and Ignace Pollet. 2005. Co-operatives and Fair Trade. In *COPAC Open Forum on Fair Trade and Cooperatives*. Berlin.

Di Domenico, MariaLaura, Helen Haugh, and Paul Tracey. 2010. "Social Bricolage: Theorizing Social Value Creation in Social Enterprises." *Entrepreneurship Theory and Practice* no. 34 (4):681–703.

Diaz Pedregal, Virginie. 2006. "Participer au développement du commerce équitable dans les pays du Nord : caractéristiques sociales du personnel des structures de commerce équitable et stratégies de légitimation de la profession." In *De l'intérêt général à l'utilité sociale—La reconfiguration de l'action publique entre État, associations et participation citoyenne*, edited by Xavier Engels, Matthieu Hély, Aurélie Peyrin and Hélène Trouvé. Paris: L'Harmattan.

———. 2007. *Le commerce équitable dans la France contemporaine. Idéologies et pratiques, Logiques sociales*. Paris: L'Harmattan.

DiMaggio, Paul. 1988. "Interest and agency in institutional theory." In *Institutional patterns and organizations*, edited by Lynne G. Zucker, 3–22. Cambridge, MA: Ballinger.

———. 1991. "Constructing an Organizational Field as a Professional Project: U.S. Art Museums, 1920–1940." In *The New Institutionalism in Organizational Analysis*, edited by Walter W. Powell and Paul J. DiMaggio. Chicago: The University of Chicago Press.

DiMaggio, Paul, and Walter Powell. 1983. "The Iron Cage Revisited: Institutional Isomorphism and Collective Rationality in Organizational Fields." *American Sociological Review* no. 48 (2):147–160.

Doherty, Bob, and Sophi Tranchell. 2007. ""Radical mainstreaming" of fairtrade: the case of The Day Chocolate Company." *Equal Opportunities International* no. 26 (7):693–711.

Dorado, Silvia. 1999. Institutional Entrepreneurs. Engineers, catalysts, and innovators. Paper read at Academy of Management Conference, at Chicago.

Dubois, François-Xavier. 2003. *Associations et Fondations*. Heule: UGA.

Eisenhardt, Kathleen M., and Melissa E. Graebner. 2007. "Theory building from cases: opportunities and challenges." *Academy of Management Journal* no. 50 (1):25–32.

Eme, Bernard, and Jean-Louis Laville. 1994. "Économie plurielle, économie solidaire ; précisions et compléments." *Revue du MAUSS* no. 1996/1 (7).

Emerson, Jed, and Fay Twersky. 1996. *New social entrepreneurs: The success, challenge, and lessons of non-profit enterprise creation.* . San Francisco: The Roberts Foundation.

Enjolras, Bernard. 2000. "Coordination failure, property rights and non-profit organizations." *Annals of Public and Cooperative Economics* no. 71 (3):347–374.

Evers, Adalbert. 1995. "Part of the welfare mix: the Third Sector as an intermediate area." *Voluntas* no. 6 (2):119–139.

Evers, Adalbert, and Jean-Louis Laville. 2004. "Defining the Third Sector in Europe." In *The Third Sector in Europe*, edited by Adalbert Evers and Jean-Louis Laville. Cheltenham, UK and Northampton, USA: Edward Elgar Publishing.

Ezzamel, Mahmoud, and Robert Watson. 1983. "Organizational Form, Ownership Structure and Corporate Performance: A Contextual Empirical Analysis of UK Companies." *British Journal of Management* no. 4 (3):161–176.

Fama, Eugene F., and Michael C. Jensen. 1983. "Separation of Ownership and Control." *Journal of Law & Economics* no. 26 (2):301–325.

Fehr, Ernst, and Klaus M. Schmidt. 1999. "A Theory of Fairness, Competition and Cooperation." *Quarterly Journal of Economics* no. 114:817–868.

———. 2002. "The Economics of Fairness and Reciprocity. Evidence and economic applications." In *Advances in Economic Theory. Eight World Congress of the Econometric Society*, edited by Mattias Dewatripont, Lars Peter Hansen and Stephen J. Turnovsky, 208–257. Cambridge: Cambridge University Press.

FLO-I. 2010. Growing Stronger Together. Annual Report 2009–2010. Bonn: Fairtrade Labelling Organizations International.

Foss, Nicolai. 1993. "Theories of the firm: contractual and competence perspectives." no. 3:127–144.

Fraisse, Laurent. 2008. "France." In *Social Enterprise in Europe: Recent Trends and Developments*, edited by Jacques Defourny and Marthe Nyssens. Liège: EMES European Research Network.

Fridell, Gavin. 2003. "Fair trade and the international moral economy: within and against the market." *CERLAC Working Paper.*

———. 2009. "The Co-Operative and the Corporation: Competing Visions of the Future of Fair Trade." *Journal of Business Ethics* no. 86 (0):81–95.

Friedland, Roger, and Robert R. Alford. 1991. "Bringing Society Back In." In *The New Institutionalism in Organizational Analysis*, edited by Walter W. Powell and Paul J. DiMaggio. Chicago: The University of Chicago Press.

Galaskiewicz, Joseph, and Michelle Sinclair Colman. 2006. "Collaboration between Corporations and Nonprofit Organizations." In *The Nonprofit Sector. A Research Handbook.*, edited by Walter Powell and Richard Steinberg, 180–204. New Haven: Yale University Press.

Galera, Giulia. 2004. "The evolution of the co-operative form: an international perspective." In *Trends and challenges for Co-operatives and Social Enterprises in developed and transition countries*, edited by Carlo Borzaga and Robert Spear. Trento: Edizione 31.

Gardner, Charles A., Tara Acharya, and Derek Yach. 2007. "Technological And Social Innovation: A Unifying New Paradigm For Global Health." *Health Affairs* no. 26 (4):1052–1061.

Gateau, Matthieu. 2008. Le changement d'échelle du commerce équitable, une réalité empirique. Analyse localisée de l'évolution de deux associations en Bourgogne. Paper read at 3rd Fair Trade International Symposium, at Montpellier, France.

Gendron, Corinne. 2004a. "Le commerce équitable: un nouveau mouvement socio-économique au coeur d'une autre mondialisation." In *Altermondialisation, économie et coopération internationale*, edited by L. Favreau, G. Larose and A. Salam Fall. Paris: Karthala.

———. 2004b. Un nouveau mouvement socio-économique au coeur d'une autre mondialisation: le commerce équitable. In *Comparaisons Internationales.* Ottawa: Chaire de Recherche en Développement des Collectivités (Université du Québec en Outaouais).

Gendron, Corinne, Véronique Bisaillon, and Ana Rance. 2009. "The Institutionalization of Fair Trade: More than Just a Degraded Form of Social Action." *Journal of Business Ethics* no. 86 (0):63–79.

Gendron, Corinne, Arturo Palma Torres, and Véronique Bisaillon. 2009. *Quel commerce équitable pour demain? Pour une nouvelle gouvernance des échanges.* Montréal & Paris: Ecosociété & Charles Léopold Mayer.

Glaeser, Edward L. 2003. *The Governance of Not-for-Profit Organizations.* Edited by National Bureau of Economic Research. Chicago: The University of Chicago Press.

González, Alma Amalia, and Flurina Doppler. 2006. "El Comercio Justo: entre la institucionalización y la confianza." *Problemas de Desarrollo* no. 38 (149):181–202.

Grenier, Corinne, and Emmanuel Josserand. 2007. "Recherches sur le contenu et recherches sur le processus." In *Méthodes de recherche en management*, edited by Raymond-Alain Thiétart. Paris: Dunod.

Grenier, Paola. 2006. "Social Entrepreneurship: Agency in a Globalizing World." In *Social Entrepreneurship. New Models of Sustainable Social Change*, edited by Alex Nicholls, 119–143. Oxford: Oxford University Press.

Gui, Benedetto. 1987. "Productive Private Nonprofit Organizations. A Conceptual Framework." *Annals of Public and Cooperative Economics* no. 58 (4):415–434.

———. 1991. "The Economic Rationale for the 'Third Sector'. Nonprofit and other Noncapitalist Organizations." *Annals of Public and Cooperative Economics* no. 62 (4):551–572.

Handy, Femida. 1997. "Coexistence of nonprofit, for-profit and public sector institutions." *Annals of Public and Cooperative Economics* no. 68 (2):201–223.

Hansmann, Henry. 1980. "The Role of Non-Profit Enterprise." *Yale Law Journal* no. 89 (5):835–901.

———. 1988. "The Ownership of the Firm." *Journal of Law, Economics and Organizations* no. 4 (2):267–304.

———. 1996. *The Ownership of Enterprise.* Cambridge: Harvard University Press.

———. 1999. "Cooperative Firms in Theory and Practice." *Finish Journal of Business Economics* no. 4:387–403.

Harrow, Jenny, and Paul Palmer. 2003. "The Financial Role of Charity Boards." In *The Governance of Public and Non-Profit Organisations. What do boards do?*, edited by Chris Cornforth. New York: Routledge.

Hatch, Mary Jo. 1999. *Théorie des organisations. De l'intérêt de perspectives multiples., Management.* Bruxelles: De Boeck Université.

Hayes, Mark. 2006. "On the Efficiency of Fair Trade." *Review of Social Economy* no. 64 (4):447–468.

Haynes, Isabelle. 2006. "Défis et tensions dans le commerce équitable : une approche bibliographique." In *Economie solidaire et commerce équitable : acteurs et actrices d'Europe et d'Amérique Latine*, edited by Claude Auroi and Isabel Yepez del Castillo. Louvain-la-Neuve: Presses Universitaires de Louvain.

Hervieux, Chantal. 2007. Le commerce équitable comme innovation sociale et économique : performance sociale et renouvellement des pratiques économiques. In *Les Cahiers de la CRSDD*. Montréal: Chaire de Responsabilité Sociale et de Développement Durable—UQAM.

———. 2008. Les enjeux de l'entrepreneurship social : le cas de Cooperative Coffees, une entreprise de commerce équitable au Nord. In *Cahier de la Chaire de responsabilité sociale et de développement durable.* Montréal.

Hiez, David. 2006. "Le coopérateur ouvrier ou la signification du principe de double qualité dans les Scop." *Revue Internationale de l'Economie Sociale (RECMA)* no. 299:34–55.

Hinings, Bob, Royston Greenwood, Trish Reay, and Roy Suddaby. 2004. "Dynamics of Change in Organizational Fields." In *Handbook of Organizational Change and Innovation*, edited by Andrew H. Van De Ven and Scott Poole. Oxford: Oxford University Press.

Hira, Anil, and Jared Ferrie. 2006. "Fair Trade: Three Key Challenges for Reaching the Mainstream." *Journal of Business Ethics* no. 63:107–118.

Hopkins, Raul. 2000. Impact Assessment Study of Oxfam Fair Trade. London: Oxfam Fair Trade Program.

Hutchens, Anna. 2009. *Changing Big Business. The Globalisation of the Fair Trade Movement.* Cheltenham: Edward Elgar.

Huybrechts, Benjamin. 2005. *L'impact du commerce équitable sur les producteurs. Le cas de coopératives de café et de cacao en Bolivie.*, DEA interuniversitaire en Développement, Environnement et Sociétés, Université de Liège, Liège.

———. 2007. "Fondements et implications de la diversité organisationnelle au sein du commerce équitable" *Annals of Public and Cooperative Economics* no 78 (2): 195–218.

———. 2010a. *Explaining Organisational Diversity in Fair Trade Social Enterprises*, HEC Management School, Université de Liège, Liège.

———. 2010b. "Fair Trade Organizations in Belgium: Unity in Diversity?" *Journal of Business Ethics* no. 92 (0):217–240.

———. 2010c. "The Governance of Fair Trade Social Enterprises in Belgium" *Social Enterprise Journal* no. 6 (2): 110–124.

Huybrechts, Benjamin, and Jacques Defourny. 2008. "Are Fair Trade Organizations necessarily Social Enterprises?" *Social Enterprise Journal* no. 4 (3):186–201.

Huybrechts, Benjamin, and Michèle Manigart. 2003. *Etude de la création du partenariat Oxfam-Wereldwinkels & Covica ; lancement en Belgique d'un vin biologique équitable chilien*, IAG, Université Catholique de Louvain, Louvain-la-Neuve.

Huybrechts, Benjamin, and Darryl Reed. 2010. "Introduction: "Fair Trade in Different National Contexts"." *Journal of Business Ethics* no. 92 (0):147–150.

Huybrechts, Benjamin, and Emilie Sarrazin-Biteye. 2008. Le nouveau paysage des acteurs du commerce équitable en France: évolutions et enjeux. Paper read at 3rd Fair Trade International Symposium, at Montpellier.

Hwang, Hokyu, and Walter W. Powell. 2005. "Institutions and Entrepreneurship." In *The Handbook of Entrepreneurship Research. Interdisciplinary Perspectives*, edited by Sharon .A. Alvarez, Rajshree Agarwal and Olav Sorenson, 179–210. Boston: Springer Science.

Immergut, Ellen M. 1998. "The Theoretical Core of the New Institutionalism." *Politics & Society* no. 26 (1):5–34.

Jackall, Robert. 1988. *Moral mazes: The world of corporate managers* New York: Oxford University Press.

Jaffee, Daniel. 2007. *Brewing Justice: Fair Trade Coffee, Sustainability and Survival*. Berkeley: University of California Press.

———. 2010. "Fair Trade Standards, Corporate Participation, and Social Movement Responses in the United States." *Journal of Business Ethics* no. 92 (0):267–285.

James, Estelle. 1990. "Economic Theories of the Nonprofit Sector: A Comparative Perspective." In *The Third Sector, Comparative Studies of Nonprofit Organisations*, edited by H.K. Anheier and W. Seibel, 21–30. Berlin: de Gruyter.

Jensen, Michael C., and William H. Meckling. 1976. "Theory of the firm: Managerial behaviour, agency costs and ownership structure." *Journal of Financial Economics* no. 3:305–360.

Jones, Stephen, Brendan Bayley, Sarah Roberts, and Nick Robin. 2000. Fair trade: overview, impact, challenges. London and Oxford: Oxford Policy Management and Sustainable Markets Group, International Institute for Environment and Development.

Kerlin, Janelle A. 2006. "Social Enterprise in the United States and Europe: Understanding and Learning from the Differences." *Voluntas: International Journal of Voluntary and Nonprofit Organizations* no. 17 (3):246–262.

———. 2008. A Comparative Analysis of the Global Emergence of Social Enterprise. Paper read at 8th ISTR Conference & 2nd EMES-ISTR Conference, at Barcelona.

Kingma, Bruce Robert. 1997. "Public good theories of the non-profit sector: Weisbrod revisited." *Voluntas* no. 8 (2):135–148.

Kraatz, Matthew S., and Emily S. Block. 2008. "Organizational Implications of Institutional Pluralism." In *Handbook of Organizational Institutionalism*, edited by Royston Greenwood, Christine Oliver, Roy Suddaby and Kerstin Sahlin-Andersson. London: Sage.

Krashinsky, Michael. 1986. "Transaction Costs and a Theory of Non-Profit Organizations " In *The Economics of Nonprofit Institutions*, edited by Susan Rose-Ackerman. Oxford: Oxford University Press.

Krier, Jean-Marie. 2005. Fair Trade in Europe 2005: facts and figures on Fair Trade in 25 European countries. edited by Fair Trade Advocacy Office. Brussels.

———. 2008. Fair Trade 2007: New Facts and Figures from an ongoing Success Story. Culemborg: Dutch Association of Worldshops.

Labie, Marc. 2005. "Economie sociale, tiers secteur, non-profit : à la recherche d'un cadre de gouvernance adéquat." In *Gouvernement d'entreprise. Enjeux managériaux, comptables et financiers*, edited by Alain Finet, 101–124. Bruxelles: De Boeck.

Lake, Rob, and Catherine Howe. 1998. The Development Impact of Fair Trade: Evidence from the work of Traidcraft and challenges for the future. Traidcraft Exchange.

Laville, Jean-Louis. 1994. *L'Economie solidaire. Une perspective internationale.* Paris: Desclée de Brouwer.

———. 2003. "Avec Mauss et Polanyi, vers une théorie de l'économie plurielle." *Revue du MAUSS* no. 2003/1 (21).

Laville, Jean-Louis, and Marthe Nyssens. 2001. "The Social Enterprise: Towards A Theoretical Socio-Economic Approach." In *The Emergence of Social Enterprise*, edited by Carlo Borzaga and Jacques Defourny, 312–332. London: Routledge.

Lawrence, Paul Roger, and Jay William Lorsch. 1967. "Differentiation and Integration in Complex Organizations." *Administrative Science Quarterly* no. 12:1–30.

Lawrence, Thomas B., and Roy Suddaby. 2006. "Institutions and Institutional Work." In *The Sage Handbook of Organization Studies*, edited by Stewart R. Clegg, Cynthia Hardy, Thomas B. Lawrence and Walter R. Nord. London: Sage Publications.

Le Velly, Ronan. 2004. *Sociologie du marché. Le commerce équitable : des échanges marchands contre le marché et dans le marché*, Sociologie, Université de Nantes, Nantes.

———. 2009. "Quel commerce équitable pour quel développement durable ?" *Innovations* no. 2009/2 (30):99–113.

Leca, Bernard, Julie Battilana, and Eva Boxenbaum. 2008. Agency and Institutions: A Review of Institutional Entrepreneurship. In *HBS Working Paper*. Harvard: Harvard Business School.

LeClair, Mark S. 2002. "Fighting the Tide: Alternative Trade Organizations in the Era of Global Free Trade." *World Development* no. 30 (6):949–958.

Lemaître, Andreia. 2009. *Organisations d'économie sociale et solidaire. Lecture de réalités Nord et Sud à travers l'encastrement politique et une approche plurielle de l'économie.*, Ecole doctorale Entreprise Travail Emploi (CNAM) & Département des sciences de la population et du développement (UCL), Conservatoire National des Arts et Métiers & Université Catholique de Louvain, Paris & Louvain-la-Neuve.

Lemay, Jean-Frédéric. 2007. *Mouvements sociaux transnationaux : le partenariat de deux organisations de commerce equitable en France et au Pérou*, Département d'Anthropologie, Université Laval, Montréal.

Lévesque, Benoît. 2004. "Commerce équitable et économie sociale : une convergence qui s'impose." In *Commerce équitable et économie sociale : le défi de construire un réseau*, edited by Geneviève Huot and Lionel Proulx, 3–19. Montréal: Cahiers de l'ARUC, Collection Transfert.

Levi, Yair. 1998. "Coopératives, entreprises sociales et lucrativité " *Revue Internationale de l'Economie Sociale (RECMA)* no. 268:36–49.

———. 2005. How nonprofit and economy can co-exist: a cooperative perspective. Paper read at ICA XXI International Cooperative Research Conference, at Cork.

Lounsbury, Michael. 2007. "A Tale of Two Cities: Competing Logics and Practice Variation in the Professionalizing of Mutual Funds." *Academy of Management Journal* no. 50 (2):289–307.

Lounsbury, Michael, Marc Ventresca, and Paul M. Hirsch. 2003. "Social Movements, Field Frames and Industry Emergence: A Cultural-Political Perspective on US Recycling." *Socio-Economic Review* no. 1:71–104.

Low, Chris. 2006. "A framework for the governance of social enterprise." *International Journal of Social Economics* no. 33 (5):376–385.

Low, Will, and Eileen Davenport. 2005a. "Postcards from the edge: Maintaining the 'alternative' character of fair trade." *Sustainable Development* no. 13:143–153.

Low, William, and Eileen Davenport. 2005b. "Has the medium (roast) become the message?: The ethics of marketing fair trade in the mainstream." *International Marketing Review* no. 22 (5):494–511.

Macdonald, Kate, and Shelley Marshall. 2010. *Fair Trade, Corporate Accountability and Beyond. Experiments in Globalizing Justice.* Farnham: Ashgate.

Maguire, Steve, Cynthia Hardy, and Thomas B. Lawrence. 2004. "Institutional Entrepreneurship in Emerging Fields: HIV/AIDS Treatment Advocacy in Canada." *Academy of Management Journal* no. 47:657–679.

Mair, Johanna, and Ignasi Marti. 2006. "Social entrepreneurship research: A source of explanation, prediction, and delight." *Journal of World Business* no. 41 (1):36–44.

Mair, Johanna, and Ernesto Noboa. 2003. The emergence of social enterprises and their place in the new organizational landscape. In *IESE Working Paper.* Barcelona: IESE Business School.

Malo, Marie-Claire, and Martine Vézina. 2004. "Governance and Management of Collective User-Based Enterprises: Value-Creation Strategies and Organizational Configurations." *Annals of Public & Cooperative Economics* no. 75 (1):113–137.

Margado, Alix. 2002. "Scic : Société Coopérative d'Intérêt Collectif." *Revue Internationale de l'Economie Sociale (RECMA)* no. 284:19–30.

Marquis, Christopher, and Michael Lounsbury. 2007. "Vive la résistance: competing logics and the consolidation of U.S. community banking." *Academy of Management Journal* no. 50 (4):799–820.

Martin, Roger L., and Sally Osberg. 2007. "Social Entrepreneurship: The Case for Definition." *Stanford Social Innovation Review* no. Spring 2007:29–39.

Marwell, Nicole P., and Paul-Brian McInerney. 2005. "The Nonprofit/For-Profit Continuum: Theorizing the Dynamics of Mixed-Form Markets." *Nonprofit and Voluntary Sector Quarterly* no. 34 (1):7–28.

Maseland, Robbert, and Albert de Vaal. 2002. "How Fair is Fair Trade?" *De Economist* no. 150:251–272.

Mauss, Marcel. 1950. "Essai sur le don. Forme et raison de l'échange dans les sociétés archaïques." In *Sociologie et Antrhopologie*, edited by Marcel Mauss. Paris: Presses Universitaires de France.

McAuley, John, Joanne Duberley, and Phil Johnson. 2007. *Organization Theory. Challenges and Perspectives.* Harlow: Pearson Education (Prentice Hall).

Mertens, Sybille. 2005. "Une explication théorique à l'existence des coopératives agréées et des sociétés à finalité sociale en Belgique " *Non Marchand* no. 2005-2 (16):13–27.

Meyer, John W., and Brian Rowan. 1991. "Institutionalized Organizations: Formal Structure as Myth and Ceremony." In *The New Institutionalism in Organizational Analysis*, edited by Walter W. Powell and Paul J. DiMaggio. Chicago: The University of Chicago Press.

Middleton, Melissa. 1987. "Nonprofit Boards of Directors: Beyond the Governance Function." In *The Nonprofit Sector: A Research Handbook*, edited by Walter W. Powell, 141–153. New Haven: Yale University Press.

Milgrom, Paul, and John Roberts. 1992. *Economics, Organization and Management.* Englewood Cliffs: Prentice Hall International.

Miller-Millesen, Judith L. 2003. "Understanding the Behavior of Nonprofit Boards of Directors: A Theory-Based Approach." *Nonprofit and Voluntary Sector Quarterly* no. 32 (4):521–547.

Miller, Danny. 1986. "Configurations of Strategy and Structure: Towards a Synthesis." *Strategic Management Journal* no. 7:233–249.

Minasian, Jora R. 1964. "Television Pricing and the Theory of Public Goods." *Journal of Law and Economics* no. 7:71–80.

Minga. 2005. *Vers un commerce équitable*. Cognac: Le Temps qu'il fait.

Mintzberg, Henry. 1980. "Structure in 5's: A Synthesis of the Research on Organization Design." *Management Science* no. 26:322–341.

———. 1984a. "Power and organization life cycles." *Academy of Management Review* no. 9:207–224.

———. 1984b. "A Typology of Organizational Structure." In *Organizations: A Quantum View*, edited by Danny Miller and Peter H. Friesen. Englewood Cliffs: Prentice Hall.

Monaci, Massimiliano, and Marco Caselli. 2005. "Blurred Discourses: How Market Isomorphism Constrains and Enables Collective Action in Civil Society." *Global Networks* no. 5 (1):49–69.

Monnier, Lionel, and Bernard Thiry. 1997. *Mutations structurelles et intérêt général*. Edited by Ciriec International, *Ouvertures Economiques—Jalons*. Bruxelles: De Boeck Université.

Moore, Geoff. 2004. "The Fair Trade movement: parameters, issues and future research." *Journal of Business Ethics* no. 53 (1):73–86.

Moore, Geoff, Jane Gibbon, and Richard Slack. 2006. "The mainstreaming of Fair Trade: a macromarketing perspective." *Journal of Strategic Marketing* no. 14 (4):329–352.

Moore, Geoff, Richard Slack, and Jane Gibbon. 2009. "Criteria for Responsible Business Practice in SMEs: An Exploratory Case of U.K. Fair Trade Organisations." *Journal of Business Ethics* no. 89 (2):173–188.

Mulgan, Geoff, Simon Tucker, Rushanara Ali, and Ben Sanders. 2007. Social innovation: what it is, why it matters and how it can be accelerated. In *Working Paper*. Oxford: Skoll Centre for Social Entrepreneurship.

Muradian, Roldan, and Wim Pelupessy. 2005. "Governing the coffee chain: The role of voluntary regulatory Systems." *World Development* no. 33 (12):2029–2044.

Nicholls, Alex. 2002. "Strategic Options in Fair Trade Retailing." *International Journal of Retail and Distribution Management* no. 30 (1):6–17.

———. 2006. *Social Entrepreneurship. New Models of Sustainable Social Change*. Oxford: Oxford University Press.

———. 2010. "Fair Trade: Towards an Economics of Virtue." *Journal of Business Ethics* no. 92 (0):241–255.

Nicholls, Alex, and Andrew Alexander. 2007. "Rediscovering Consumer-Producer Involvement: A Network Perspective on Fair Trade Marketing in the UK." *European Journal of Marketing* no. 40 (11–12):1236–1253.

Nicholls, Alex, and Albert Hyunbae Cho. 2006. "Social Entrepreneurship: The Structuration of a Field." In *Social Entrepreneurship. New Models of Sustainable Change*, edited by Alex Nicholls, 99–118. Oxford: Oxford University Press.

Nicholls, Alex, and Charlotte Opal. 2005. *Fair Trade. Market-driven Ethical Consumption*. London: Sage Publications.

Nizet, Jean, and François Pichault. 1995. *Comprendre les organisations. Mintzberg à l'épreuve des faits*. Paris: Gaëtan Morin.

———. 2001. *Introduction à la théorie des configurations : du "one best way" à la diversité organisationnelle, Collection Management*. Bruxelles: De Boeck Université.

North, Douglass C. 1990. *Institutions, Institutional Change and Economic Performance*. Cambridge: Cambridge University Press.

———. 1991. "Institutions." *Journal of Economic Perspectives* no. 5 (1):97–112.

Nyssens, Marthe. 2006. *Social Enterprise. At the crossroads of market, public policies and civil society.* London: Routledge.
———. 2008. "Belgium." In *Social Enterprise in Europe: Recent Trends and Developments*, edited by Jacques Defourny and Marthe Nyssens. Liège: EMES European Research Network.
O'Regan, Katherine M., and Sharon M. Oster. 2000. "Nonprofit and For-Profit Partnerships: Rationale and Challenges of Cross-Sector Contracting." *Nonprofit and Voluntary Sector Quarterly* no. 29 (1):120–140.
Oliver, Christine. 1992. "The antecedents of desinstitutionalization." *Organization Studies* no. 13:563–588.
Olson, Mancur. 1965. *The Logic of Collective Action.* Cambridge: Harvard University Press.
Ortmann, Andreas, and Mark Schlesinger. 1997. "Trust, repute and the role of non-profit enterprise." *Voluntas* no. 8 (2):97–119.
Ostrower, Francie, and Melissa M. Stone. 2006. "Governance: Research Trends, Gaps, and Future Prospects." In *The Nonprofit Sector. A Research Handbook.*, edited by Walter W. Powell and Richard Steinberg. New Haven: Yale University Press.
Otero, Ana Isabel. 2007. Étude de cas de l'organisation de commerce équitable IDEAS. In *Cahiers de la CRSDD.* Montréal: Chaire de Responsabilité Sociale et de Développement Durable—UQAM.
Özçağlar-Toulouse, Nil, and Amina Béji-Bécheur. 2008. *Le Commerce équitable : entre utopie et marché.* Paris: Vuibert.
Özçağlar-Toulouse, Nil, Amina Béji-Bécheur, Matthieu Gateau, and Philippe Robert-Demontrond. 2010. "Demystifying Fair Trade in France: The History of an Ambiguous Project." *Journal of Business Ethics* no. 92 (0):205–216.
Özçağlar-Toulouse, Nil, Edward Shiu, and Deirdre Shaw. 2006. "In search of fair trade: ethical consumer decision making in France." *International Journal of Consumer Studies* no. 30 (5):502–514.
Pache, Anne-Claire, and Felipe Santos. 2010. "Inside the Hybrid Organization: An Organizational Level View of Responses to Conflicting Institutional Demands." *INSEAD Working Paper* no. 2010/57.
Peattie, Ken, and Adrian Morley. 2008. "Eight paradoxes of the social enterprise research agenda." *Social Enterprise Journal* no. 4 (2):91–107.
Petrella, Francesca. 2003. *Une analyse néo-institutionnaliste des structures de propriété "multi-stakeholder".* Une application aux organisations de développement local, Faculté des sciences économiques, sociales et politiques, Université Catholique de Louvain, Louvain-la-Neuve.
Pfeffer, Jeffrey, and Gerald Salancik. 1978. *The External Control of Organizations: A Resource Dependence Perspective.* New York: Harper & Row.
Phills, James A. Jr., Kriss Deiglmeier, and Dale T. Miller. 2008. "Rediscovering Social Innovation." *Stanford Social Innovation Review* no. Fall 2008:34–43.
Platteau, Jean-Philippe. 1987. La nouvelle économie institutionnelle et la problématique coopérative. In *Cahiers de la Faculté des Sciences économiques et sociales de Namur, Série recherches.* Namur: Université Notre-Dame de la Paix.
Polanyi, Karl. 1944. *The Great Transformation.* New York: Rinehard & Company.
Poncelet, Marc, Jacques Defourny, and Patrick De Pelsmacker. 2005. A fair and sustainable trade, between market and solidarity: diagnosis and prospects. Brussels: Belgian Science Policy.
Poos, Samuel. 2008. Le commerce équitable en 2008. Bruxelles: Fair Trade Centre—Coopération Technique Belge.
Powell, Walter W. 1991. "Expanding the Scope of Institutional Analysis." In *The New Institutionalism in Organizational Analysis*, edited by Walter W. Powell and Paul DiMaggio. Chicago: The University of Chicago Press.

Powell, Walter W., and Paul DiMaggio. 1991. "Introduction." In *The New Institutionalism in Organizational Analysis*, edited by Walter W. Powell and Paul DiMaggio. Chicago: The University of Chicago Press.

Purdy, Jill M., and Barbara Gray. 2009. "Conflicting logics, mechanisms of diffusion, and multilevel dynamics in emerging institutional fields." *Academy of Management Journal* no. 52 (2):355–380.

Radbourne, Jennifer. 2003. "Performing on boards: The link between governance and corporate reputation in nonprofit arts boards." *Corporate Reputation Review* no. 6 (3):212–222.

Raynolds, Laura T. 2008. "Mainstreaming Fair Trade Coffee: From Partnership to Traceability." *World Development*.

Raynolds, Laura T., and Michael A. Long. 2007. "Fair/Alternative Trade: historical and empirical dimensions." In *Fair Trade. The challenges of transforming globalization*, edited by Laura T. Raynolds, Douglas L. Murray and John Wilkinson. London: Routledge.

Raynolds, Laura T., Douglas L. Murray, and John Wilkinson. 2007. *Fair Trade. The challenges of transforming globalization*. London: Routledge.

Raynolds, Laura T., and John Wilkinson. 2007. "Fair Trade in the agriculture and food sector." In *Fair Trade. The Challenges of Transforming Globalization*, edited by Laura T. Raynolds, Douglas L. Murray and John Wilkinson. London: Routledge.

Reed, Darryl. 2009. "What do Corporations have to do with Fair Trade? Positive and Normative Analysis from a Value Chain Perspective." *Journal of Business Ethics* no. 86 (0):3–26.

Reed, Darryl, and J.J. McMurtry. 2009. *Co-operatives in a Global Economy: The Challenges of Co-operation Across Borders*. Newcastle upon Tyne: Cambridge Scholars Publishing.

Reed, Darryl, Bob Thomson, Ian Hussey, and Jean-Frédéric LeMay. 2010. "Developing a Normatively Grounded Research Agenda for Fair Trade: Examining the Case of Canada." *Journal of Business Ethics* no. 92 (0):151–179.

Renard, Marie-Christine. 2003. "Fair trade: quality, market and conventions." *Journal of Rural Studies* no. 19:87–96.

———. 2005. "Quality certification, regulation and power in fair trade." *Journal of Rural Studies* no. 21 (4):419–431.

Renard, Marie-Christine, and Victor Pérez-Grovas. 2007. "Fair Trade Coffee in Mexico: At the Center of the Debates." In *Fair Trade. The challenges of transforming globalization*, edited by Laura T. Raynolds, Douglas L. Murray and John Wilkinson. New York: Routledge.

Ronchi, Loraine. 2000. Fair Trade in Costa Rica: an Impact Report In *Economics Subject Group*: University of Sussex.

———. 2002. The impact of fair trade on producers and their organizations: a case study with Coocafé in Costa Rica. In *PRUS Working Paper* edited by Poverty Research Unit at Sussex: University of Sussex.

Roozen, Nico, and Frans van der Hoff. 2001. *L'aventure du commerce équitable. Une alternative à la mondialisation*. Paris: JC Lattès.

Rose-Ackerman, Susan. 1987. "Altruism, Ideological Entrepreneurs and the Nonprofit Firm." *Voluntas* no. 8 (2):120–134.

———. 1996. "Altruism, Nonprofits, and Economic Theory." *Journal of Economic Literature* no. 34 (2):701–728.

Rouleau, Linda. 2007. *Théories des Organisations*. Québec: Presses de l'Université du Québec.

Saidel, Judith R. 1998. "Expanding the Governance Construct: Functions and Contributions of Nonprofit Advisory Groups." *Nonprofit and Voluntary Sector Quarterly* no. 27 (4):421–436.

Samuelson, Paul A. 1954. "The Pure Theory of Public Expenditure." *Review of Economics and Statistics* no. 36:387–390.

Sarrazin-Biteye, Émilie. 2009. Les réseaux d'acteurs du commerce équitable. Exemple de l'Ile-de-France. In *Rapport final du PICRI Commerce Equitable*. Paris: Plate-Forme pour le Commerce Equitable—Institut d'Etudes sur le Développement Economique et Social.

Schneiberg, Marc. 2005. "Combining New Institutionalisms: Explaining Institutional Change in American Property Insurance." *Sociological Forum* no. 20 (1):93–137.

Schneiberg, Marc, Marissa King, and Thomas Smith. 2008. "Social Movements and Organizational Form: Cooperative Alternatives to Corporations in the American Insurance, Dairy, and Grain Industries." *American Sociological Review* no. 73 (1):635–667.

Schümperli Younossian, Catherine. 2006. "Le commerce équitable sous tension." In *Economie solidaire et commerce équitable. Acteurs et actrices d'Europe et d'Amérique latine*, edited by Claude Auroi and Isabel Yepez del Castillo, 49–69. Louvain-la-Neuve: Presses Universitaires de Louvain.

Scott, W. Richard. 1991. "Unpacking Institutional Arrangements." In *The New Institutionalism in Organizational Analysis*, edited by Walter W. Powell and Paul DiMaggio. Chicago: The University of Chicago Press.

———. 2003. *Organizations: Rational, Natural and Open Systems*. Fifth edition ed. Upper Saddle River: Prentice Hall.

Scott, W. Richard, and John W. Meyer. 1991. "The Organization of Societal Sectors: Propositions and Early Evidence." In *The New Institutionalism in Organizational Analysis*, edited by Walter W. Powell and Paul DiMaggio. Chicago: The University of Chicago Press.

Selznick, P. (1996), "Institutionalism "Old" and "New"", *Administrative Science Quarterly*, 41, 270–277.

Seo, Myeong-Gu, and W. E. Douglas Creed. 2002. "Institutional contradictions, praxis, and institutional change: a dialectical perspective." *Academy of Management Review* no. 27:222–247.

Skloot, Edward. 1987. "Enterprise and commerce in nonprofit organizations." In *The nonprofit sector: a research handbook*, edited by Walter W. Powell, 380–393. New Haven: Yale University Press.

Slitter, Gary, and David A. Spencer. 2000. "The Uncertain Foundations of Transaction Costs Economics." *Journal of Economic Issues* no. 34 (1):61.

Smith, Sally. 2010. "For Love or Money? Fairtrade Business Models in the UK Supermarket Sector." *Journal of Business Ethics* no. 92 (0):257–266.

Sobel, Joel. 2005. "Interdependent Preferences and Reciprocity." *Journal of Economic Literature* no. 43 (2):392–436.

Spear, Robert. 2000. "The Co-operative advantage." *Annals of Public and Cooperative Economics* no. 71 (4):507–523.

Spear, Roger. 2004. "Governance in Democratic Member-Based Organisations." *Annals of Public and Cooperative Economics* no. 75 (1):33–59.

———. 2008. "United Kingdom." In *Social Enterprise in Europe: Recent Trends and Developments*, edited by Jacques Defourny and Marthe Nyssens. Liège: EMES European Research Network.

Spence, Laura J., and Robert Rutherfoord. 2001. "Social responsibility, profit maximization and the small owner-manager firm." *Journal of Small Business and Enterprise Development* no. 8 (2):126–139.

Steinberg, Richard. 2006. "Economic Theories of Nonprofit Organizations." In *The Nonprofit Sector: A Research Handbook*, edited by Walter W. Powell and Richard Steinberg, 13–31. New Haven: Yale University Press.

Steinrücken, Torsten, and Sebastian Jaenichen. 2007. "The Fair Trade Idea: Towards an Economics of Social Labels." *Journal of Consumer Policy* no. 30 (3):201–217.

Suchman, Mark C. 1995. "Managing Legitimacy: Strategic and Institutional Approaches." *The Academy of Management Review* no. 20 (3):571–610.

Tadros, Catherine, and Marie-Claire Malo. 2002. "Commerce équitable, démocratie et solidarité : Equal Exchange, une coopérative exceptionnelle au Nord." *Nouvelles pratiques sociales* no. 15 (1):76–97.

Tallontire, Anne. 2000. "Partnerships in Fairtrade: Reflections from a Case Study of Cafédirect." *Development in Practice* no. 10 (2):166–177.

Thompson, John L. 2008. "Social enterprise and social entrepreneurship: where have we reached?: A summary of issues and discussion points." *Social Enterprise Journal* no. 4 (2):149–161.

Thornton, Patricia H., and William Ocasio. 1999. "Institutional Logics and the Historical Contingency of Power in Organizations: Executive Succession in the Higher Education Publishing Industry, 1958–1990." *The American Journal of Sociology* no. 105 (3):801–843.

———. 2008. "Institutional Logics." In *The SAGE Handbook of Organizational Institutionalism*, edited by R. Greenwood, Christine Oliver, Kerstin Sahlin and R. Suddaby. Los Angeles: Sage.

Tolbert, Pamela S., and Lynne G. Zucker. 1996. "The Institutionalization of Institutional Theory." In *Studying Organization. Theory & Method*, edited by Stewart R. Clegg and Cynthia Hardy. London: Sage Publications.

Townley, Barbara. 2002. "The role of competing rationalities in institutional change." *Academy of Management Journal* no. 45:163–179.

Utting, Karla. 2009. "Assessing the Impact of Fair Trade Coffee: Towards an Integrative Framework." *Journal of Business Ethics* no. 86 (0):127–149.

Vienney, Claude. 1997. "Le maintien et le renforcement de la réciprocité entre l'entreprise et le mouvement." In *Desjardins : une entreprise et un mouvement ?*, edited by Benoît Lévesque. Montréal: Presses Universitaires de Québec.

Viganò, Elena, Michela Glorio, and Anna Villa. 2008. *Tutti i numeri dell'equo. Il commercio equo e solidale in Italia*. Roma: Edizioni dell'Asino.

Warrier, Meera. 2011. *The Politics of Fair Trade. A Survey*. New York: Routledge.

Weerawardena, Jay, and Gillian Sullivan Mort. 2006. "Investigating social entrepreneurship: A multidimensional model." *Journal of World Business* no. 41 (1):21–35.

Weisbrod, Burton A. 1975. "Toward a Theory of the Voluntary Nonprofit Sector in a Three-Sector Economy." In *Altruism, Morality and Economic Theory*, edited by E.S. Phelps, 171–195. New York: Russel Sage Foundation.

———. 1998. "Conclusions and Public-policy Issues : Commercialism and the Road ahead." In *To profit or not to profit—The commercial Transformation of the Nonprofit Sector*, edited by Burton A. Weisbrod, 287–305. New York: Cambridge University Press.

Wilkinson, John. 2007. "Fair Trade: Dynamic and Dilemmas of a Market Oriented Global Social Movement." *Journal of Consumer Policy* no. 30 (3):219–239.

Williamson, Oliver E. 1979. "Transaction cost economics: The governance of contractual relations." *Journal of Law and Economics* no. 22:245–246.

———. 1985. *The Economic Institutions of Capitalism: Firms, Markets, Relational Contracting*. New York: The Free Press.

———. 1995. *Organization theory: from Chester Barnard to the present and beyond*. New York: Oxford University Press US.

———. 2000. "The New Institutional Economics: Taking Stock, Looking Ahead." *Journal of Economic Literature* no. 38 (3):595–613.

———. 2002a. "The Lens of Contract: Private Ordering." *American Economic Review* no. 92 (2):438–443.

———. 2002b. "The Theory of the Firm as Governance Structure: From Choice to Contract." *Journal of Economic Perspectives* no. 16 (3):171–195.

Yin, Robert K. 2009. *Case Study Research. Design and Methods*. Thousand Oaks: Sage Publications.

Zehner, David C. 2002. "An Economic Assessment of 'Fair Trade' in Coffee." *Chazen Web Journal of International Business*.

# Index